Ilan Stavans

Ilan Stavans

Eight Conversations

Neal Sokol

Amherst,
Mayo 2004

Para Martín Espada —

Queridísimo amigo
y partícipe de
conversaciones instrumentales

Ilan Stavans

The University of Wisconsin Press

The University of Wisconsin Press
1930 Monroe Street
Madison, Wisconsin 53711

www.wisc.edu/wisconsinpress/

3 Henrietta Street
London WC2E 8LU, England

Printed in the United States of America

A Cataloging-in-Publication data record for this book
is available from the Library of Congress.
ISBN: 0-299-19910-x *cloth*

Contents

"But about this interview. You know it is the custom, now, to interview any man who has become notorious."

"Indeed! I had not heard of it before. It must be very interesting. What do you do it with?"

"Ah, well,—well,—well,—this is disheartening. It ought to be done with a club in some cases; but customarily it consists in the interviewer asking questions and the interviewed answering them. It is all the rage now. Will you let me ask you certain questions calculated to bring out the salient points of your public and private history?"

Mark Twain, An Encounter with an Interviewer

Preface

The first time I read the work of Ilan Stavans, I was perusing the pages of a favorite literary journal of mine, *Transition*. His witty and biting essay "Two Peruvians" played the personality of novelist Mario Vargas Llosa off against the persona of Shining Path leader Carlos Abimael Guzmán Reynoso. Like scores of other readers before and after, I was struck by Stavans's touch with words: his prose was luminous, noncondescending, and thought provoking. Indeed, the way he dished out the "snapper" reminded me of Mark Twain. Like Twain, he cut his teeth in journalism, and, just like the author of *Huckleberry Finn*, he employs a sharp, argumentative style that makes the reader's ride less bumpy when traveling to the payoff.

Stavans also knows his postmodernism inside out, and his magic prose is filled with humor, trickery, and sleight of hand. He draws into a bag of tricks again and again on subjects ranging from Subcomandante Marcos to Selena to Elián Gonzáles.

But for all his style and playfulness, Stavans is a man of letters and ideas with electricity at his fingertips—a man at once committed to the ancient double life represented by the pen and the sword. In an age where we have abandoned the page-turner for the channel changer, his oeuvre is a passport back into the universe of Jorge Luis Borges, Edmund Wilson, and Isaiah Berlin, all of whom had a formative influence on him. Through his essays, Stavans journeys into the realm where the intellect always tests itself anew. He is a fiercely independent critic: he might throw down the gauntlet when he feels that a piece has been marked up way beyond its real value; or he will praise a manifestation of pop culture if it appears to him to be an allegory or perhaps a symptom of a larger human issue. We are invariably inspired by his courage and conviction.

After reading "Two Peruvians," I didn't return to Stavans again until 1996 when I found his collection *The One-Handed Pianist and Other Stories.* I later went out and bought his other books as quickly as they hit the press. I took them with me on a research trip to Brazil. On my return, I worked up the conviction to write to him—the first of many such letters. I was then on staff at Steven Spielberg's Survivors of the Shoah Visual History Foundation. I was also deeply involved in a personal exploration of Jewish life in America and abroad, and in the way the memory of the Holocaust lives on. Those demands took me all over Europe and into North Africa and Israel. I examined the Jewish past in prewar Europe, and the Jewish present of survivors who had rebuilt their lives in Israel, America, Europe, Latin America, and South Africa. Those experiences inevitably informed my discussions with Stavans as our correspondence accumulated. I still vividly recall an early exchange with him: a discussion of Irving Howe's *World of Our Fathers,* on our "fathers," or what we consider to be the "official" Jewish-American approach to history. His comments were unpredictable, radical, and enlightening. "We have much to learn from the period of *cohabitation* in medieval Spain," he said. "Jews then understood the concept of 'tolerance' in less manipulative a fashion than we do today. American Jews have a monolithic, Eurocentric viewpoint. Diversity for them is comfortable when it occurs outside their realm, but not in the comfort of home." The conversations in this book are filled with such comments, and collectively they inspired me to complete a book of my own conversations with Stavans.

The dictionary defines the word "conversation" as "informal or friendly talk; exchange of ideas and opinions by talking informally." Recorded and transcribed, conversations, might of course be far from leisurely paced, especially when they are destined for print. We want to put the best face on our words. The result is often a stiffness and dogmatism that is unappealing. This is because, after months on the lecture circuit or press junket, a writer's responses become polished and rehearsed. But the reader of this volume is likely to be surprised. Stavans is what the French describe as a *conversateur:* his answers to my questions—questions that I hope are a map of and a compass to his peripatetic mind—are candid, panoramic, even artful. They defy expectations and, as such, they constantly pushed me, as the interviewer, to break with convention and improvise, improvise, improvise.

The popularity of the literary conversation genre has exploded since the late nineteenth century. The format is a far cry for readers from Johann Peter Eckermann's indispensable dialogue with Goethe, *Gespräche mit Goethe in den letzten Jahren seines Lebens, 1823–1832*. This newly minted tradition is both widely revered and frequently lampooned. Many times the interviewer attempts to sketch authorial intention and meaning. The readers use this dialogue an instruction manual. Quite frequently the warning label is the same—fragile: handle with care.

A literary conversation can also be volatile or stale. Twain's "1601: Conversation as It Was by the Social Fireside in the Time of the Tudors" explored the easily forgotten scatological heritage of the word "conversation." Twain uses a dialogue among Queen Elizabeth, William Shakespeare, Ben Jonson, Francis Bacon, and other luminaries of the day to mock the absurdities of conversation. Twain's crude satire allows us to flash forward to a glimpse of our new century; it is a mirror of modern American obsessions complete with its "who-said-whats" and "whens." But then again, Mark Twain would know a bit about this firsthand. After all, he was the most interviewed celebrity of his age. His essay "An Encounter with an Interviewer" was a send-up of this grand pageant of egoism. Literary legends are now processed through mass-market consumerism. As a result, conversation of the literary kind that appears in print might either be a blessing or a curse. I've tried to avoid these customary trappings. Instead, for inspiration, I looked at the transcripts of literary conversations from the tradition's more salubrious examples, starting with Eckermann and progressing to Richard Burgin's conversations with Borges and Isaac Bashevis Singer. To top it off, I consumed anything and everything recorded by the interviewing pioneer and master of the form: Studs Terkel.

So, after an engaging epistolary exchange, I eventually proposed the idea of a series of conversations to Stavans. He agreed to reflect on a handful of topics and delineate eight distinct areas of discussion: his background as a Mexican, an American, and a Jew; the role of intellectuals in society; translation as a form of life and the beleaguered concepts of originality and authenticity; his passion for dictionaries and his interest in Spanglish, the hybrid encounter of Spanish and English spoken not only in the United States but around the globe, as the epicenter of a cultural earthquake of global proportions; the responsibilities of the public intellectual; the literature of *la hispanidad* (that is, things Hispanic); and the rabbinical tradition of critical thought; and the uses of tragedy in individual and collective life. A number of leitmotifs jump from one conversation to another. I have sought to be nonschematic: translation, for instance, is at the core of the fourth conversation, yet ruminations on the topic appear elsewhere too. The exchanges took place during tête-à-têtes between 2001 and 2003 in Los Angeles, Amherst, and New York City. I used a tape recorder and accumulated almost a dozen cassettes. The fine-tuning of responses was done by e-mail and in person.

No doubt I caught Stavans by surprise at times. More often than not, though, he forced me to rethink the set of *idées fixes* all of us carry along with us. In reaction, so as to test his views—and also, his consistency—I reread all of Stavans's oeuvre, which is, needless to say, quite substantial: more than half a dozen nonfiction books that include the polemical classic *The Hispanic Condition,* the bestselling memoir *On Borrowed Words,* as well as the collections of essays *Art and Anger, The Riddle of Cantinflas,* and *The Inveterate Dreamer.* I also revisited various widely known canonical anthologies of his, like *The Oxford Book of Jewish Stories* and *The Scroll and the Cross,* the latter an odyssey through one thousand years of Jewish-Hispanic literature. Not to let the present tense flee evasively, I sought out uncollected articles and commentary published in periodicals such as the *Times Literary Supplement* and the *Guardian* in England, and the *Nation,* the *Boston Globe,* and the *Los Angeles Times Book Review* in the United States. I wore no blinders and kept in mind the lessons of William Hazlett's stinging essay, "On the Conversation of Authors": the art of conversation, he announced, "is the art of hearing as well as being heard." Taking this lesson to heart, I listened enough to see if his views doubled back on themselves, to see how far he could go with the rope without creating the proverbial noose. As far as I'm concerned, that is the only way available to challenge a first-rate mind. (A brief note on style: the first time a book, essay, or TV show by Stavans is mentioned in the following pages, I've inserted in brackets the original date of publication.)

I want to thank the many people who were at my side during the preparation of this book for their incredible support and suggestions for this project. First and foremost, my gratitude to Ilan Stavans himself, whose friendship is an asset that has transformed me. My expressed gratitude to Irene Vilar, originally an acquisitions editor at Syracuse University Press, whose initial excitement never decreased; to John J. Fruehwirth and Mary

Selden Evans and her staff for the embrace; to Robert Mandel, director of the University of Wisconsin Press, for his enthusiasm and support; to Renee Steinke at the *Literary Review* as well as Donna Stein and Walter Cummins of *Tiferet* for a space to plant these words; to Bobbie Helinski at Amherst College, always ready to help with accommodations; and to the staff of Frost Library, for their guidance. I would also like to thank my brother Brent D. Sokol for being a bedrock of ideas and Olufemi Dawah Terry for off-the-cuff manuscript suggestions. Beth Marchese, Sara Carreras, and Kathy Fernando all deserve thanks for their extraordinary transcription efforts and their patience. Finally, my heartfelt gratitude to M. J. Devaney for her sharp, diligent, meticulous copyediting job and to Sue Breckenridge, managing editor at the University of Wisconsin Press, for her care while overseeing the editorial process.

On occasion, Stavans has been described by others, pejoratively, as an interloper. This adjective, the reader will soon realize, is, actually, a compliment. He is, indeed, an intruder, a trespasser, an outsider looking in. He once suggested to me that his condition as a Jew in the Hispanic world is that of an encroacher—"I'm an impostor, a chameleon." He added that "Chameleons adapt to the environment by incorporating its patterns, by making themselves at home. But home for them is . . . where? Nowhere and everywhere." This, then, is a book about imposture. It is also yardstick for measuring the evolution of Stavans's thought. He is, in my eyes, a truly global thinker, with an erudition that ranges from Flavius Josephus in ancient Rome to Maimonides in Córdoba, from Noam Chomsky to comic strips south of the Rio Grande. "God is in our silences," he said to me once in Manhattan. And then: "It isn't the actual destination but the journey itself, with all its perils and achievements, that matters—not where it is that one is going, but why is it that we're in motion." How is that for an attitude toward life?

—N. S., 5764

Ilan Stavans

I

The Self and the World

I. S.   My ancestors lived in Poland and the Ukraine for centuries. They were poor and uneducated merchants, although my mother's ancestors maintained a prominent standing within the Jewish community. In the late nineteenth century, as pogroms erupted and anti-Semitism spread, various members of the family decided to immigrate to the New World: a few came to the United States, others traveled as far as Brazil. As a result of immigration quotas, a portion ended up in Mexico. My father's mother, Bela Stavchansky, arrived in the early decades of the twentieth century from Nove-Brudno, a small town near Warsaw.

The process of adaptation was rough, but they succeeded marvelously. Their genealogical talent to assimilate into new environments proved to be as effective as it had been many times in the past. In some cases, the accepted strategy seemed to be to altogether cut ties with Europe: not to speak a word of Polish again, not to invoke relatives' names. . . . For a while I thought this attitude to be cruel to the degree of being inhuman. I didn't think highly of one of my grandmothers because of it. But as I grow older, I realize that every immigrant, to survive, needs to find his own tactics. I too forced myself not to phone the Mexican family too often by long distance when I moved to New York City. I put their photos in my room, but sometimes quietly hid them under the mattress.

N. S. Were you afraid to cave in to nostalgia?

I. S. I remember the period as one filled with moments of intense longing.

N. S. Ellis Island holds a firm nostalgic grip on the American Jewish imagination both in literature and film. Is there an equivalent iconic port of entry for Jewish immigration to Mexico?

I. S. Not really. . . . Veracruz was a port of entrance, but immigrants also arrived at other sites, including Central America. Keep in mind that, unlike the massive immigration through Ellis Island, the newcomers to Mexico were just a few hundred, and at times a couple of thousand a year.

N. S. New York is part of your spiritual and intellectual center of gravity. For example, in your memoir *On Borrowed Words* [2001] you wrote: "No matter where I live, no matter where I travel, the only place I feel I truly belong is New York." New York has been transformed by the tragic events of 9/11.

I. S. The events have had a deep impact on me, as they have on most everyone I know. It is a date that will live in history as a watershed: before it we enjoyed life with a naïveté that today seems almost obscene. It was Billy Collins who said that New York in particular, and the United States in general, lost their virginity on that date. If so, it was rape that brought it along: a violent act of submission.

N. S. One passage in your memoir eerily foreshadows these troubled times: "New York is a city that is omnipresent in literature, so much so that if a catastrophe ever occurred one would be able to re-create its sidewalks, dance clubs, and subway stations, its love affairs and robberies, even the shadow projected by a restless fly on a rain-soaked umbrella, through what its inhabitants write about." Do you still feel that literature can re-create life formerly existing in Manhattan or is it part of a past we know we can't return to?

I. S. Obviously, no one ever imagined such a catastrophe. But surely literature is a way to overcome death and oblivion. Masterpieces will emerge from the ashes.

N. S. Let me return to the perception of the Jewish experience in Mexico. How is it different from that in the United States?

I. S. America, in the mind of Eastern European Jews, was a Promised Land. Mexico, on the other hand, wasn't even on the map. If anything was known about it, it was marred with distortion: primitive, barbaric, uncivilized. . . .

N. S.   Still, Mexico City became a small-scale center of secular Yiddish culture and learning. As a young boy you attended Mexico City's oldest Yiddish day school, the Colegio Israelita de México. How did your education impact or expand the way in which you see the world?

I. S.   I describe in some detail my "Yiddish days" in my memoir *On Borrowed Words*. I remember those days with ambivalence. I was conscious of the fact that I was a member of a tiny religious minority and I resented the fact that my parents wanted me to learn Yiddish, a language that, after World War II, seemed to be dying worldwide. Today I look back with endearment to those experiences and feel grateful to my parents for the choice they made in my education.

The *Yidishe Shule* was a Bundist institution. It saw language and culture as fountains of Jewish continuity, although, by the time I was an adolescent, Hebrew and Zionism had almost replaced Yiddish and Bundism as the accepted ideology.

N. S.   What are your strongest recollections of your student days at the Colegio Israelita de México?

I. S.   It was a self-enclosed, protected environment. Mexico was always outside the window, not inside the school. Several of our teachers were *mestizos,* but the moment they passed the threshold of the school, they became like us: aloof, Europeanized dwellers.

N. S.   Were you conscious of that aloofness?

I. S.   No, age has granted me perspective. I was a happy child in a blissful environment, unconcerned with *lo mexicano.*

N. S.   The secular Yiddish school movement in America, orchestrated by the International Workers' Order, the Jewish National Workers' Alliance, Left Poale Zion, the Sholem Aleichem Folk Institute, and the Workmen's Circle, ostensibly collapsed in the fifties. The curriculum was progressive in tone and orientation (socialism or communism was a staple part of the educational diet). Was your education at the Colegio Israelita de México also a progressive one? What was your reaction when you heard the school had slashed the number of hours Yiddish is used in the classroom?

I. S.   It wasn't as progressive as one might have wished. In spite of its Bundist roots, the teachers were conservatives, and so was the

5

administration. Their mission was to make us "culturally Jewish." Ideology was never discussed seriously. Zionism was a fixture in the classroom, but it was seen as a source of kitschy adoration. We were trained to idolize the early He-Halutz generation.

Am I sad that Yiddish is finally being pushed out of the classroom? No, not really. I love my Yiddish, but I see no practical purpose in teaching children to read, write, and speak a language that is, for all purposes, a fossil.

N. S.   A fossil?

I. S.   Yes: a relic, much like Latin, Aramaic. . . .

N. S.   Wouldn't it be better if future generations were functionally literate in the Yiddish classics?

I. S.   Better perhaps, but impractical. Languages rise and fall as a result of historical circumstances. Few have suffered as severe a blow as Yiddish did at the hands of Hitler, though. The result of that blow is that we are doomed to approach the Yiddish classics through translation.

N. S.   You were taught Yiddish at an early age.

I. S.   Yes, in kindergarten, primary school, and onwards. It was also the language spoken by the immigrant generation. My parents early on communicated with their own parents in Yiddish.

N. S.   And Spanish?

I. S.   Spanish was the public language—the language of the street. It was the nation's language. As Jews, we spoke it with others. It was our primary vehicle of communication.

N. S.   When did you learn Hebrew?

I. S.   As Zionism began to take hold as an ideology among Mexican Jews, from the fifties onward, Hebrew became a threat to Yiddish. Kids heard Hebrew in the mouth of envoys from Israel hired in school as principals, music teachers, and language instructors. In the sixties, Israel was a source of pride for Mexican Jews. Israeli folk songs, Israeli kitsch, and Israeli memorabilia were everywhere. A relative traveling to Jerusalem would invariably return with a little bottle of dessert sand from the Negev, a *kova tembel*, an illustrated book with images of the Damascus Gate, the Golan Heights, the Wailing Wall. . . .

N. S.   What was it like for you to be immersed in a world of many languages at such early age?

6

I. S.   Polyglotism was a way of life. Eastern European Jews had spoken far more languages than we did. Our view of the immigrant generation was infused with admiration for their linguistic talent. People in Warsaw in the twenties spoke Hebrew, Yiddish, Polish, Russian, German, and French, to offer only a partial list. Jews have been prone to this verbal multiplicity as a result of their diasporic journey.

To be honest, I don't remember thinking as a child: "How exciting it is that I speak various tongues!" I wasn't an exception. Everyone around me did it. It was a natural response to the environment.

N. S.   In your lyrical essay, "The First Book" [*Art and Anger* (1996)], you explain that as a child you disliked books, preferring the outdoors instead. But, as you note, your "irreverence and disrespect for books ended abruptly the day of my first encounter with what I think of as the Book [the Torah]." How deep was your exposure to Jewish religious civilization?

I. S.   Mine was a secular family. My parents were perceived as bohemians by the Jewish establishment. As a family we lived far away from the Jewish neighborhoods in Colonia Hipódromo, Colonia Polanco, and Colonia Tecamachalco. Our house, built when I was little, was in the southern part of the city, in a region considered then to be on the fringes of civilization. There were no synagogues nearby. The Colegio Israelita de México, in Colonia Narvarte, wasn't close either; our school bus took an hour or more to get there every morning. The centers of study and prayer, then, were distant from us. This is exactly as my parents wanted it. My mother's home was Orthodox, but she moved away from it when she married my father. Religion for them was a source of continuity, but it was also perceived as a manifestation of primitivism.

N. S.   Why primitivism?

I. S.   My mother perceived orthodoxy as rigid, undemocratic, and intellectually awkward.

N. S.   Your father, Abraham Stavans, is a veteran film, TV, and theater actor in Mexico. He was in the cast of numerous soap operas, including *Mi destino eres tú, Mi querida Isabel,* and *Baila conmigo.*

I. S.   He once convinced a friend of his to cast me in a small soap-opera part. It was a catastrophe!

N. S.   What happened?

I. S.   I simply couldn't deliver the lines.

N. S.   What did your father's career inspire in you as a child?

I. S.   Envy. . . . In *On Borrowed Words* I included a section on looking behind the curtains, on seeing the audience mesmerized by the performance he was giving. An hour before the show, in the dressing room, he would put on make-up, a toupee, a fake moustache, a fedora hat. . . . Slowly, the transformation would take place before my eyes: the man who was my father would become someone altogether different. Yes, "envy" is the word that comes to mind. For approximately two hours, the audience would get the better of him—not me, not my brother and sister. The feeling of envy was infused with a sense of astonishment. How could someone I knew so well borrow another personality? Once the show was over, the original body and soul would be reunited again: my father would regain control of himself—he would become the person I always knew. . . . While witnessing one of those transformations, I must have realized, for the first time ever, the power of art to liberate us but also to take away an integral part of who we are.

N. S.   Did your father ever lose sight of who he was as a result of spending so many years in character?

I. S.   He never lost sight of who he was and how the other personalities could threaten to take over. In retrospect, though, I believe there were many selves inside him, on- and offstage. I have a vivid recollection of a particular performance. It must have been the mid-seventies. My father was on the cast of the *Line,* by the American-Jewish playwright Israel Horowitz. In the play, half a dozen characters are supposedly standing on line, waiting . . . to do what? The audience never finds out where these people are going or why they want to be on a queue. One of the actors, Arturo Beristáin, suddenly forgot he was part of the play. He got so involved in his role that he lost sense of time, space, and self. I remember what my father said after the show: *"Arturo se disasoció"*—he got himself disassociated. He forgot he was simply pretending to be someone else. If memory serves me well, my father never lost himself, though: *nunca se disasoció.* I had *confianza* in him—I trusted his instinct.

N. S.   When your father is out on the street do people stroll up to him and address him as one of the characters that he performed on stage or TV?

I. S.   People don't always remember his name, but they immediately recognize him in public spaces. If he happens to be playing the role of the evildoer that week, they might abuse him verbally. Still, people know the difference between life and fantasy. Although on occasion, somebody would say, "Oh, can you do this little gesture that you do on camera that is so funny or that is so appealing?" and, as a form of compliance, perhaps generosity, he would do it. In other words, he would act just for a tiny second, offstage. He's a wonderful jester. When telling you a joke, he will impersonate all the characters in a way that transports you to another universe.

N. S.   Did your father ever dream of being Broadway bound?

I. S.   He would have loved to. . . . In fact, he would at times joke that the shape and size of his nose had become his major obstacle. Sooner or later, though, he understood he had been born in an altogether different context.

N. S.   Did your father influence your literary career?

I. S.   Unquestionably.

N. S.   A few days ago I reread the essay "September 19, 1985" [*Las Mamis,* edited by Esmeralda Santiago and Joie Davidow (2000); also in *The Inveterate Dreamer* (2001)].

I. S.   It was done at the invitation to be part of an anthology about mothers.

N. S.   Your mother must have been a crucial influence on you, too.

I. S.   More important perhaps than my father.

N. S.   How so?

I. S.   My mother is a supremely rational person, whereas my father is impulsive. His moods are mercurial. My mother responds to whatever challenge she has ahead of her with extensive research. Only after she knows everything about the problem, every single facet of it, is she ready to act.

N. S.   Has your mother's attitude towards religious Judaism softened over the years? Is she even slightly religious?

I. S.   Not in the traditional sense. Sometime in the late seventies and early eighties, she underwent a profound transformation. She became interested in Martin Buber's form of existentialism, as well as in the philosophy of Franz Rosenzweig, in particular in his book *The Star of Redemption.* That led her to the Hasidic movement of the Ba'al Shem Tov, and from there she became attracted to Kabbalah.

Not from the viewpoint of a scholar like Gershom Scholem. In fact, Scholem's approach makes my mother cringe. She thinks that Scholem emptied the vessel of Kabbalah of all beauty. What attracts her is mysticism, an inner road to the knowledge of the divine.

N. S.   Why does she dislike Scholem?

I. S.   She believes Scholem dissected the Kabbalah the way one dissects a rabbit in a high-school lab. She believes in a Spinozean form of mysticism. This might appear a contradiction in terms, but she is at once a hyperrationalist and a seeker of *union mystica*. With her encouragement, I first read the Zohar and Buber's *Tales of the Hasidim*. It was also through her that I encountered the work of Carlos Castaneda. Castaneda's *The Teachings of Don Juan,* a cult volume in the seventies about mushroom culture in Oaxaca and alternative levels of consciousness, left a deep mark on me. It brought mysticism home.

N. S.   So your learning and love for the Kabbalah were sparked by your mother. . . . Eventually, you studied Kabbalah at the Jewish Theological Seminary [JTS] under the scholar Moshe Idel.

I. S.   My mother introduced me to Buber, Heschel, Rosenzweig, and the medieval ascetic Bahya Ibn Paquda. She gave me books to read. She is the rationalist in the family, although she has a mystical part to her personality too. Although she always functions in society, friends of hers, also inclined toward mysticism, have given up on secular life and have entered a Yeshiva, a monastery, or another sanctuary devoted to contemplation and seclusion. To this day, my mother keeps a volume of the Zohar near her. She also decorates her environment with symbols and paraphernalia from the Kabbalah.

N. S.   Did you ever share with equal intensity her passion for the Kabbalah?

I. S.   I never became a student of Kabbalah in any serious fashion. Moshe Idel was an encyclopedia in motion: his knowledge of the thirteenth-century mystic Abraham Abulafia, of the Zohar, of crucial messianic mystics, was magnificent, but he was an uninspired public speaker and mediocre teacher. Like Hannah Arendt and Walter Benjamin, Scholem was a byproduct of Berlin's *weltanschauung:* he was bookish, cosmopolitan, and ideologically oriented. Idel, in contrast, is an Israeli. His book *Kabbalah: New Perspectives,* published in 1988, shortly after I graduated from JTS, is proof of it. The faculty at JTS organized a symposium on it prior to its release. I remember Idel's participation: engaged yet morose. He had been born in Romania in 1947, just as the Zionist State was about to become created. His perspective fits the Israeli worldview of the generation that came of age in the seventies: self-centered, aloof, arrogant. . . . His opinions on Hasidism are attractive, but he remains a specialist not quite able to branch out to other disciplines of knowledge. At any rate, the mere personal contact with him invigorated me.

N. S.   How old were you when you first read the Zohar?

I. S.   In my early twenties. But it isn't until one turns forty that mystical literature should be tackled in depth, and then only by those about to be initiated. I read the treatise with enormous interest. The first encounter left me numb. I understood a minuscule part of it. But my curiosity peaked and I felt the need to read about it: about Moisés de León, its author, about the book's pseudoepigraphic origins and the rumors that the true author was Rabbi Yohanan ben Zakai.

N. S.   Why isn't your mother more central in *On Borrowed Words*?

I. S.   The memoir is about the quest to find my own individual language. The influence of my mother on my education is palpable not in language but in other ways.

N. S.   What other types of mystical literature did your mother introduce you to?

I. S.   I remember reading Leone Ebreo's *Dialoghi d'Amore,* not a mystical book per se, but one that springs from the tradition. I also read the stories of Rabbi Nakhman of Bratslav and the legends of the Ba'al Shem Tov.

N. S.   Thinking it over, I noticed that your sister Liora doesn't feature prominently in the memoir either. How come she also escaped a starring role? Is this just a matter of extra material being left on the cutting room floor or was the choice deliberate?

I. S.   For the same reason. Liora is five years younger than I. Although we shared much together, my intellectual quest took roads that kept me away from her. Only later, already as adults, did the two of us reconnect.

N. S.   Did you experience anti-Semitism in Mexico? You have answered this question in *On Borrowed Words,* but I want you to elaborate a bit on the topic.

I. S.   Only tangential experiences: verbal attacks, for instance.

N. S.   You've written that your years at the Universidad Autónoma Metropolitana-Xomilico [UAM-X], in the southern section of Mexico City, were a "turning point" ["Unmasking Marcos," *The Riddle of Cantinflas* (1998)]. How so?

I. S.   Having graduated from an all-day Yiddish high school, UAM-X is the environment where I first came in touch with non-Jews. Ours was a radical campus. The faculty was made of left-wing South American—mostly Argentine—exiles and émigrés, as well as native Mexican academics and activists. My class included students who would eventually become prominent photographers, advertising agents, filmmakers, as well as people who joined the Zapatista uprising in Chiapas. The world of politics was new to me. It was at UAM-X that I wholeheartedly experienced Mexico as a fractured, unbalanced society in which I was not only a member, but also a participant and witness.

N. S.   While in Strand Books, I recently stumbled across a slim volume of translated poetry by the Mexican-Yiddish poet Isaac Berliner, entitled *City of Palaces,* illustrated by Diego Rivera. It led me to think about Jewish literary role models. In the early stages of your career, did you have role models in the local Jewish community, whether writing in Yiddish or Spanish? Have you heard of Berliner's book? Was it part of a larger, vibrant subculture of Jewish writing in Mexico City?

I. S.   *City of Palaces* is an intriguing collaboration. Berliner was not an inspired poet, but his sympathies with the oppressed hit inspired notes in the volume. Rivera, it appears, made the engravings as a sign of admiration for his friend.

No, there were no concrete role models in the early eighties. I was acquainted with Esther Seligson and Angelina Muñiz-Huberman, two Mexican writers whose work, linking Jewish and Mexican themes, was eye opening. But neither of them was my kind of writer. My breakthrough in this area was my discovery of Isaac Goldemberg's novel *The Fragmented Life of Don Jacobo Lerner.* I found a copy in a mediocre bookstore, called Librería de Cristal, and read it in a matter of hours. It was proof, at least to me, that one could be Jewish and Latin American and that these two cultures could be explored lucidly through literature. My subsequent admiration, and my quest to find Goldemberg himself, is chronicled in my introduction to the 1998 English edition of the book, released by the University of New Mexico Press. I had a similar reaction when, already in the United States, I encountered the novels of the Brazilian fabulist Moacyr Scliar. As the years went by, both Goldemberg and Scliar became friends.

But let me return to Berliner: he was a proto-model, one I didn't know about until a few years ago. Many of these precursors wrote in Yiddish. I didn't know much about crypto-Jewish authors in Mexico either—such as Luis de Carvajal the Younger—until the mid-nineties, when I made it my duty to explore this period in earnest. I find it perplexing that there is little or no connection whatsoever between Ashkenazic Jews in the Americas today and their colonial counterparts. It is as if the *shtetl* dwellers arrived in a land that had never seen Jews before, which, as you know, is not the case.

N. S.   Before we go any further, how much privacy did you forfeit in your autobiography, *On Borrowed Words?*

I. S.   Every autobiography is an act of betrayal. I don't mean this in regards to one's own family and friends; they too are betrayed, of course. After all, memory is a most fragile, malleable human faculty. The act of betrayal, really, is against oneself. When I saw the early copy of *On Borrowed Words* in my mailbox, I thought: "I have become a book." And then: "But is this the book I was destined to become?"

N. S.   Autobiographies can drag family and friends into the spotlight. What was your family's reaction to *On Borrowed Words?* In the *New York Times,* the reviewer said you were "often unsparingly critical" of your brother and father. Did they view the memoir as too revealing?

I. S.   For months I feared their reactions. A writer's family, to safeguard sanity, learns to read the writer without reading him. The portraits I offer of my father and brother were shaped by love—wounded love, no doubt, but love nonetheless. In the end, these portraits, I'm convinced, are more about my own shortcomings than about theirs.

N. S.   Did you need permission from your family to be frank and so honest?

I. S.   No one should need to request such permission.

N. S.   But people are susceptible. . . .

I. S.   Literature is about truth. I wanted the chapter entitled "On My

Brother's Trail," about my brother Darián, to be less his history than my own history as his brother. In any case, if he ever drafts his own version, it would probably look as if I'm from Mars and he is from Venus.

N. S.   This discussion reminds me of a legendary story involving the German poet Heinrich Heine's perpetual need of money. Once, while flat-out broke, he apparently threatened his family and relatives with including them in his nonfiction work and memoirs, unless they paid him a tidy fee.

Anyway, talk to me more about your political apprenticeship. . . .

I. S.   Essentially, I still hold on to an ideological viewpoint not too different from the one I first developed in those years. My elite education had built a bubble in which I and those around me lived. UAM-X was a revelation. It is impossible to come from Mexico and not recognize, as an intellectual voice, the discrepancies in the milieu. One would need to be either dumb or blind. My arrival the United States in 1985 only confirmed those beliefs, for I came at a time when the Latino community was—unfortunately, to a large extent it still is, although there is a growing Hispanic middle class that holds the key to a better future—at the bottom of the social pyramid.

In the early eighties I was looking for ways to leave Mexico. After fruitless attempts to settle in Spain and Israel, I came to the conclusion that the best—the only—place for me was New York City. My mother's interest in Franz Rosenzweig, Buber, and Heschel led me to study Jewish philosophy and thought more earnestly. At the suggestion of a teacher of mine from Argentina, I wrote essays on Rosenzweig and the medieval ascetic Bahya ibn Paquda. My teacher suggested that I pursue my studies at JTS and sent one of my essays to a colleague of his there. The result was a scholarship that allowed me to leave Mexico.

The institution had two schools: a rabbinical one and a graduate one. I enrolled in the latter. The academic standards were loose, mainly as a result of the poor quality of students from the rabbinical school, who were in the majority and whose presence was ubiquitous. But I keep very fond memories of the place because it allowed me to embark on a journey of self-discovery. I spent endless hours in the library, reading everything I could find, from the Zohar to Spanish and Hebrew poetry. I wasn't interested in faith but in the intellectual history of ideas that shaped the Jewish people from rabbinical times to the present. I studied under a couple of luminaries—Moshe Idel, among them.

Socially the place was filled with awkward, maladjusted people looking for answers to their existential questions. American Judaism at the time was undergoing a profound transformation: coping with feminism, with interfaith marriages, with an increasing ideological polarization of the Jewish community, with black-Jewish relations, and the out-of-hand situation in the Middle East. In retrospect, my years at JTS were perhaps the most exciting in terms of learning deeply and widely. I guess I became an "outsider at home" there, as a roommate of mine used to say.

For a while I dreamed of making *aliyah* and in the mid-1980s I sold my belongings and tried to fulfill my dream. But Israel wasn't for me: it was too political a place. Jews in it were not a minority and I quickly realized that, in spite my ambiguity toward Mexico, I enjoyed then—and I enjoy now—being in the minority.

The Israel I came across in the late seventies and early eighties was a postcard Promised Land made of sunsets at the Damascus gate, old Arabs on donkeys, the peaceful waters of Lake Kinneret, and soldiers dwelling on the Wailing Wall—in short, a hallucination. The tension between Israelis and Palestinians was constantly underplayed. Hatred was lurking underneath, of course.

N. S. Instead of an *aliyah,* though, you chose to move to New York. Why did you choose Columbia University to pursue a doctorate?

I. S. I wanted to stay in Manhattan. Upon arrival, I worked as a journalist, sending dispatches for a couple of Mexican dailies: *La Jornada* and *Excélsior.* But I wanted to solidify my legal status and graduate school was the easy path to achieve the objective. JTS wasn't an option, since I didn't see myself in Jewish Studies per se, since the discipline had a normative American perspective that I lacked. Hispanic culture attracted me: I knew it inside out. I also felt there was much to be done in this area, where faculty seemed invariably parochial. NYU was an option, since I was offered a scholarship to attend. But I preferred the Upper West Side. I felt more akin to Morningside Heights.

N. S.   You've described your journey as a student in Columbia's Spanish Department—also known as *Casa Hispánica*—in the essay "A Critic's Journey" [*Chronicle of Higher Education* (9 August 2002)].

I. S.   It was a suffocating, erratic place. The professors appeared to me to be from another planet. They were Chileans, Argentines, and Spanish-speaking Americans with a stilted vision of Hispanic civilization. Some felt contempt for the United States. The academic trifles constantly overwhelmed the place. Absolutely no connection with the Caribbean immigrant life that populated the streets of Harlem was ever established. What mattered was a dead Iberian culture invariably described as the Golden Age (Lope de Vega y Carpio, Cervantes, Luis de Góngora y Argote, Francisco de Quevedo y Villegas) and nineteenth- and twentieth-century south-of-the-border figures studied in isolation, without connection to the *fin de sèecle* in which we all, students and teachers, were actors. I invariably left the classroom dissatisfied.

N. S.   Early on in *On Borrowed Words* you write that when your grandmother, Bela Stavchansky, was in "distress," she returned to her "homeland," e.g., her first tongue. Did you frequently return to your "homeland" for refuge while in New York?

I. S.   At Columbia I lived a disassociated life: I was bilingual, bicultural, binational. . . . I continued to write in Spanish for *Excélsior* in Mexico, and *Diario 16* in Spain, and *El Nacional* in Venezuela, as well as for a handful of other American newspapers, including *El Diario/La Prensa* in Manhattan. I published reviews, essays and stories under my own name, but I used a number of different pseudonyms, too. I also began to write in English for the *New York Times Book Review*. In those years I got married, and soon after had my first child. Since the beginning I used Spanish and English—and eventually Spanglish—at home.

N. S.   In my research, I found your literary outpouring in those early days in New York City to be prolific. I found material under the pseudonyms of Zuri Balkoff, Nino Ricssar and Melquíades Sánchez. I'm sure there is more than meets the eye.

I. S.   It was a period of intense experimentation for me.

N. S.   Balkoff is an *alter ego* for you. In fact, in its Mexican edition, your novella *Talia y el cielo* [1989] was co-written by Zuri Balkoff and Ilan

Stavans. The book has a prologue by the Guatemalan Alcina Lubitch Domecq. When did the idea for Zuri Balkoff come about?

I. S.   I first used the pseudonym in an essay I wrote in Spanish, for a magazine called *Aquí estamos,* sponsored by the Mexican Jewish community. Hiding behind pseudonyms and *noms de plume* and *de guerre* is a device that is appealing to some, perhaps because I feel that our own name is also, in some way, arbitrary, e.g., an accident of life. In fact, I reviewed work of mine, sometimes critically, under a pseudonym. Anyway, "Talia in Heaven" is about a Canadian Jewish woman who travels to an imaginary Latin American country where she falls in love with a bipolar Hispanic Jew: the two extremes of the male protagonist are represented by Balkoff and Stavans. In order to make the fictional account tangible, the two sides of my self needed to have a role as authors. [*Laughter.*]

N. S.   Why hide behind a pseudonym?

I. S.   It is not always about hiding, but about letting parts of your mind free. Fernando Pessoa described his multiple personalities as "heteronyms": Ricardo Reis, Alberto Caeiro, Alexander Search, and Alvaro de Campo. Each has an individualized personality. Each holds a secret to the mystery of Pessoa's overall identity. In some sense, mine were also heteronyms. Zuri Balkoff is far more ideologically radical, more clamorous, than I am. For several years, I published in the Mexican newspaper *La Jornada* a number of literary pieces (reportage, essays, reviews) marked by their political syncopation under the *nom de guerre* of Zuri Balkoff. At the same time, I contributed to other newspapers with my own name or with other pseudonyms.

Over the years, I've also developed a female pseudonym that allows me to explore feminine sides of my self.

N. S.   Can I ask you what that pseudonym is?

I. S.   I'd rather keep it secret.

N. S.   The *New York Times* profiled you in November 13, 1999. They mention a couple of detective novels you've published, also under pseudonyms.

I. S.   True.

N. S.   Do you want to say more about them?

I. S.   Not really.

N. S.   Speaking of detective fiction, your doctoral dissertation at

Columbia University was *Antiheroes: Mexico and Its Detective Novel* [1990]. This is a genre not particularly well liked by some highbrow literati. Edmund Wilson, as you know, detested it.

I. S.   Borges and Nabokov knew much about detective fiction, to the extent of altogether renewing the genre made famous by Edgar Allan Poe and Arthur Conan Doyle and later on Dashiell Hammett and Raymond Chandler. Wilson, on the other hand, was a snob, as is evident in his infamous essay "Who Cares Who Killed Roger Ackroyd?" In any case, what I most enjoy about detective novels isn't the clockwork as much as the ethics—the extent to which these artifacts are an expression of the tension between civilization and barbarism, between order and chaos.

N. S.   There are scores of international authors articulate in more than one tongue: Vladimir Nabokov, Samuel Beckett, and Joseph Conrad come to mind. The critic Steven G. Kellman describes these literary artists as possessing "a translingual imagination." They inhabit two or more universes. . . .

I. S.   On the other hand, there are those, of course, who claim that no one is able to fully express his mind in a language other than the mother tongue.

N. S.   It isn't your case, obviously.

I. S.   Well, I tend to think of the authors you've listed as owners of two minds. A bilingual, I once was told, is really two monolinguals stuck at the neck.

N. S.   Do you like that definition?

I. S.   It is false. A bilingual has only one mind, which manifests itself through different shades.

N. S.   Shades. . . .

I. S.   When I speak in English, I'm aware of facial and body gestures that are different from those activated when I speak Spanish, Yiddish, and Hebrew. Just like an actor: depending on the language, a slightly different personality emerges. . . .

N. S.   Even when that language is not oral but written.

I. S.   Sure. I have a foreign accent in the written page as well. As for my oral skills, these days I have an accent in Spanish too. The translingual journey has pushed me to the abyss: I no longer know which is my first, second, and third tongues. . . . They have equal value for me. I use them as the context dictates. In writing, of course, one is able to "shape" sentences with a patience and care.

No other item in the universe holds my attention more steadily than books. I open them to make sense, to reflect on the time in which I live, to escape from my milieu. . . . I find the gallery of words that is a language extraordinarily attractive: I want to know their origin, their conflicting meanings, and the potential they have to express an idea. I don't know what comes first, language or thought; I do know, though, that, as the saying goes: I only know what I mean when I see what I say. . . .

N. S.   In the early stages of your career you worked in theater and screenwriting. Do you intend to return to either medium?

I. S.   I still nurture a love for theater, although from the dramatic perspective only. In the last few years I've been very curious about TV and have begun to work on a documentary series and perhaps on ways to make room for ideas on the small screen. As for cinema, I would like to make a film or two one day. I've been at work on a screenplay based on a story of mine, *El Ultimo*. It is an examination of family life during the seven days of shiva after a Mexican Jewish patriarch passes away. As I mature, I grow more convinced that as a public intellectual it is my duty to explore various forums, not only the printed word.

N. S.   You wrote a musical in 1979 entitled *Genesis 2000*. Musicals seem so different from your writing now. What motivated this side of your creative oeuvre? Is it a biblical pageant for the new millennium? In 1992 an off-Broadway theater performed your one-act play, *Vals triste*. Can you talk to me about your experiences in writing for the stage?

I. S.   *Genesis 2000* is a piece of juvenilia. It was written in Yiddish and it was the first work of mine ever reviewed—also in Yiddish. It was a parable inspired by Saint-Exupéry's *The Little Prince*. I wrote it, I guess, because my father was in theater and I daydreamed of gaining his admiration. Soon after I wrote another play, *Mujeres*, about three women of various ages who, the public finds out at the end, are one and the same. Then came *Vals triste:* it is a monologue my father commissioned—an adaptation of a novel by the German author Patrick Süskind, responsible for *Perfume*. It was performed by him across Mexico, in the United States, and, if I am correct, in Central America as well.

I have always felt close to theater and I find actors fascinating people. But I also feel ambivalent toward them. This ambivalence, no doubt, finds its source in the figure of my father. .

N. S.   In the essay, "The First Book," you also talk, to a lesser extent, about literature as a parallel world—a "Leibnitizan cosmos."

I. S.   From my childhood I remember a book entitled *Un automóvil llamado Julia,* about a pair of siblings who buy an old car and fix it up in a neighbor's shed. I also remember a volume called *El soldadito de plomo.* That was, I think, the first full-length picture book I read fully on my own.

In the seventies and early eighties I admired the adventure novels of Jules Verne and Emilio Salgari. Later on I was mesmerized with *The Hunchback of Notre Dame*—which my mother had in an edition she herself had sent to a special binder—and Tolstoy's *War and Peace* and *Anna Karenina.* This was the period in which I discovered the Russian novelists. Along with Tolstoy came Dostoevsky and Turgenev. I remember discovering their oeuvre and in no time at all reading everything by them that I could put my hands on. Chekhov, whom my father adored, also became a favorite. I find most of his short stories to be veritable gems. [*Laughter.*]

I read far and wide in those years: I remember, for instance, the impact that Faulkner's *As I Lay Dying* and *Light in August* had on me. I was just simply hypnotized by them. Faulkner, to me, has accomplished something miraculous: he has twisted language in order to penetrate, without reservations, the mind of simple-minded people in the Deep South. I also encountered Hemingway, for whom I had less of a disposition. I found him overpraised: a writer desperately trying to impress me as a reader.

It was only after I read the Russians and the U.S. authors that I came to the Latin American ones: Borges, Gabriel García Márquez, Julio Cortázar, and Mario Vargas Llosa. . . . But that was already toward the mid-eighties.

N. S.   What about science? Do you think that to be a complete writer that it is important to be scientifically or mathematically literate and understand the basic physical principles of the universe: our genetics, our cosmology, and our evolution?

I. S.   I haven't been a reader of too many scientific volumes. I've read

Darwin voraciously and find him an alluring author. A. R. Luria, the Russian psychologist responsible for *The Mind of a Mnemonist* and *The Man with a Shattered World,* whom Oliver Sacks took as his model, is superb. Sigmund Freud, of course, whose case studies are veritable literary gems. And Stephen Jay Gould, at his most relaxed, was the owner of an engaging style. I've also read *The Double Helix* and the polemical *Two Cultures* by C. P. Snow. Sacks himself I love. How many times have I reread *The Man Who Mistook His Wife for a Hat, Awakenings, A Leg to Stand On,* and *The Island of the Color-blind*? I visited Sacks in the mid-eighties at his home in Fire Island, before he began contributing to the *New Yorker.* It was a period in which he still indulged in essays decorated with copious footnotes, thus maintaining a dialogue with himself within the essay. Our conversation was memorable. We talked about Darwin and the shaping of *The Origin of Species,* about Aldous Huxley's experiments with mushrooms, about Borges and Luria. That dialogue continued in the form of correspondence for some time.

I understand little by way of science. . . . I sit at Amherst College sometimes at the same table with colleagues in economics, chemistry, and biology. I could invoke a dictionary definition of what an atom is, or even a microchip, but I could not really explain to you what they are. Sometimes working my VCR or my tape recorder, it's a trip for me that becomes a nightmare. Technology I know how to handle, because I kind of teach myself, force myself to understand the commands of the word processor; but I have no idea how a telephone works, how e-mail makes my message appear instantaneously somewhere else, how a mere light bulb works.

On the other hand, I have deep admiration for doctors such as Anton Chekhov, Somerset Maugham, Arthur Conan Doyle, William Carlos Williams. . . . I find compassion and humanity in their oeuvre. I don't see a description of what a molecule or antibiotics are or how the body reacts when one has gonorrhea, or when the character has gonorrhea, in very scientific language. Unquestionably the most appealing of all scientists in terms of his storytelling talents is Sigmund Freud. I find his theories uninteresting but his narrative style hypnotic. Something similar happens with Oliver Sacks: while reading *The Man Who Mistook His Wife for a Hat,* you're likely to forget that it is a compilation of case studies that you have in hand. Of course, on occasion a certain encyclopedic book—*The Sleepwalkers* by Hermann Broch or *The Man without Qualities* by Robert Musil—gives the author free range to dump in every bit of available knowledge about a particular topic at his reach. Usually this results in excesses that overwhelm my attention. Another such instance is *Palinuro of Mexico* by Fernando del Paso, in which the homonymous protagonist is a doctor-in-training. This facet of the protagonist becomes the excuse for all sorts of disquisitions on the history and practice of medicine.

N. S.   Sherwin Nuland said that for doctor-writers "their words are a natural extension of their healing." In rereading *The Collected Stories of Moacyr Scliar* [2000], I came across somewhat similar descriptions of the body, certain subtle mannerisms and flourishes that give away his training as a physician.

I. S.   In Scliar's work, these descriptions never upstage the narrative. They can be an invitation to take a microscopic trip into the body or a certain reaction that one has to the elements. And that can only come by profession. The same thing happens with law, with legal writers who would include all sorts of references to codes and rejoinders within the judicial system.

N. S.   Let me return to the topic of names. Your full name is Ilan Stavchansky Slomianski. When did you decide to shorten your name to Stavans? Why did you do it? Do people perceive the surname Stavans as Jewish? Was changing your name part of a social trend, much like Bashevis Singer and other Jewish writers who Americanized their names in the United States?

I. S.   My father uses Stavans when he acts on the professional stage, although his passport still says Stavchansky. He did it, he told me, because nobody in the Mexican theatrical circles was able to pronounce his actual patronymic. His older brother, my uncle, Tío Isaac, did change his last name officially to Stavans when he committed himself to a career in painting. My brother, a musician, uses Stavans too. In my case, it was simply an endorsement of family policy. My wife, Alison, thoroughly dislikes Stavans: she finds it unappealing, insipid. She claims Stavchansky is far better as a literary name: one can write epic novels with a last name like that, she says. What am I to do? I've grown accustomed to Stavans. Besides, I'm not the type of writer who can produce an epic novel. Although, it is true, Stavans sounds like the name of a minimalist author, and I am not that either.

N. S.   You're miraculously prolific. By age forty, you had authored and edited published works at an astounding rate. How have you stayed motivated?

I. S.   In my case, it isn't a question of motivation. In a twenty-four hour period, I find myself overwhelmed with ideas: book reviews, stories, essays. . . . It is a question of time: How can I make good use of my hours to allow for these ideas to flourish and not annihilate one another and then bury me with exhaustion? Happily, I am most productive when saturated with deadlines: the more, the better. . . . Also, I write better when I'm exhausted.

N. S.   Why?

I. S.   Ideas appear to flow freer then.

N. S.   Tell me about your personal habits when it comes to writing. . . .

I. S.   I have a rigorous routine: when the family is around, I don't work; I do find myself thinking about an essay or story while at dinner, but I try to escape those temptations. No sooner are the kids on the bus, though, than I'm hooked to the computer. When I'm not teaching, my working day then goes from 8:30 AM to about 1 PM. After that, my free time is spent in reading and writing letters for a couple of hours. At night I read again for several hours, and if a deadline is upon me, then I finish the piece that is due. But very seldom do I steal hours from sleep. My habit is to go to bed at 11 PM and wake up at 6 PM, jog for an hour, and then prepare the kids for school. When I'm teaching, then I devote my free time to correspondence and to prepare for the classroom.

N. S.   Do you keep books nearby when you write?

I. S.   My office is on the third floor of our house. It has windows and tons of books. I write alone, without music. No talismans are needed—unless you count the books as such. Indeed, I've tried to write in empty rooms and I find myself empty too. For me writing and reading go hand in hand. My advice to young writers is simple: read, read, read. . . . Or better: read and envy the authors you most admire. [*Laughter.*]

N. S.   Do you read surrounded by books, too?

I. S.   I do, indeed. I'm of the opinion that literature is a most elitist activity. It is made by the few for the few. The books that matter are
often read by only a handful of people, at least initially. How many
readers did Whitman's *Leaves of Grass* have? Not many. . . . This is
particularly true in poetry, but it also occurs in fiction and even nonfiction. Kafka, Bruno Schulz, Elias Canetti are the property of a
small cadre of initiated readers. In the United States, driven as we are
by the democratic spirit, the objective is to make everything for
everyone. But literature was never for the masses. It could entertain
with serialized novels and pamphleteering treatises, but the literature
that survives might often be ignored in its own time. When I'm told
about the decline of readers in our age, I always reply "but the decline has been going on for centuries."

N. S.   Have you ever composed poetry?

I. S.   In Mexico in the early eighties, I published a handful of Byzantine
poems in the tradition of Lope de Vega and Quevedo. These exercises were utterly anachronistic. They should remain forgotten
forever.

N. S.   Your students say that you know a vast amount of poetry by heart.

I. S.   Not much. A handful of poems by Góngora, Quevedo, Sor Juana
Inés de la Cruz, Rubén Darío, Neruda. . . .

N. S.   And I hear that you also memorized large portions of Spanish
prose, too.

I. S.   Again, not much: several stories by Borges, Cortázar, and Au-
gusto Monterroso, fragments by Domingo Faustino Sarmiento and
Gabriel García Márquez, a handful of pages from *The Labyrinth of
Solitude*. . . .

N. S.   I've also read some children's riddles — in bilingual format — that
you've done in recent years. I understand you wrote approximately
two dozen for a folklore volume in celebration of the Mexican bingo
game *¡Lotería!* Might I persuade you to recite one or two of them?

I. S.   This one is a riddle about *El Torito,* the little bull:

Con cuernos elude,	With horns it defies,
al torero sacude.	a bullfighter's sighs.
Nada lo asusta,	It finds nothing scary,
la vaca lo busca.	the cow it will marry.
¿Qué es?	What is it?

24

Another one to *Las Estrellas,* the stars in the firmament:

De noche dedican	They sprinkle with light
la luz que salpican.	the infinite night.
Si sigues su tino,	Follow them straight,
verás tu destino.	to find your own fate.
¿Qué son?	What are they?

And one more to *La Calavera,* the character of the skull that is ubiquitous in the *Día de los Muertos:*

Que el mundo se ría,	The end might be scary.
cabeza sin guía.	Take one and be merry. . . .
Los dientes corrompes,	Don't laugh at Death's jest.
de un golpe te rompes.	Remember: you're next.
¿Qué es?	What is it?

N. S.   Cervantes is a role model for you.

I. S.   He is among my favorite authors, alongside Flaubert and Sholem Aleichem. I've reread *Don Quixote, Madame Bovary,* and *Tevye the Dairyman* so many times, I know entire portions by heart. Borges is also part of this list. In nonfiction, my idol is Edmund Wilson, whose entire oeuvre I've been collecting for years. One day I want to write a eulogy for Wilson—a eulogy in the form of a reflective essay. I did that not long ago in *Octavio Paz: A Meditation* [2001]. Paz had played a formative role in my career as an essayist. I've read his books since my early twenties. Wilson, on the other hand, is an acquired taste: I came across him in my mid-thirties. . . . His intellectual odyssey I find immensely gratifying, though. He is a metronome through which one is able to understand the ups and downs of almost the entire twentieth century.

N. S.   When did you first read *Don Quixote?*

I. S.   I don't remember finding the humor the first time around. It must have been the late seventies. Somehow, I have an early vivid memory of Gustave Doré's illustrations, included in a deluxe edition a Russian friend of mine had given me along with a copy of Dante's *Divine Comedy.* I still have these volumes. I remember browsing through the *Quixote* alone in my room late one afternoon and reacting negatively to the gothic images: they had a macabre, supernatural quality to them, more akin to Poe than to Cervantes. Then I read the book, quite slowly, and was hypnotized by its rhythm, but the images made me feel as if I had entered a forbidden universe.

In time, I've collected editions of Cervantes's masterpiece in various languages: thirteen different full English renditions, dozens of Spanish versions, as well as variations of different kinds: straight translations made, for example, in the Elizabethan, Victorian, modern and postmodern ages, also, children's books, critical editions, etc. I also have at home French, Portuguese, and Hebrew translations, and I have in the original *The Travels of Benjamin the Third,* the parody that Sh. Y. Abramovitsh, the so-called grandfather of Yiddish letters, made of the *Quixote.* I once put together, as a present to a group of friends, a small anthology that includes some hundred illustrations of *Don Quixote* by scores of artists, such as Salvador Dalí and Doré.

N. S.   It evolved into a special issue of the magazine *Hopscotch* [fall 2001].

I. S.   True.

N. S.   You've been involved in widely publicized polemics on the theatrical approach to Latino identity as well as on the fate of American Judaism, Sandra Cisneros, Spanglish, Octavio Paz, etc. In an interview with Dan Cryer in *Newsday* [8 August 2001], you stated that "I don't think the role of the intellectual is to please. . . .Controversy is very positive. Polemics are crucial. Democracy survives precisely because we can debate and we can be controversial."

I. S.   Ongoing, modulated dialogue is crucial. Voltaire once said: "I disapprove of what you say, but I will defend to the death your right to say it."

N. S.   Have you enjoyed the polemics in which you've been involved over the years, especially the one on the fate of *la hispanidad* in the United States?

I. S.   Each and every aspect of them. [*Laughter.*]

N. S.   Do you read reviews of your books?

I. S.   No, I don't.

N. S.   I want to talk about your initiation as writer. Can you pinpoint the exact moment you absolutely knew you wanted to become one?

I. S.   I enjoyed composition class in middle school—especially the morning a teacher of mine praised a story I had submitted for that week's assignment. I forget the exact content of the story, but it included a reference to the Mexican anthem and also a passing scene in a cemetery. I also remember submitting, for another class, perhaps when I was thirteen or fourteen years old, an impressionistic essay about the journey of a number—any digit, say 597—as it travels *within* a calculator from one command to another. The teacher thought the piece was ingenious and suggested that I might want to devote more time to literature.

But I wasn't an avid reader in my childhood and adolescence. Instead, I always longed for outdoor activities. It wasn't until my late teens and early twenties that I began to read in earnest. To me reading is the precondition for writing. It must have been somewhere along those years that I began to dream of becoming an author and writing the type of books that I enjoyed, which in those years were novels and travel essays.

Add to all this the fact that my mother frequently said—invoking the Talmud—that any Jew has three duties on this earth: to plant a tree, to have a child, and to write a book.

N. S.   Was this type of career choice favored within your family?

I. S.   As an actor, my father has struggled against the will of his family, which stood steadfast against the idea that acting is a venerable career. My paternal grandmother used to make his life miserable way into my father's adulthood. In fact, in my adolescence I remember her asking me, in private, if my father was capable of supporting us—a strange comment to be said to a grandchild, no doubt. The effect was that I knew, and my siblings did too, that she never had faith in him as an artist. Even when he became successful, with TV shows and regular theater seasons, she still wondered if he was suitable enough to have a stable family. My father, of course, would make fun of her in the open: to have embraced his aspiration of acting was in and of itself a triumph for him.

N. S.   Did you experience pressure to go into a more conventional, stable occupation often associated with Jews, such as doctor, lawyer, or merchant?

I. S.   I did. . . . When time came for me to choose a career, my father's struggles became a lesson. He was sympathetic, and so was my mother. I didn't have to fight the same battle. But my father did establish a limit for me: when I told him I wanted to become a writer, he said we had to write a contract between us. In the contract I would promise to finish a BA degree so that, should my writing not allow me to support my family and myself, I would always have an alternative. And indeed, I finished a bachelor's in psychology, in large part to fulfill the contractual requirements we set for ourselves. I can't tell you if he actually drafted a contract: I don't have a solid memory of the piece of paper itself. But I do remember, without any doubt, that we made a formal agreement.

I thank my father for that prerequisite. I've never practiced as a psychologist, but the undergraduate studies I embarked on were enlightening. And I've always taken a similar road when approaching a decisive choice: I want to leave myself an alternative door open.

N. S.   Did your experiences as a journalist have an influence on you?

I. S.   There is no better school, I believe. Journalism teaches you to compress sentences, to be straightforward and persuasive, and to make up your own mind about the world at large. Also, it teaches the power of words: journalists are chroniclers of the present. Plus, in Latin America, as much as one desires to be objective, subjectivity always gets in the way. When I was young, people in Mexico knew that the media delivered only the official story. Truth, spelled with a capital "T," was always beyond TV screens and newspaper pages. Then again, much that is purposefully untruthful is channeled through the media. An example: in *La Jornada,* at times I reviewed nonexistent films and books. Press time was upon us and the pages needed to be filled.

N. S.   You have shifted gears from writing fiction, which you showcased early on in your career with *The One-Handed Pianist and Other Stories* [1996], to writing nonfiction, such as the memoir *On Borrowed Words.* You have lived in the United States sixteen or seventeen years. How has life north of the Rio Grande impacted your writing? Has your writing gone from "resisting the confessional mode" to fully embracing it?

I. S.   *On Borrowed Words* refuses to be straightforward autobiography. It doesn't follow a chronological format. In terms of verb tenses, all chapters begin in the present, quickly go back to the past, only to return again to the present tense in the end. And the focus is language per se, not events in life. For instance, in chapter 2, "The Rise and

Fall of Yiddish," I reflect on the existential and linguistic odyssey of my grandmother Bela Stavchansky. As soon as she found out that I would write a memoir, she wrote down her own forty-page-long autobiography and sent it to me. "This is what you are allowed to say about me, Ilan," she said in a note. Aside from her intransigence, it puzzled me that she had written her narrative, not in her mother tongue, Yiddish, but in Spanish. The answer is clear: her choice of language determined the readers she wanted to reach. She chose Spanish instead of Yiddish not only for me but for my children to be able to understand her. Was she a traitor to her own tongue? Likewise, I chose English—not Yiddish, not Spanish, not Hebrew—to be accessible to my present readers, who constitute the universe in which I find myself today. But am I a traitor too?

N. S.   The stories in *The One-Handed Pianist and Other Stories* were principally written between 1989 and 1994. *Talia y el cielo* ["Talia in Heaven"] was first drafted in the late seventies. In the latter half of the nineties you seem to have lost interest or become increasingly less involved in your own fiction. . . .

I. S.   I always wanted to be a novelist. Not an essayist, not an autobiographer, but a novelist. . . . In my early twenties, my idols were Vargas Llosa and García Márquez, whose reputations were a result of their talent in fiction. I always wanted to sit down and write novels. Instead, in adulthood I find myself allured by the essay. But I haven't given up on fiction altogether. I've published a couple more than a dozen stories and a novella under my own name. And I've made a commitment—to myself, to my publisher—to finish a novel soon. [*Laughter.*]

2

The Uses
of Catastrophe

N. S.   In the "Letter to a German Friend" [*Art and Anger*], you recount how you explored your family roots, Jewish memory, and mythology, while on honeymoon in Poland and Czechoslovakia. You and your wife visited Kafka's Prague and several former concentration camps sites. What kind of preconceptions on those subjects did you carry with you to Europe?

I. S.   It was 1988 and I was looking for my roots in the Old Continent— the path various ancestors had taken from Lithuania, the Ukraine, and Poland across the Atlantic Ocean. Alison was also in search of her family past in Czechoslovakia. We visited Auschwitz and Birkenau, too. By that time, American Jews were already at the peak of their genealogical fever to find the *shtetl* at all costs.

In Prague I visited Kafka's gymnasium and the various sites where he and his family lived. The allure of the place also involved Rabbi Judah Loew, known as the Maharal, and his famous Golem. Besides the Old Jewish Quarter, the Jewish cemetery is a tourist attraction. It is there that the Maharal is buried. Hundreds of devotees visit his tomb annually, placing pebbles and scribbled messages on the surface—to him and to G-d. I intended to write one but wasn't able to find a piece of paper. So I decided to draft it on the back of a business card, which I took from my wallet. Shortly after doing it, I felt guilty: a business card? Is there anything more Jewish?

Months later, already back home, I received a personal letter from a youngster in East Germany, which at the time was still under Communism. He had been wandering around the Jewish cemetery and found my message. He asked me: what does a Jew at the end of the twentieth century say to G-d after the Holocaust? In retrospect, that, in and of itself, was the crowning moment of our journey: a non-Jewish German intercepting a Jewish message to the divine.

N. S.   Did you consider the message to be private—your own communication with G-d? Or did you leave it behind believing that the message was both private and public at the same time?

I. S.   I guess it wasn't a fully private endeavor. I remember sticking the paper deeply in between the stones of the tomb. I've done something similar—though not with a business card—in Jerusalem, at the Western Wall.

N. S.   What interests me is the fact that there was a two-sided epistolary exchange, although the recipient is not necessarily the one you originally intended. Up until the medieval ages, the epistolary genre was considered a public affair.

I. S.   There are multiple exchanges, the most famous among them being the tormented one between Abelard and Eloise. In any case, *me sentí traicionado*—I felt betrayed. In retrospect, *betrayal* strikes me as a strong word, although the German youngster did intercept my communication with the divine.

N. S.   In what language did you write your message to G-d?

I. S.   I don't remember. . . . Was it in Yiddish? No, I believe I wrote it in English. Alison was next to me and I have the vague recollection that, although I was the one that put pen to paper, it was a joint letter. By contacting me, the youngster was manifesting his curiosity. It was a gesture of compassion, understanding, and solidarity. Upon receiving it, my reaction was of disbelief, even shock.

N. S.   You wrote him back. . . .

I. S.   I wrote to him in English, the language he had chosen for his correspondence. The exchange went on for some time. Eventually, I breached the tacit contract that existed between us and published my original letter. At that point, the bizarre friendship became public.

Cynthia Ozick wrote a letter about my letter, in which she described how offended she was at the fact that I would engage in dialogue with a second- or third-generation German. In her mind, Jews should have minimal contact with the descendants of their victimizers. That is why she'll never agree to visit Germany.

N. S.   Where was the exchange published?

I. S.   In *Midstream*.

N. S.   Do you feel that the epistolary art is in decline?

I. S.   The genre of correspondence goes beyond the usual how-do-you-do. It has become a standard narrative device. Think of *The Guide for the Perplexed* by Rabbi Moshe ben Maimon, known in Latin as Maimonides and in Hebrew by the acronym Rambam. It was shaped as a letter to a perplexed former student of his, Joseph ben Judah. Maimonides also communicated through correspondence with the Jews of Yemen and Morocco, about such topics as *Kiddush Hashem* (e.g., suicide in the name of G-d). Happily, through his letters he opened up a window to his mind the future would otherwise not have available.

Is the age of correspondence gone? No, I believe it to be more emphatic today than ever. Personally, I have been using e-mail for about a decade and can't conceive of my life today without it. To think about my life a decade ago is to think of an impoverished period. If each e-mail is a letter—sometimes I have trouble using the word "letter" for an e-mail even though electronic mail is exactly that: an electronic message—but if an e-mail is a letter, then I must write forty, fifty, sometimes sixty letters a day, with a length that varies from a single line to dozens of paragraphs. The single line is often an immediate, instantaneous reaction. The longer, essayistic correspondence allows me a full openness in front of others in which I might reflect on my circumstances. We have many more letter writers than ever before, but letters don't survive. Letters disappear as fast as we send them out. And very few people save them. I save correspondence, I save e-mails. I don't save all the e-mails that I get, but I save some of them and print them out, and sometimes need to go back to them. Because for me, it's a statement of where you've been and who you were before you become the person that you are today. And also, the carelessness with which people use e-mail today, in syntactical and grammatical terms, is obvious and has been repeated a thousand times. It has many drawbacks. People don't use capitals anymore, people use "emoticons," e.g., the dwarfish signs that look like inverted faces. Exclamations are overused, too. At the end of a sentence you might have ten exclamation marks. Not to say a word about typos, misspellings, and so on. Conversely, it is safe to say that e-mail has liberated people from the rigidity of syntax. . . .

N. S.   We won't have books about correspondence like those between Walter Benjamin and Gershom Scholem, Hannah Arendt and Heinrich Blücher, Paul Celan and Nelly Sachs?

I. S.   Not at the same level. Those were full-blown letters sent out by postal service. They were carefully prepared, in most cases at least. They would take two weeks to a month to reach the addressee, who would in turn take one or two weeks to answer and then send it back. You would see the difference of styles, there would be a degree of separation between the sending and the receiving of the letter and the process that one takes to meditate on what content to include. Today, e-mail correspondence is automatic. One gets an e-mail and through the reply digit, one answers quickly. We might have, in the future, some correspondence that was saved in e-mail form by some savvy person, who has a librarian or an archivist's soul, but not as many as before. And also, I think the pleasure of reading them will be very different. It isn't a beautiful experience, not to the degree that it used to be. There are letters by Paul Celan, for instance, that you mentioned, or by Benjamin. The letters that Benjamin sent to Adorno, Scholem, and Brecht are revealing. By offering us personal information that serves as context, they enable us to map out his *Arcades Project* and essays such as "The Task of the Translator" and "Art in the Age of Mechanical Reproduction."

N. S.   You've engaged in electronic dialogues that serve an equal function. Take, for instance, the discussion on anthologies published in the *Forward* [30 October 1998], upon the release of *The Oxford Book of Jewish Short Stories* [1998]. Indeed, I've read transcripts of interviews with Blake Eskin, Melvin Jules Bukiet, Leila Ahmed, Anita Desai, Caryl Phillips, and Morris Dickstein that you've participated in. How does that differ from the kind of exchange we are having now?

I. S.   In cases where e-mails have been printed, obviously there has been a care and concentration in the preparation of those e-mails. That is unlike any or most other e-mails that one sends a day—one knew that the target was a printed page and that one needed to be more concerned, more dedicated, that sentences needed to be more stylized, and so on. I believe e-mail has a key to certain chambers of the mind that you don't have when you have the person sitting in front of you. You're alone in your office, often late at night, and you get e-mail and respond to it. . . .

N. S.   You've also written other forms of *"J'accuse,"* such as the public letter to President George W. Bush in *AGNI* 54 [spring 2001] about capital punishment in America. And *World Literature Today* [summer–autumn 2001] brought out an epistle of yours about 9/11, in which you detail your immediate personal reaction to the terrorist attacks to the World Trade Center and the Pentagon.

I. S.   For a democracy to work fully and successfully, the dialogue between the citizenry and its leaders has to be ongoing and kept afresh.

N. S.   You've said you were at the Auschwitz concentration camp memorial with your wife, Alison. What was your emotional state? Did the two of you share the same reaction?

I. S.   I remember thinking how incredible it is that the grass in Auschwitz was green the morning we visited the place. And I recall going through the barracks with Alison, entering the museum galleries, seeing the piles of glasses, soap, shoes, and hair, and knowing that those piles were tourist artifacts designed to create a particular type of emotion. That obscene thought disgusted me. Museums, in general, make me uncomfortable. Still, I visit them obsessively. [*Laughter.*]

N. S.   That is the topic of the essay "Museum Fever" [*Forward* (21 May 1999); also in *The Inveterate Dreamer*].

I. S.   Jewish museums are strange places. I've gone to ones in Greece, Spain, Ireland, England, Germany, Poland, Czechoslovakia. . . . What function do they serve? My impression is that they turn the Jews into archetypes. Also, they appear to be designed to ease the guilt of a non-Jewish population that acted cowardly in times of trouble.

N. S.   But did you find that the museums at Auschwitz and Bergen-Belsen were effective in preserving memory?

I. S.   In and of themselves, museums are institutions that appeared on earth with a particular purpose. They are the result of the French

Revolution and the Enlightenment. Napoleon was one of the first promoters of museums as temples where those cultures that he had conquered could be preserved. But today we have turned museums into shopping markets and the store often is the first and last stop for many of these tourists. We've turned history into a tourist shrine. Think about it: no culture before ever turned stones and landscape, not into consecrated, religious sites, but into amusement parks: Auschwitz, Gettysburg, the Peloponnesus. . . . Not far from Amherst is Sturbridge Village, where the staff is paid to behave as if it was still 1638.

Take a pottery utensil—decorated with colorful Inca scenes—from Machu Picchu in Peru. Its purpose at home, if any, is domestic: it is used to heat stew. The moment it leaves Peru in a tourist box, its value is transformed: it becomes folklore. People appreciate it as a manifestation of a specific culture. They say: "Look, its design is dramatically different from the utensils we use." Exactly the same happens with Jewish shrines: curators contextualize them in order to emphasize a period in time, a pattern in tradition, etc. It all takes place as in the classic story by Delmore Schwartz—whose title comes from John Keats: "In Dreams Begin Responsibilities"—on a distant screen, before our eyes, not only to entertain us but to enlighten aspects of our past that might be dormant.

N. S.   In other words, these museums are like institutional biographies. The exhibition panels tell the story of the fate of the Jewish people. Holocaust museums in Europe are, to varying degrees, confessions of a host culture's complicity and participation in genocide.

I. S.   Exactly. . . . Why have these Holocaust museums in major cities in Europe, in Latin America, in the United States, emerged in the last fifty years? Who are these museums meant for? Are they meant for the non-Jews to see what the Jews went through? Are they, as you are suggesting, and I think you're right, are they monuments of guilt? It's the guilt that that host country has of the atrocities that were committed that has erected this huge museum. And who's going to come? Non-Jews are going to come and some Jews are going to come and feel proud and happy that the host country that was once evil has now turned to good. Has it turned to good? It is that kind of a psychoanalytical approach of let's rid ourselves of guilt by erecting a big temple. What do we Jews feel about it and how do we turn our past into a big shrine? Jews are professionals in extracting every possible juice from the past. Although Diaspora life precludes us from turning concrete places into shrines—we always need to be on the go, so no attachment to a particular place is acceptable—the nostalgia that connects us to where our forefathers lived is unavoidable. And in Israel today, for obvious reasons, the device has become a national obsession. The stones become monuments to the War of Independence, the Yom Kippur War, the Lebanon invasion, this or that, and now that everybody can travel freely in Europe, those places, those museums, become shrines too, to the Dreyfus Affair. Is the Dreyfus Affair a way to enable the French to feel less guilty about the whole case? Is it for us just to feel closer to the French because finally they have enabled the whole event to be explored? Who is the U.S. Holocaust Museum in Washington, D.C. meant for? I've heard often repeated that the Holocaust has become an American institution and that most American kids in school know more about it than about the decimation of the Native American population or even about the Vietnam War. At least, people are able to come up faster with approximate numbers: six million. And how many Native Americans perished at the hands of the colonialists?

Post–World War II Jewish culture makes me uncomfortable.

N. S.   "March of the Living" and the Israeli government send school children to visit the concentration camp memorials. What kind of lessons do you feel these students walk away with? Would you send your own children on these very same programs?

I. S.   They look at it through the dictum sometimes attributed to Winston Churchill and by others to Hegel: "If one does not learn from the past, one is condemned to repeat it." But, unfortunately, in Israel today, kids are sent to Europe to see those shrines when the terrible situation in the Middle East is such that the tension between Israel and the Palestinians is in and of itself a subject of bloodshed and disaster and on both sides. In other words, these kids don't have to go very far to see how history, if it doesn't repeat itself, at least doesn't cleanse itself altogether from evil on both sides, at both ends. I won't send my kids. I went there to see them. Our generation has turned the Holocaust into an excuse to hide behind. My own family went through the Nazi atrocities and since I was a child I've felt connected to the events of 1939 to 1945. But Jews are a people with a propensity to fall into the abyss of history.

N. S.   You've written eloquently about *Zakhor: Jewish History and Jewish Memory* by Yosef Hayim Yerushalmi ["Memory and Literature," *AGNI* 48 (fall 1998); also in *The Inveterate Dreamer*].

I. S.   I'm quite fond of that slim volume. It makes a beautiful distinction between Jewish memory and Jewish historiography. And Jewish memory in the Talmud is not chronological: the Schools of Hillel and Shammai live hundreds of years apart, and in different places too; yet in the rabbinical Responsa they appear to be contemporaneous. This creates an effect of a historical dialogue. It makes one think that Jewish time isn't progressive but static—a single moment, experienced in full by millions of people *simultaneously* as they receive the Torah from Moses in Mount Sinai. These events are stored horizontally—that is, contiguously—in Jewish memory, a stunning receptacle in which Moses the Egyptian, Moses Maimonides, Moses Mendelssohn, and Moses Hess, author of *Rome and Jerusalem,* find themselves in conversation, *face to face,* each a contemporary of the rest. But Jewish history is an altogether different item. A consequence of the Emancipation, it seeks to place Jews *in* concrete time. Jewish history is about the Phoenicians, the Babylonians, the Greeks, the Romans, the Byzantians, and so on. It is about the Bible as an archeological document, about Flavius Josephus as a compass . . .—about sequence, and sequence is about progress, and progress is about justifying one's means through actions. Our present conundrum as Jews is the result of the emphasis we've placed on history over the last 250 years. You wouldn't have Zionism today were it not for nineteenth-century nationalism, would you? Zionism is a messianic movement not in the religious sense of the term, outside history, but in *precise* time, within history. American Jewish life is experienced in the same sense: as the result of a clear-cut development.

N. S.   What can students learn from Holocaust memoirs?

I. S.   A lot.

N. S.   Do they learn to prevent the mistakes of the past?

I. S.   Skepticism is useful. Ours is the age of Kosinski and Wilkomirski, the age of the hyperinflated Elie Wiesel. Wiesel who has become a guru, a Hasidic master for the ages. Holocaust testimony is invaluable in that it lets us know what we went through at an atrocious time in history. I remember a lucid piece by Irving Howe: "Writing and the Holocaust," included in his *Selected Writings, 1950–1990*. In it Howe argues that judging as a critic, Holocaust literature puts you in a difficult position of judgment. Could one argue that, on the basis of style and content, a particular Holocaust memoir is without merit? Likewise, think about the *Diary of Anne Frank*. Otto Frank rescued the manuscript from oblivion, but agreed to publish it in a sanitized version. Then came the Broadway and Hollywood version. Somehow, posterity has cheapened the message of this little innocent girl.

N. S.   In response to all the controversy over Anne Frank, Cynthia Ozick stated that she felt the book would have been better if it had been burned.

I. S.   The idea is excessive. . . . Ozick is a "posture" writer.

N. S.   In what way?

I. S.   She is needlessly baroque—a show-off.

N. S.   To my knowledge there are at least ten versions of *Anne Frank* made for TV or film. There is even an animated *Anne Frank*. Ultimately, I think that filmmakers don't aim for scene-by-scene precise recreations that are faithful to history. For one, these projects are saddled with budget, time, and production restrictions. For example, Jon Avnet's *Uprising* was filmed in Bratislava instead of Warsaw. A recent made-for-TV *Anne Frank* was filmed in Prague instead of Amsterdam. Tim Blake Nelson's adaptation of Primo Levi's "The Grey Zone" used some village outside Sofia as a stand in for Auschwitz-Birkenau. The extras work cheap. You can only have fidelity to tone and mood. That is the dilemma in recreating Bergen-Belsen and Auschwitz on film.

I. S.   The journey from one medium to another is laborious. In general, though, events like the Holocaust might be invoked more powerfully through the written word, where much is left to the imagination. In art, violence is better insinuated. . . .

N. S.   There is also this issue of whether or not the audience can handle graphic content. In America, some people have complained when Holocaust-related films are shown on TV. There was a Republican Congressman from Oklahoma, the co-chairman of the Congressional

Family Caucus, who complained about the nudity in *Schindler's List*. He argued, to my understanding, that the film had no place on prime-time TV.

I. S.   Preposterous.

N. S.   Filmmakers themselves also impose their own rules in treating the Holocaust. To return to Tim Blake Nelson—he told the *New York Times*, about his film, *The Grey Zone*: "A lot of Holocaust films have a lot of moping, but that's not what this film is about. It's not a movie about mournful, flogged, tortured Jews. I don't want to show the familiar images of Jews as victims. There aren't any Jews praying in this movie, weeping submissively. I don't have them using Yiddish words." This to me is another spin on the Holocaust but an illogical one. What is Blake Nelson saying? Jews weren't victims at Auschwitz, they didn't silently pray or weep? And not one word of Yiddish uttered?

I. S.   It is a self-inflicted backlash that American Jews are immersed in. They ask: how much longer can we accept the image of victims? The answer of the incoming generation is straightforward: let us cleanse history of its own excesses.

N. S.   Tzvetan Todorov, the Bulgarian philosopher, argues that the public needs to acknowledge and sympathize with the victims of violence. There is a need for society to publicly condemn violence. This I feel is important. We must acknowledge victims and condemn the violence. But we must never lose sight of the victims' humanity or else we run the risk of exposing victims to further injury by those critics and deniers who would condemn their right to speak. This is what the eminent historian Christopher Browning emphasizes— that human suffering, not heroism, is the preeminent feature of Holocaust testimonies and memoirs: he once stated "One of the saddest 'lessons' of the Holocaust is confirmation that terrible persecution does not ennoble the victims. A few magnificent exceptions not withstanding, persecution, enslavement, starvation, and mass murder do not make ordinary people into saints and heroic martyrs. The suffering of the victims, both those who survived and those who did not, is the overwhelming reality. We must be grateful for the testimonies of those who survived and are willing to speak, but we have no right to expect from them tales of edification and redemption."

I. S.   I agree.

N. S.   In "The Holocaust in Latin America" [*Chronicle of Higher Education* (25 May 2001)], you laid out a very interesting premise that for most Latin Americans the Holocaust is "still little acknowledged."

I. S.   The Holocaust remains unacknowledged south of the Rio Grande. This is in sharp contrast with the so-called "Shoah business" in the United States, Israel, and even Europe. Hispanics feel altogether unattached to the period. The reason might have to do with the small-scale participation of Latin America in World War II. Still the region became a safe haven for refugees, especially Nazis, Communists, and Jewish survivors. This is expressed in literature. Take for instance *Under the Volcano* by Malcolm Lowry, with a hellish scene that comes as the conclusion. It takes place in Cuernavaca, some sixty miles from Mexico's capital, on *Día de los Muertos*. There are other examples: *You Will Die in a Distant Land,* by José Emilio Pacheco, a handful of stories by Borges, *A Change of Skin* by Carlos Fuentes. . . . Latin America holds the fifth largest concentration of Jews in the globe and yet there is no relevant Holocaust memoir industry to speak of.

N. S.   Why not?

I. S.   Perhaps because no one is interested.

N. S.   Talk to me about the your experiences dealing with the scandal surrounding the publication of *Man of Ashes,* the memoir by Salomón Isacovici and Juan Manuel Rodríguez. It started, if memory serves me well, with your essay "Novelizing the Holocaust" [*Hopscotch: A Cultural Review 1:2* (1999); also in *The Essential Ilan Stavans* (2000)].

I. S.   My own role in some of these cases has been to pave the way for a reflection on the role the Holocaust has played in Latin America. I said earlier that the region seems unconcerned, even detached from the incidents of World War II. It is true, but this didn't stop survivors from arriving onto these trans-Atlantic shores and, also, from narrating their assimilation into the societies that opened their doors to them. After Auschwitz-Birkenau, after Buchenwald and Dachau, what did it mean to end up in Quito, Sao Paolo, and Buenos Aires?

N. S.   This is where *Man of Ashes* comes in . . .

I. S.   Its last chapter invoked the moment in which he arrives on a plane to Quito and he comes across for the first time people who are not like him: darker in skin, speaking a different language, but generous from day one. And he talks about his experience with *ladinos* and *mestizos*. (In this context, *"ladino"* refers to the Indians of Ecuador and not to the Judeo-Spanish language.) The author of *Man of Ashes,* at least originally, was Salomón Isacovici, who immigrated to Ecuador in 1948 and died of cancer in 1998. Isacovici was born in Sighet, the same town in Romania where Elie Wiesel is from. In Quito he became a businessman and raised a family. Then, in his old age, he decided to write a memoir. He didn't do it alone, though. After drafting a handful of pages, he showed them to his granddaughter. In turn, the granddaughter showed the material to a schoolteacher who in turn suggested to the grandfather that he should get a ghostwriter because there was a story there and clearly he needed help. Isacovici ended up connected to a former Jesuit priest, Juan Manuel Rodríguez, a novelist in his own right. Rodríguez became a kind of ghostwriter of sorts—or better, a scribe.

N. S.   What was Rodríguez's reputation up to that point?

I. S.   He was born in Bilbao, Spain, in 1945. He published a series of books, including *El Espantapájaros* [Scarecrow], a novel, released in Mexico in 1990. In Ecuador he was primarily known as a Jesuit priest, an educator, university administrator, and literary figure. In any case, the feud began as *Man of Ashes*—in Spanish, the full title is *A7393: Hombre de Cenizas*—reached its final stage. Essentially, Rodríguez's argument was that his role was more than a ghost writer: he had actually conceived and developed the entire narrative, on occasion adding fictional accounts; thus, he should be featured in the title and in publicity material as a co-author. Then, upon publication, he took it a step further, suggesting that *Man of Ashes* was a novel, not a memoir; that it was his own brainchild more than Isacovici's. He said that his own experience growing up in Bilbao and elsewhere in Spain were crucial in the development of the protagonist. . . .

The scandal was clear-cut: a Holocaust memoir written by a Jesuit priest? When time came for the translation, done by Dick Gerdes, then a professor of Spanish at the University of New Mexico, to be released by the University of Nebraska Press, Rodríguez threatened to sue the publisher if he wasn't introduced as the co-author of the volume. Also, he would not allow the work to be reprinted in Mexico or anywhere else in the Hispanic world. With the permission of Ricardo

Isacovici, Salomón's son, Gerdes sent me the manuscript. I quickly became fascinated by the affair.

N. S.   You've spoken with Rodriguez.

I. S.   For an assignment in the *Forward,* I interviewed the related parties and uncovered Rodríguez's complicated sham. I engaged him in an e-mail exchange that began on a positive note but ended in a sour way. He was unhappy with the fact that he was being portrayed as the villain. He denounced me and procured a lawyer in the United States. But then he stopped suddenly. . . . Before my essay was published, lawyers had to make sure that the material was not subject to libel.

In any case, as soon as the Ecuadorian edition of *Man of Ashes* materialized, it became clear to him that this was his ticket to immortality. He blackmailed Isacovici. Shortly before his death, Isacovici wrote an affidavit in which he stated that nothing in his memoir was "fictional," that every single anecdote was true to his memory.

N. S.   How was the book received in Spanish?

I. S.   Ecuador has a small Jewish community. I discuss the reverberations of *Man of Ashes* in my essay "Novelizing the Holocaust." In Mexico, the memoir was published by Editorial Diana. It won the Fernando Jeno Prize. I read it, but I didn't know the tale behind it. It was never reprinted, though. The first edition sold, and then it disappeared from sight.

N. S.   Is this the most prominent Holocaust memoir to be published in Latin America?

I. S.   There is the *Long Voyage,* by Jorge Semprún, a non-Jewish Spaniard who during the Felipe González government served as Minister of Culture. Also, *Las cartas que no llegaron* [Letters without destination] by Mauricio Rosencof and *Unbroken: Testimony of a Holocaust Survivor from Bueno Aires* by Charles Papiernik. In 1995 Katherine Morris edited a volume called *Odyssey of Exile: Jewish Women Flee the Nazis for Brazil,* which included some mesmerizing accounts, especially one by Renée–Marie Croose Parry. Plus, *Prisoner without a Name, Cell without a Number,* by Jacobo Timerman, the Argentine journalist, also addresses the Holocaust, albeit tangentially. Still, when compared to the United States and Europe, the number of autobiographies by survivors is minuscule south of the Rio Grande.

N. S.   It might be enlightening to compare Wolfgang Koeppen's Jakob

Littner's notes from a hole in the ground [*Jakob Littners Aufzeich-nungen aus einem Erdloch*] to Salomón Isacovici's *Man of Ashes*. *Man of Ashes* is a Holocaust memoir that is dogged by claims that it is an invention of fiction. Koeppen's purportedly fictionalized book turns out to be based on fact. Earlier we talked the scandals surrounding the writings of Binjamin Wilkomirski and Jerzy Kosinski. How is the reader challenged by such debates in fiction and nonfiction Holocaust writing?

I. S.   For the most part, the debate surrounding *Man of Ashes* took place in the United States. The echoes in the Southern Hemisphere were few and far between.

N. S.   Is that because, as you've said before, the Holocaust, as a topic of conversation, flies relatively below the radar of the average reader in Latin America?

I. S.   Yes, but ultimately the answer has to do with context. . . . In the United States, Cynthia Ozick wrote an important essay on the topic for *Commentary,* reprinted later on in her collection *Quarrel and Quandary.* In it she discussed the Wilkomirski and Isacovici cases. In her essay she attempts to delineate the border between fact and fiction. That endeavor is irrelevant in Latin America, where dreams and reality blend in more easily. Take the case of Rigoberta Menchú, the Guatemalan Indian awarded the Nobel Prize for Peace in 1992. Not too long ago, David Stoll, a Stanford-trained anthropologist on the faculty at Middlebury College, accused her of distorting the truth in her autobiography *I, Rigoberta Menchú.* North of the Rio Grande, the controversy was enormous, particularly in left-wing academic circles; but not in the Spanish-speaking world, at least not to the same degree. She had embellished some aspects of her life, so what? The fact that the most famous advocate for the Indians in Central America, a freedom fighter, resister, and rebel was branded a liar, a charlatan, made little impact.

N. S.   You published the essay "Truth or Dare: Rigoberta Menchú" [*Times Literary Supplement* (23 April 1999); also in *The Essential Ilan Stavans*].

I. S.   It was all about the cultural clash between north and south. In the end, David Stoll made Menchú more humane in people's eyes. It is evident that there were problems in the shaping of *I, Rigoberta*

Menchú. As it happens, Menchú had been on tour in Europe when she worked with Elizabeth Burgos-Debray, a Venezuelan reporter and then-wife of the French intellectual Régis Debray. Once the transcription was finished, Burgos-Debray apparently sent the transcription to Menchú. But did she read it? Or did a committee she worked with at the time assume that responsibility? It's all up in the air. In the end, Burgos-Debray was given permission to publish it. Soon after, the volume became an international bestseller. True, there are aspects that make *I, Rigoberta Menchú* suspicious. For instance, how would an uneducated Indian woman from the countryside deliver her narrative in so crystalline a format, complete with biblical and political quotations? Was Burgos-Debray more than the mere transcriber, also? Personally, I haven't heard the tapes. Stoll calls attention to the discrepancy, and rightly so. Still, Latin America let the issue pass by without remorse. After all, factual information packaged in scientific fashion is a quality of the European mind—a product imported from abroad. South of the border, people prefer to be dreamers. . . .

N. S.   A lot is at stake in that cultural clash, though: Holocaust survivor's experiences are either subject to outright denial or ennobled and imbued with superhuman powers. Either way, it is unfair to the survivors because it robs them of their own humanness.

I. S.   Sure. But in our industrialized societies, we've also turned survivors into saints. They are the keepers of the past, and as such, they are superior to us—beyond good and evil. Or are they? Elie Wiesel first drafted his classic *Night* in Yiddish. Understandably, it includes aggressive comments about the Nazis. He sought to publish it, to no avail. But when he turned it into French and gave it to André Malraux for advice, these comments had been wiped out. Today, Wiesel is the ultimate American Jewish icon.

N. S.   Survivor memoirs are generally read with a greater degree of sanctity than the scandalous memoirs of an actor or politician. We tend to expect corruption as native to the politician's personality or occupation. The religious or quasireligious character of a life story presents larger obstacles. The *New York Review of Books* explored Martin Luther King's life story and found that some of his sermons borrowed judiciously from other people's sermons. The stature of a religious man, a hero, is called into question by his very humanness. For some of us, it might be irrelevant. For others, though, it is the subject of gruesome fascination: to watch the holy become mundane.

I. S.   Suffering isn't quantifiable. It isn't that people are above good and evil, but that they have suffered more. How can you quantify how much a person has suffered? Is the suffering of three days worse than the suffering of two days and a half? Or the suffering of a pain in your toe better than the suffering of surgery that you undergo for stomach cancer? Suffering is relative: a single moment of pain might perpetuate itself forever. In contrast, a lifelong descent to hell might be, in the end, more easily overcome. Therein the trap: no two acts of suffering are comparable. For the suffering of a single individual is unbearable enough.

To return to my earlier thought, Stoll makes Rigoberta Menchú more human because you could see that she could make mistakes. When you think of César Chávez, when you think of Martin Luther King, when you think of figures like Gandhi for instance, you think of people who did not commit any evil. But no, these are people that lapse into everyday evil in the very same mundane way we do. Not evil in the sense of killing another person, but the garden variety type: a little lie, cheating on an exam, beating your sibling over the head. . . . Should we extricate those elements in our autobiography in order to turn the narrative into a sanitized version of human affairs?

N. S.   Also in the *Times Literary Supplement,* historian Saul Friedländer wrote that all testimonies should be taken as fact until proven false. The complications hatched by Rigoberta Menchú, Wilkomirski, and Kosinski's writings should not discourage us from reading. . . .

I. S.   Of course. These controversies are positive: they help us understand the boundaries of the times in which we live and how these differ from those of other cultures and other eras.

N. S.   I want to return for a moment to your point about the relative lack of interest about the Holocaust in Latin America. Readers and filmgoers in the United States and parts of Europe have certainly been fascinated with the historical connection of Nazism to South America: Ira Levin's *The Boys from Brazil,* Peter Malkin's *Eichmann in My Hands,* Marcel Ophul's *Hotel Terminus,* and even comic books like *Captain America.* These are films and books that deal with fugitive

Nazis hiding out in South America or plotting the resurrection of the Reich. There was a recent documentary called *Forgotten Fatherland* where a British film crew was sent into the jungles of Paraguay to find the last remnants of the Aryan colony founded by Nietzsche's sister, Elizabeth. Are Latin Americans fascinated with the idea of Aryan ideologues and Nazi fugitives in South America?

I. S.　　They unquestionably are. Nazis live in the popular imagination of Latin America through comic strips and B-movies. They might show up as evil, but certain groups also idealize them. The ambivalence is the result of the lack of understanding of what the Third Reich was about: its scope, its ideology. The Third Reich was intolerant of racial difference, and had Hitler not been defeated by the Allies, he would have entered Africa and Latin America, and his approach to the *mestizo* race, this so-called cosmic race, would not have been very positive. He didn't detest *mestizos,* the way that he despised the Jews, because he never encountered one. History would be dramatically different had the Third Reich conquered Europe and Northern Africa, and then moved to the Americas. How would he have approached "the other" this side of the Atlantic? No doubt the region would have been fertile ground for further military and political expansion. Aryan superiority attracts a number of fascist groups in places like Argentina and Chile. But these people are on the fringes of society. There have been a number of dictators—Pinochet, Trujillo, Straussner, and in Argentina during the Dirty War, the various Juntas—but their regimes were not justified by a philosophy of racial supremacy, as Nazism was, but by issues of class.

N. S.　　Samuel Rawet's *The Prophet and Other Stories,* Leo Spitzer's *Hotel Bolivia,* and Isaac Goldemberg's *The Fragmented Life of Don Jacobo Lerner.* . . . These volumes explore Jewish émigré acceptance, ambivalence, and transience in Latin America. You have written essays on Goldemberg's play *Hotel AmériKKa* and Spitzer's academic study *Hotel Bolivia.* Can you talk about the idea of the hotel, for example, of Jewish transience in the "other America"?

I. S.　　The term "hotel" recurs in a number of intellectual writings and with landscape artists who paint hotels or little motels or passing a *posada,* as sites where the Jew will stop, rest, find some recreation, pray, and then move onward. The hotel as a metaphor is in contrast with that of the root. The rooted tree. You are in one place and you become that place. In this case, the Jews are there, but the Jews are not of there. They are not of that place. I don't think that everybody would agree with this point of mine in Latin America. Aren't we as Mexican as any Mexican? Still, perhaps with the exception of Argentina, and to a lesser extent, of Brazil, Jews in the region live with several degrees of separation from the mainstream population. Think of the bankruptcy in Argentina. It has resulted in the formation of the so-called "*nuevos pobres*," a growing class of impoverished people whose standard of living has decreased dramatically since 2000. They survive by performing four, five, sometimes six jobs. They can't survive any longer today, though. A lot of Ashkenazi Jews are in that segment of the population. Philanthropic organizations in the United States, even in Russia, send money to help them. The Jewish immigration to Argentina started with communes in the countryside that housed penniless dwellers from Eastern Europe. Eventually, these dwellers moved to urban centers. They prospered. But they are hungry and poor again. In fact, since Poland is slated to enter the European Union by 2004, hundreds are requesting permission to relocate to where their ancestors started from. Isn't it ironic? The descendants of Polish-Jewish immigrants are returning to their genealogical roots, the same nation that aborted them more than a hundred years ago. The hyphenated identity of Argentine Jews is breaking apart. Again, the hotel as metaphor is clear. You are at home, *en casa,* as long as the place is plentiful and you're welcome. But the moment the welcome is revoked, you must depart. There are between 220,000 and 240,000 Jews in Argentina. Many are unlikely to leave: after all, they are Argentines first and foremost, and Jews second. The mere idea to relocate is anathema. Still, others are already in Israel, the United States, and Europe. And there's a flux of Jews eager to move to Spain and Mexico too.

N. S. Argentina's place in the history of twentieth-century anti-Semitism has been a hot topic for exploration. Your historical introduction to *Tropical Synagogues* [1994] touches upon the 1919 pogrom in Argentina, the *Semana trágica.* Later, we have the "Dirty War," where Jews *desaparecieron*—disappeared—in amounts disproportionate to their number within the general overall population.

The recent economic collapse has created a new tidal wave of Jewish immigration.

I. S.   Consider also the brain drain of Jewish intellectuals from south of the Rio Grande: scientists, lawyers, doctors, artists fleeing to the United States, Spain, France, and Israel. But mainly to the United States: Mexican, Cuban, Puerto Rican, Argentine Jews have built communities in Massachusetts, Arizona, California. . . . My hope is that my children will be grateful for what America has given us, although I also hope they remain somewhat detached from the core of *la americanidad*. Jews travel from one hotel to the next, don't they?

N. S.   In *On Borrowed Words,* you wrote: "In Mexico I was, am, and will always be a welcome guest in a rented house, one I can never fully own." Could we say that a "rented house" is a step up from a "hotel"?

I. S.   Yes: a borrowed space.

N. S.   In your article "The Resurgence of Anti-Semitism" [*American Jewish Congress Monthly* (April 2002)], you explore ideas that I haven't seen in your writing before. You state that "It's time to realize, in a very conscious fashion, the extent to which American Jews are satanized in the globe and to explore strategies of self-defense—physical and intellectual."

I. S.   American Jews have grown complacent. They are America and America is them. This is but a mirage. Anti-Semitism today is strong in France, Germany, England, the Arab states, Latin America. . . . Ours is a rowdy, noisy world. What scares me personally is the naiveté of American Jews. There might come a time when the concept of tolerance in the United States is questioned, which might entail the temporary suspension of liberty. American Jews might find themselves against the wall. Nothing is forever. Self-defense, even escape, might be the only response. History, after all, is a laboratory and it has happened before. German Jews didn't think their end was in sight, did they? Instead, they were convinced they had reached the end of the Diaspora as a possibility. Full assimilation, full participation in society . . . since the Emancipation, they had fought for these ideals. What an innocent dream! It took the ascent of Adolf Hitler in 1933 to shatter the utopian belief of several generations. 9/11 might also be a wake-up call. If so, it strikes me that, as American Jews, we refuse to recognize the message. As far as the majority is concerned, 9/11 was an anti-American attack, not necessarily an anti-Jewish one. This, in my view, is a mistake. As a people, we are yet again tested. Are we able to read the present properly? Do you know what the difference is between a pessimist and an optimist? The pessimist believes things cannot get worse. The optimist, instead, believes they can.

N. S.   "Self-defense" is also a topic in *On Borrowed Words*. You were a member of an organization called *Bitakhon*.

I. S.   "*Bitakhon*," in Hebrew, means "security." The experience of belonging to a paramilitary organization, a secret one, orchestrated by the Mexican Jewish community with, I suspect, the advice of the Israeli government, was enlightening to me. It was a call for self-defense among the youth, which, in return, was trained in secret intelligence and martial arts. I don't know the full details of how such an organization was put together. I know what I saw and how I participated. The experiences in the dead of night frightened us. It also made us aware that, at some point in the future, we might receive a coded phone call in which we would be asked to perform more sophisticated tasks. This wouldn't be the type of call an Israeli citizen in the reserve battalions receives to return to the Army. Ours was a different type of war: an undeclared, mysterious war. Who was our enemy? Everybody and nobody.

N. S.   Did aggressions occur?

I. S.   In 1982, Mexico's President José López Portillo nationalized the bank industry, claiming that that was a way to solve the problem of *la fuga de dólares,* the dollar drain leaking vast amounts of money outside Mexico to the United States, Switzerland, the Cayman Islands, and elsewhere. There were all these anti-Semitic comments in the form of graffiti about *sacadólares,* a term referring to people who had taken their money out of Mexico. At one point the government threatened to release a list in the newspapers that would include people who were *sacadólares.* Anxiety was in the air. By then I was already out of *Bitakhon.* Still, I knew people whose job it was to go out in the middle of the night and erase the graffiti. Some friends, I believe, were also in charge of beating an anti-Semitic figure active in the media. In any case, I wasn't a protagonist in the endeavor. I participated in exercises, but was perceived as a brainy boy. Others were far more active, physically speaking, than I ever was. *Bitakhon,* by the way, wasn't made up of solely men. Women were also active.

N. S.   Is Mexico's Jewish community still vulnerable?

I. S.   As a result of its wealth, it is a target of kidnappings. Every time I return to Mexico, my mother briefs me on recent happenings in the Jewish community. Ironically, the community itself often silences the crimes. Since it doesn't want public attention, it is better to sweep them under the rug. For instance, I have family in Guadalajara, which is the third largest city in Mexico after Mexico City and Monterrey and in the seventies, a cousin of mine was dating another Jewish member of the community who was kidnapped by an extreme right *Opus Dei* group of the University of Guadalajara. He was murdered, his corpse left in a parking lot, stuffed with hay. It was a traumatic experience for the family. The fact that it had been kept quiet left me puzzled.

N. S.   When you say "self-defense," the term has such strong connotations post-9/11.

I. S.   I'm suggesting alertness. Time shall come when the Israelis will laugh at American Jews and say: "You thought you're living a comfortable life, eh? Now you too have to defend yourselves." And yes, the defense will be physical—*Bitakhon*-like. More than a year ago, would anyone have thought that the World Trade Center could disappear suddenly from the face of the earth? I don't believe the internal peace enjoyed in the United States today is likely to last forever.

N. S.   Since the bombing of the AMIA, the Argentine Israelite Mutual Aid Association building in Buenos Aires, we've seen a gradual increase in the need for security measures for Jews in the Americas.

I. S.   In the seventies, I remember attending Yom Kippur and Rosh Hashanah services while police cars waited outside the synagogues to defend us. That vigilant approach was in contrast with the sixties when you would go to the synagogue and nobody would even know what a synagogue was. By that point, Mexican Jews had professionalized their fear, so to speak. Security was needed. We were under a watchful eye, at least from the authorities. In the early nineties, everything changed: the AMIA and the Israeli Embassy in Argentina were the target of terrorist attacks. Dozens of people died. More than ten years later, the perpetrators have not been brought to justice.

Mexico is thousands of miles away from Buenos Aires. Still, echoes of the explosions were felt. It was obvious there was suddenly an extension of the Middle East. That enlargement of the map was again proven on 9/11. The West Bank and Gaza, the Israeli border with Lebanon, the war in Afghanistan, have tentacles worldwide.

American Jews easily forget their double identity: American *and* Jewish. They make no distinction between these two facets of their self. However, outside the United States, people increasingly discern one from the other. Or else, in places like the Arab world they are deliberately confused: American *and* Jewish, one and the same condition. In those eyes, George W. Bush is a Jewish president.

N. S.   How did leading literary lights in Latin American respond to 9/11?

I. S.   Anti-Americanism runs deep in the Hispanic world. Intellectuals who have benefited from a leisurely existence in the United States wrote angry comments about America. South of the Rio Grande, demonstrators against Washington were pervasive in the months after the 9/11 attacks. The voices of wisdom have also been present, though. For instance, Mario Vargas Llosa, in his column for *El País,* stood on the side of reason.

N. S.   How can we respectfully mark or honor the thousands of lives swept away in the beastly crimes of 9/11?

I. S.   I've always been uncomfortable with memorials: architectural (museums, sites, etc.), temporal (holidays), and symbolic (a ribbon, a photo, etc.). Still, I understand, and even sympathize with, the need to safeguard in collective memory. Not only a fresh building to replace the World Trade Center but a full-fledged memorial is probably a fitting response. On the other hand, the most appropriate way to honor the victims of terrorism is to promote and protect liberty and tolerance.

N. S.   A decade from now, how will we publicly remember this tragedy?

I. S.   The future will remember 9/11 as the day that marked a new chapter in global history. What we're about as Jews, Americans, and Westerners is coded in the fateful hours of that sunny Tuesday morning. It will be our test to live up to the challenge: to respond suitably to the clash of values that that tragic day represents.

N. S.   How have you explained these tragic events to your children?

I. S.   It has been difficult, mainly because I still don't know how to explain to myself—and control—the fear and uncertainty that invades me. My two boys came back from school on 9/11 with knowledge of what had happened in New York, Washington D.C., and Pennsylvania. Somehow, the five-year-old knew more the ten-year-old, perhaps because they were told what happened at different times during the morning. But the five-year-old is too young to be concerned. My ten-year-old, on the other hand, talks a lot about what terrorism means, about Middle Eastern politics, about the hatred of America that is alive in the Muslim world.

I am scared for them: is the world they are inheriting one in which they will be able to move at ease, to be happy, the way we did? In many ways, the interim between 1945 and 2001, between Nazism and Muslim fanaticism, now seems as a relatively benign period in history.

N. S.   Do you find the responsive groundswell of flag waving and patriotism disquieting?

I. S.   In my own case, 9/11 ratified my embrace of the United States as *mi hogar,* my home. That night and on a couple of successive nights, I cried inconsolably as I watched the response of millions of Americans, and of billions of people around the world. But the multiplication of American flags on our soil has also distressed me. Patriotism is the ideology of the wicked and insecure. When a flag becomes an artifact of defiance, it ceases to be a symbol and becomes a weapon. The war that ensued after the tragic events has much to do with the impasse in the Middle Eastern conflict and with the excesses of American foreign policy since World War II. "Hyphenated Americans" need not be blind to the nation's imperfections; on the contrary, their duality ought to be a tool they use to understand the impact the United States has on the rest of the world, which at times is pernicious. I for one love America but I'm not blind: the Muslim world feels betrayed by our diplomats, and with good reason. While I am a full supporter of Israel, I believe the approach to the decades-long Arab-Israeli conflict needs to be evenhanded.

N. S.   For the moment, intellectual fare in the public arena has been in turns both erudite and inane. The left (if we can even speak of it in such monolithic terms) has been enlivened by a few rounds of sparring between Christopher Hitchens and Noam Chomsky. Both Bill Maher (host of ABC's *Politically Incorrect*) and Susan Sontag have taken serious heat for their public statements. Maher even lost commercial sponsors and his show was dropped by some ABC affiliates in Midwest. Should we brace ourselves for a bruising, government sanctioned countercritique and silencing of dissent?

I. S.   It is our duty to express our consent and dissent in the clearest, most responsible fashion. This country is based on tolerance and free debate. The duty of intellectuals is for them not to become easy supporters of a manipulative government. Even if it is difficult to be objective in times like this, we should do everything in our power to understand why the two sides are acting as they do. As for the three intellectuals you've listed, I find Chomsky a dinosaur of sorts: he is the one Jewish-American intellectual who refuses to grow up. Hitchens, in turn, often strikes me as an opportunist with an array of surprises up his sleeve. As for Sontag, I find her much more convincing when compared to Chomsky and Hitchens, although at times she thrives by overintellectualizing the ideas she tackles, and also getting lost in a maze of semantics.

N. S.   Sontag's early take on the events—presented in the *New Yorker*—were certainly confrontational. She compared the terrorists' actions to the U.S. bombing of Iraq: "The disconnect between last Tuesday's monstrous dose of reality and the self-righteous drivel and outright deceptions being peddled by public figures and TV commentators is startling, depressing. The voices licensed to follow the event seem to have joined together in a campaign to infantilize the public. Where is the acknowledgment that this was not a 'cowardly' attack on 'civilization' or 'liberty' or 'humanity' or 'the free world' but an attack on the world's self-proclaimed superpower, undertaken as a consequence of specific American alliances and actions? How many citizens are aware of the ongoing American bombing of Iraq? And if the word 'cowardly' is to be used, it might be more aptly applied to those who kill from beyond the range of retaliation, high in the sky, than to those willing to die themselves in order to kill others. In the matter of courage (a morally neutral virtue): whatever may be said of the perpetrators of Tuesday's slaughter, they were not cowards." How did you understand Sontag's analysis? Do you see the assault on the World Trade Center as "a consequence of specific American alliances and actions"?

I. S.   I think the word "coward" isn't appropriate. The word is used to describe disdainfully someone who displays ignoble fear of lack of courage. But the terrorists had no fear to commit suicide so as to proclaim what it seemed to them to be a "higher value." In my eyes they are bastards, even though I see where they come from: a Muslim world that has been sidestepped by Western countries. There is much to learn from 9/11, including the fact that American foreign policy has planted poisonous seeds now grown into full-fledged trees.

N. S.   Is there is less public tolerance for opposing viewpoints in times of crisis? If so, is that dangerous for democracy? Or is it necessary to maintain unity and confidence in the face of a real and deadly threat?

I. S.   Tolerance for opposing views is low today, but we should not desist. The Soviets used intellectuals to manufacture consent. Chomsky has used that description, "the manufacturers of consent," to describe Western intellectuals as well. But not all among us are factories of consent. In the West we at least have the chance to disagree. That is something neither the Soviets nor the Muslim fundamentalists make room for. Intellectuals play a crucial role: they are the voice of conscience. Conscience is not about endorsement of military or economic sanctions that our leaders want us to embrace. Instead, it is about a higher state of affairs, about the moral life of society. In the minds of American Jews, 9/11 brought back memories of the Holocaust.

Hitler saw the Jews as his enemies. Osama bin Laden does the same.

N. S.   But 9/11 wasn't strictly against Jews.

I. S.   Jews symbolize capitalism. The World Trade Center was, in the eyes of Al Qaeda, a Jewish temple.

3

The Task of
the Intellectual

N. S.   What is an intellectual?

I. S.   An enabler of ideas.

N. S.   What role does the intellectual play in public life here in the
United States? I ask you because the lion-mane-coifed, French-
Jewish media darling, philosopher-activist, Bernard-Henri Lévy,
once edited a book where he posed a simple question to intellectuals
worldwide: *What Good Are Intellectuals?*

I. S.   I tend to see the role of intellectual as that of a traveler to a distant
land whose mandate is to offer a comprehensive report on what his
eyes see. Except that the journey taken is not miles away but around
my desk—not a physical journey per se but a journey of the mind.

N. S.   I recall that in your book *Octavio Paz: A Meditation* you penned
"[I]n Latin American literati are seen as a voice for the oppressed and
silenced." Why has this understanding of intellectuals predominated
in Latin America?

I. S.   Yes. South of the border, the tradition is to approach the intellectual as an opponent to the status quo. South of the Rio Grande there
has always been a large segment of the population that has been
voiceless. By "voiceless" I mean dispossessed of any power. It has fal-
len on the intellectual to become their speaker. I feel a note of caution

is needed, though. Although the intelligentsia in Latin America gravitate typically to the left, there have always been intellectuals seated comfortably across the ideological spectrum.

N. S.   Do public intellectuals in Latin American have a limited audience?

I. S.   Literature is an elitist endeavor south of the Rio Grande.

N. S.   In the volume on Paz you explain that Fidel Castro's defiant rise to power was a "veritable rite of passage" for an entire generation of Latin American thinkers and artists. In what way?

I. S.   Intellectuals, at least those with even a slight interest in history, are often messianic: their dream is to make ideas influential, to change the course of events. But do ideas have edge? On the one hand, Auden said, rightly so, that "poetry makes nothing happen." On the other hand, Heinrich Heine, the German poet, once warned the French—as Isaiah Berlin indicated—never to underestimate the power of ideas: philosophical concepts nurtured in the stillness of a professor's study could destroy a civilization. The Cuban Revolution of 1958 to 59 was a template onto which the intelligentsia in Latin America projected its own messianic dreams. It was also the rite of passage to evidence, in the eyes of many, that politicians are, by definition, corrupt.

N. S.   Many of that Castro-era generation came to the United States. Eventually, they became prominent in various disciplines, including academia. Your essay "Against the Ostrich Syndrome" [*The Essential Ilan Stavans*] critiques the intellectual warfare waged within Spanish-language departments of American universities. One of the points you made was that "the exiled intellectuals barricaded in Spanish departments" were living in a universe still ruled by "the anachronistic radicalism of the Cuban Revolution." How well did these intellectuals fare here? What was the reaction to your essay by your Spanish-language department colleagues?

I. S.   For the first generation of Cuban exiles, the United States was a temporary stage. Sooner or later, Castro would fall and their return to the island would take place. With that attitude they built a culture of nostalgia. Their children and grandchildren were educated in that culture. Some broke away from it. They realized that their status as Cuban-Americans was an invitation to reflect on another set of questions that only tangentially dealt with Castro and the island. But some sort of nostalgia prevails in them too.

All in all, exiled Cuban intellectuals, such as Heberto Padilla and Antonio Benítez-Rojo, fared quite well in the United States. Padilla benefited tremendously from the welcoming hand of people like Susan Sontag and Robert Silver. He devoted the rest of his life to poetry and journalism. Of course, one could argue that, as soon as he left the island, his élan disappeared: he became a shadow of himself. This might be the reason why, in spite of the success he accomplished—his books were published by Farrar, Straus and Giroux; he was often invited to speak on the lecture circuit—he gave in to alcohol and eventually died, lonely and somewhat forgotten, in a Midwestern hotel room. Benítez-Rojo, on the other hand, refashioned himself as an academic, publishing a groundbreaking volume of theoretical reflections: *The Repeating Island*. He built a solid career as a college professor and continued to write essays on Afro-Cuban art and music, as well as novels and stories. He was never one to be overwhelmed by ideology. Over the years, he and I have spent much time together: Cuba is in his heart and mind, but never as a source of nostalgia.

As to the essay "Against the Ostrich Syndrome," it was controversial from the moment it appeared in *Academic Questions* [11.1 (winter 1997–98)]. Spanish departments are among the most morose. It has taken years for the faculty to be at a syncopated pace with the rapid changes of the Hispanic population in the United States and the rest of the globe. More often than not, these departments devote their energy to romanticizing the culture of the so-called Spanish Golden Age and of the *Generación del '98*. I meant the essay to agitate the waters, to question the complacency of tenured professors with an unavoidable disdain for things *Latino*.

N. S. You've written that in the nineties the literature of Latin America was in crisis. Does the younger generation of writers from Latin America still embrace the old guard's marriage of art and politics?

I. S. There is a new group that defines itself as the *Generación McOndo*. In its attempt to move away from *lo real maravilloso,* as Magical Realism was originally known in Spanish, it has embraced a form of urban realism (drugs, pop culture, the Internet) that some middle-class readers south of the Rio Grande feel a kinship with, but that the largest segment of the public find unattractive. That segment finds this generation too Americanized.

N. S.　Again, in "Against the Ostrich Syndrome" you describe, albeit tangentially, your dissatisfaction with the Department of Spanish at Columbia University, where you completed your doctoral degree in 1990. This dissatisfaction is also featured in your essay "A Critic's Journey." In the latter essay, though, you speak with admiration of a single teacher: Gonzalo Sobejano.

I. S.　He was a Spaniard who specialized in Quevedo and Lope de Vega, Benito Pérez-Galdós and Leopoldo Alas "Clarín." On the face of it, there was little room for enchantment: his pedagogical style was old-fashioned (he read from notes in the classroom and assigned standard reports to students) and aloof in his demeanor. But he was committed reader of literature whose mission in this world was to let the power of words open up as wide as possible. Sobejano was not possessed by the deeply-seated envy that inhabits the academic's heart. He was honest and persuasive in his argument. His dislike for empty theoretical systems was well-known. His methodical approach to a text had little to do with science and much to do with passion. When a student offered an insightful, original commentary on a sonnet by Góngora, for instance, Sobejano was genuinely pleased. He would allow himself to be surprised by his student's interpretations. Literature doesn't grow old, he used to say; it is simply eclipsed. . . . I cherished his friendship and support. From him I learned to appreciate the relationship between teacher and pupil as a companionship in which the two parts are always changing.

N. S.　Today's ambitious intellectual has plenty of crossover potential in media such as film, TV, even music (Cornel West cut a rap–spoken-word music album entitled *Sketches of My Culture*). You have branched out into film — *El Ultimo* is in development with director Alejandro Springall, responsible for *Santitos* — and TV, hosting a critically praised interview show, already in its second season, airing on the PBS flagship station WGBH. How often do intellectuals break out of the academy and really influence or sway the terms of public discourse here in America?

I. S.　The academy has hijacked intellectual debate, castrating it. Academics are domesticated intellectuals: they are complacent in their tenured positions, dreaming of freedom of speech but rarely exercising it. It is a sad state that American academia finds itself today in its relationship to literature and to democratic debate. Much of what takes place within the four campus walls is masturbatory, self-serving liberal, blah blah blah. Conservative voices are quickly pushed out of the ring. Also, the way creative writing programs have "bought" the talent of writers (poets, essayists, novelists), domesticating it, is troubling. Literature thrives by not turning into an idol-worshiping endeavor, but that is exactly what literature within the academy has become today.

N. S.   The *Boston Globe* highly rated your TV show, *Conversations with Ilan Stavans*. The newspaper described it as "refreshingly un-Rose-like." You've hosted people like Junot Díaz, Jorge Ramos, Richard Rodríguez, Linda Chávez, Rubén Blades, and Ron Untz. How has TV impacted the way you consciously shape and contour dialogue?

I. S.   I love the medium of TV as a forum of ideas. To engage in a conversation on screen isn't difficult. The secret is to forget—and make your guests forget too—that the eye of the camera is a witness.

N. S.   How about the pitfalls of interviewing. . . .

I. S.   You might be better qualified than I to answer that question, don't you think?

N. S.   In your critique of Philip Roth's *Shop Talk* published in the *Forward* [26 October 2001], you pointed out that the dialogue was more about his ego than the people he was interviewing.

I. S.   *Shop Talk* is a series of interviews that he made with important writers, mostly Jewish: Mary McCarthy, Saul Bellow, Bashevis Singer, Primo Levi, Aharon Appelfeld, and others. Roth is an extraordinary novelist whose latter work I admire profusely, especially *Operation Shylock, American Pastoral,* and *The Human Stain.* Nevertheless, he's an egomaniac, a factor that impels him to manipulate his interviewees, to make the dialogue inflexible. I get the impression he is eager to upstage them. A fine interview is about the concatenation of ideas, about exploration and discovery. The interviewer must consider oneself the brush, whereas the interviewee is the canvas. An explosion of shape and color results from the relationship between them.

N. S.   In your opinion, do intellectuals within minority groups here in America feel pressured into demonstrating a united front to the general public?

I. S.   They surely do feel the pressure. As a member of a minority, the moment you become famous you are immediately turned into a "representative" of your group. But who appointed you? And what are your responsibilities? These are difficult questions, of course. In truth, even as members of a minority intellectuals have no duty other than to themselves. That in and of itself is an intimidating task, of course.

N. S.   Turning to your own experience, how much of a critical role does ancestry play in establishing the bona fide credentials of intellectuals to comment on minority affairs?

I. S.   It plays a decisive role. At the personal level, though, my Jewishness for me is the crucial link. I feel part of a long chain of generations devoted to understanding the role they play on earth. I'm only one of the many who have come before and will come after me. My work only has meaning when read against this transhistorical parade.

N. S.   Is there a presumption that to be a qualified critic of Hispanic affairs in the United States, a writer must pay dues in, or homage to, the Chicano movement? Does your acknowledgement of your Jewish heritage work for or against you as a cultural critic of Latino affairs?

I. S.   In 1998, as I finished *On Borrowed Words,* the need to articulate my own role as a public intellectual forced me to reread the works of the so-called "New York Jews," e.g., Irving Howe, Alfred Kazin, Daniel Bell, and others who agglutinated around magazines such as *Partisan Review.* They served a fundamental function in the forties and fifties: that of bridge builders. The death of Kazin that same year prompted many in the media to talk about him as "the last of the public intellectuals." I was puzzled by the finality: why the last one? In the age of multiculturalism, is there no longer room for the likes of him and Lionel Trilling?

Their Jewishness, of course, was of the utmost importance. In an open society, ideas, always in fair competition, need to be digested critically, and these intellectuals understood themselves as a sort of Dante's Virgil. In the age of Stalinism and the atomic bomb, theirs was an irreplaceable task: to examine the relationship between the individual and the group, and between art and politics, and to make sense of history. Ideas for them were a most treasured item: they studied them with admirable patience, analyzing their roots and applicability at the present time. Mexico, where I came of age, has a very different understanding of intellectuals and their place. They have been, from the age of independence to the present, anti-establishmentarians—a voice for the voiceless, refuseniks by profession. But their "responsibility," to invoke the approach of Dwight Macdonald, often verges on the pathetic: their easy left-wing politics are predictable and, thus, inefficient.

N. S.   Another important figure is Noam Chomsky.

I. S.   Chomsky strikes me as a "non-American" American intellectual, one closer to this type of dissent. A "tester" of *idées fixes* to the degree that even the term "intellectual" is unacceptable to him—intellectuals, as he puts it in an influential essay of 1984, are sheer manufacturers of consent. He is part of the tradition of Mikhail Bakunin. This is not by chance, of course. He descends from anarchists and Hebraists. But even though he comes from Philadelphia, ought Chomsky be considered a "New York Jew"? The answer is a rotund "no." It is intriguing, nonetheless, to explore why this is so. His background is not too different from that of Howe, for instance.

At any rate, these figures, some more and others less, have been an inspiration to me. I've already told you about my passion for Wilson. I've stopped counting the books by him I own; I reread them religiously. Wilson's prose is a model of clarity and conviction. His arguments are invariably forceful, but they are delivered with grace. He was a true Renaissance man, delving into almost every aspect of culture: Marxism, the Dead Sea Scrolls, the "Lost Generation," Europe after World War II, the Iroquois, the American Civil War, Vietnam, Vladimir Nabokov, translation, consumerism, income tax, etc. For Wilson, to be a critic was to serve as a conduit between society and ideas, to provoke people's imagination, to read the world as a never-ending book, to find meaning in the complications of life. The job carried along a strong dose of controversy and envy, especially from his pulpit in the *New Yorker;* but therein lies its importance: ideas only have meaning when one weighs their significance.

Wilson admired the Jews because they manage to see culture through a double vision: inside out and outside in. To me that binary self is essential. As a Mexican active in both Spanish- and English-language mediums in the United States, I feel there is a job that is clamoring to be done: to investigate the crossroads where Jews and

Hispanics come together, not only today but yesterday and tomorrow. To do so, one needs to approach the topic from a cosmopolitan, democratic viewpoint, for no civilization lives in isolation. In today's culture wars, the easiest way to undermine democracy is to dismiss someone's argument as invalid because "the person in point has no ethnic credentials and doesn't come from an experience of depravation." The holes in this thesis are plentiful: where would we be if we could only talked about our own immediate experience? An open society invites its citizens to share in a banquet of possibilities. To reduce oneself to a single aspect of life is to choose blindness.

I write about what interests me, without requesting permission from anyone.

N. S.   A debate raged at the turn of the millennium: certain cliques of academics and literary critics needlessly fawning over public intellectuals. In his *New Republic* essay "Real Wounds, Unreal Wounds: The Romance of Exile," Ian Buruma explained how literary and academic circles presently tend to glamorize exiled writers: "Now it is exile that evokes the sensitive intellectual, the critical spirit operating alone on the margins of society, a traveler, rootless and yet at home in every metropolis, a tireless wanderer from academic conference to academic conference, a thinker in several languages, an eloquent advocate for ethnic and sexual minorities-in short, a romantic outsider living on the edge of the bourgeois world." But not all exiled writers have lived a hard life in exile. So Buruma takes issue with that slippery breed of politically engaged, well-to-do writer who "live[s] in a closed world of theory, in metaphorical exile, far from the problems of real victims, of people who are forced to live in real exile." In your opinion, do literati and academics abuse the "exile" concept in this way?

I. S.   Exile has indeed become a fashionable state of mind, and academics, more than anyone else, romanticize it. They see in it a metaphor of restlessness, although most of them live a most sedentary life. Indeed, the restlessness springs precisely from the fact that academics live a most comfortable life, politically uncommitted, detached from earthly matters. The university system, especially in England and the United States, has evolved to create this dangerous state of isolationism. Few academics—increasingly, the word itself, "academic," makes my skin crawl—have an active role in world politics. People like Edward Said, whom I admired thoroughly, are an exception.

N. S.   Actually, Said is part of my next question. Ian Buruma makes an example of the legendary Columbia University literary critic. In the late nineties, Said threw what amounted to "symbolic" stones at the Lebanese-Israeli border after Israel's withdrawal from Lebanon. According to Buruma, writers like Said, a boarding-school educated, ivy-league professor, "trivialize actual suffering" and "transform victimhood into a fashion accessory" by donning "the bloody mantle of real victims." Was Said in fact guilty of these charges or was he merely an easy target in a politically explosive atmosphere? What risks is a writer exposed to when he or she stakes out a highly public position on a sensitive political issue and acts in a loosely appointed role as the spokesperson for a group of dispossessed people?

I. S.   Said was as imperfect a man and an intellectual as anyone else, and he shouldn't be free of criticism. In fact, he was quite controversial, to the point that his office at Columbia University was burned once, and he received more death threats than all other academics today combined. The conservative monthly *Commentary* has published one too many attacks that are nothing short of libelous. In an conversation collected in the volume *Interviews,* edited by one of Said's former students, he explained his reaction by saying that rather than engage monthly in a lawsuit that would waste his energy for years, he chose to focus that energy in more productive endeavors. It is no doubt the right approach, although I'm sure Neal Kozodoy, the editor at *Commentary,* would have loved a more direct engagement. You simply cannot take those attacks too seriously, all the more if they come from the *New Republic.* The reason, again, is simple: the magazine's literary editor, Leon Wieseltier, is a pro-Zionist defender incapable of allowing any criticism whatsoever of Israel's political and military stakes. He's been after Said for longer than I can remember, much in the way he has been after Cornel West. But Said earned my full respect. Even when I disagreed with him, as I often did, he was a consummated stylist, and passionate reader, and a courageous intellectual. Zionism has undergone many stages since the late nineteenth century, and especially since the Six-Day War. Said was at the forefront of a serious opposition from the Palestinian perspective, as serious and "civilized" as any true Israel supporter should dream of being. Did Said "trivialized actual suffering"? I don't think so. The Palestinians are victims, and so are Israelis. To ignore one in favor of the other strikes me as unfair and nearsighted. Said, whose oeuvre I've read for years and is a man I had meaningful conversations with, was not anti-Jewish. In fact, he went as far as to describe himself as "the last Jewish intellectual."

N. S.   Your political writings on Latin America ["Two Peruvians," "Mexico: Four Dispatches," "Unmasking Marcos" *(The Essential Ilan Stavans)*] don't create a hyperbolic persona in order to pander to populist or nationalist concerns. In fact early on in your career you matter-of-factly stated: "I grew up in an intellectually sophisticated middle-class, . . . secure, self imposed[,] Jewish ghetto (a treasure island) where gentiles hardly existed." Yet you don't sentimentalize your Jewish identity. Nor do you sentimentalize your Mexican identity; in the very same essay, entitled "Lost in Translation," you candidly wrote "I must confess never to have learned to love Mexico . . . I only love my country when I am far and away. Elsewhere—that's where I belong: the vast Diaspora." Yet, even in the United States you seem to stand independent of narrow allegiances. Given your prominence as a writer, isn't it tempting to transform your life saga into a rhetorical device that promotes political change?

I. S.   The responsibility of the intellectual, if he has any, should be to himself. Making easy political alliances is a fault many have paid for, especially during and immediately after World War II. To be a critic is to keep one's eyes wide open, and not to fall victim to this or that system of thought. Independence of thought has its price. The position, of course, brings you enemies. In the end, though, a person should be judged not only by the quality of his friends but, equally, by the honesty and dignity of his enemies.

N. S.   Do you believe the rigor and quality of thought of public intellectuals has declined?

I. S.   I don't. . . . Literature, as I mentioned, is for the few, not for the many. Intellectuals used to have a larger impact on society. If that influence has diminished, it is because intellectuals have not found ways to use technology to their advantage.

N. S.   Can you compare the stature and public reputation of intellectuals in Mexico with their peers in the United States and Europe?

I. S.   Intellectuals in Mexico have always been seen as the speakers of the silent minority. They oppose the status quo and, as such, become the consciousness of society. A similar role was played by European intellectuals until World War II. But the last third of the twentieth century, with its unyielding embrace of capitalism, turned intellectuals into a sheer marketing commodity: entertainers in a society obsessed with leisure. That is what the United States turns intellectuals into: versions of Jerry Lewis. Their success is measured by the amount of books they sell and whether they are published by the *New Yorker* and reviewed in the *New York Review of Books* and if they appear on Oprah. They neither talk to the lay reader, nor represent alienated segments of society.

N. S.   Pablo Neruda was one of Latin America's most public intellectuals. In 2003 you edited *The Poetry of Pablo Neruda* for Farrar, Straus and Giroux. The compilation contains a nearly six hundred-poem bounty rendered in English by a cast of thirty-six translators. How many poems did Neruda pen in his lifetime?

I. S.   Several thousand. . . . Think of it: the edition of 1973 of Neruda's *Complete Works* totals 3,522 pages; but in the five-volume set of 1999, the first three tomes, in which his poetry is contained *in toto,* are 1,279, 1,453, and 1,067 pages respectively.

N. S.   What brought you to this project?

I. S.   I've been a reader of Neruda for years, but my interest in him was eclipsed by other figures, particularly Borges. This changed when a former student of mine, Jesse Lytle, invited me to read a poem in his wedding. He handed me *The Captain's Verses* and pointed to "Your Laughter" as his choice. I approached the invitation with trepidation. I remembered the political Neruda far more than the romantic Neruda. I was swept away by the poem. I immediately reread his marvelous odes. A few weeks before the ceremony, as if by G-d's will, I saw my friend Jay Parini in Manhattan. We were both attending the planning session for the Mercantile Library's John Steinbeck centenary celebration. At the intermission, I told him about my "rediscovery" of the "passionate" Neruda. Parini immediately said: "We're in desperate need of a volume that sideboards the Chilean's poetry *in toto*—a holistic picture." I remember returning home with a sense of mission. I then called Jonathan Galassi, by far the best poetry editor in the New York publishing industry. He was thrilled with the idea.

N. S.   What are the most notable contrasts and similarities between the various translators' approaches to Neruda's poetry?

I. S.   Each translator—from Alastair Reid and Margaret Sayers Peden to John Felstiner and Robert Bly—approaches Neruda's originals quite differently. Some seek to reproduce the cadence of the original, while others are more literal. I can't think of an author with a more numerous cadre of translators. Unfortunately, there is much bad blood between them.

N. S.   What drew Ricardo Eliezer Neftalí Reyes y Basoalto [Pablo Neruda's given name] to the work of Czech poet Jan Neruda?

I. S.   Nothing more than sheer chance. He heard the name and liked it. Curiously, Latin America doesn't have a solid pseudonymical tradition.

N. S.   Early in his career, Neruda traveled on behalf of the Chilean government throughout Burma, Ceylon, Java, and Singapore. How did the few years he spent as a diplomat in the Far East influence him?

I. S.   They pushed him to understand exile and colonialism as conditions of modernity. It is impossible to understand *Residence on Earth* and *Canto General* without knowing about these journeys away—far away—from home. Actually, Neruda spent most of his life on the move: he is the ultimate nomad. Sometimes exile was a job, other times it was a forced situation.

N. S.   *Canto General* was his breakthrough work. . . .

I. S.   Indeed. An astounding oeuvre drafted between 1938 and 1949, in it Neruda revisits the flora, fauna, and human history of the entire continent. The Oronoco River and the entire Amazon jungle are described through luminous stanzas, Time and space are protagonists and poetry is simultaneously presented as witness and participant.

N. S.   What was the U.S. government's reaction, if any, to Neruda's book *Incitement to Nixoncide*?

I. S.   Although he sought to distinguish between the American people and their government, for much of his life Neruda was a *persona non grata* in the U.S. Remember: he was close to Salvador Allende and thus an enemy of the American-backed General August Pinochet. The full and accurate title of the volume, composed between 1972 and 1973, is *A Call for the Destruction of Nixon and Praise for the Chilean Revolution*. In Neruda's view, the collapse of Allende's efforts were brought about by American foreign policy. In response, he sought to use poetry to indict the American president.

N. S.   In *The Hispanic Condition* [1995], you wrote about Neruda's deep sympathies with Chicanos and Puerto Ricans.

I. S.   In the 1960s, during the Civil Rights era, he was a hero of the American Left. *Song of Protest,* composed between 1958 and 1968, is a celebration of the Cuban Revolution and an attack against American imperialism in Puerto Rico. Likewise, he sympathized with the Chicano movement. He also wrote a play about the nineteenth-century border outlaw Joaquín Murrieta, whom Neruda described not as a Mexican but as a Chilean.

N. S.   Which of Neruda's work stands out among your own personal favorites?

I. S.   Hard to say. *The Heights of Macchu Picchu,* perhaps. Or maybe "I Explain a Few Things," "I Ask for Silence," the odes to the onion and dictionary, "I Wish the Woodcutter Would Wake Up," various poems in *The Captain's Verses. . . .*

N. S.   Despite some change in viewpoint, you still employ many of the vehicles favored by Latin American intellectuals. For example, in your book-length meditation on Octavio Paz's literary gifts, you write that "literary supplements and journals of opinion have always played a major role in the shaping of [Hispanic] culture." Your quarterly magazine *Hopscotch,* published by Duke University Press, draws from that very same tradition. Its web site states that "the title of *Hopscotch* is an invocation of the spirit of the path-breaking Argentine novelist Julio Cortázar." Why was Cortázar chosen as the spiritual center of this endeavor? Is Cortázar invoked because his writings, like your journal, attempt to be "experimental" and "courageous" in nature?

I. S.   I first read Julio Cortázar's novel, originally released in 1963, when I was in Houston, Texas, around 1982. It was a revelation. This is a novel that approaches literature playfully and, at the same, time injects it with a strong dose of spirituality. The Argentine made the dangerous distinction of "male" and "female" readers: the first is a reader who doesn't take anything for granted, who is involved in the process of creation along with the author; the second is a receptive reader, one who simply assimilates information. Cortázar was attacked, and rightly so, by feminists that claimed he typified women as torpid. Eventually he changed the categories to "active" and "passive." The objective of *Hopscotch,* a quarterly review, is to engage readers vigorously in the act of reading, to make them think with skeptical eyes; not to take anything for granted. My goal, since its inception, has been to present Hispanic culture from a cosmopolitan perspective, as a communicating vessel that points everywhere all the time. Hispanics today—be they in San Juan or Madrid, Buenos Aires or Chicago—are the result of a long historical process that has been nurtured by Greek, Roman, Byzantine, Muslim, Jewish, Berber, Visigothic, French, English, and scores of other civilizations.

N. S.   You have written about Cortázar's "use of the salamander, the *axólotl,* as a symbol to describe Latin America's popular soul, always ambiguous and in mutation." Do the articles assembled in and selected for *Hopscotch* draw strength from this literary metaphor?

I. S.   The image of the *axólotl* is dear to me. Other images I use—life in the hyphen, the duality of Dr. Jekyll and Mr. Hyde, and so on—also draw attention to the never-ending mutability of the human self. Not surprisingly, my favorite animals since childhood have been amphibians, creatures of two habitats.

N. S.   By comparison, what animal would represent the Jewish popular soul? Spiegelman's mouse? Malamud's *Jewbird*? Or perhaps the birdlike human beings that decorate the famed thirteenth-century *Bird's Head Haggadah*? Or should it be the scapegoat sacrificed in the book of Leviticus?

I. S.   The scapegoat invokes the wrong images. Jews, in spite of what modern Judaism never tires to emphasize, have also been victimizers. Authority in the Talmudic and rabbinical periods was used unsparingly, with catastrophic results. Think, for instance, about figures like Elisha ben Abuyah in the first and second centuries of the Common Era. Or Rabbi Nakhman of Bratslav. Or the countless Kabbalists that were marginalized in Spain by the rabbinical establishment. At the heart of Jewish history there has always been a tension between the establishment and the counterestablishment, between authority and rebellion. I would be more inclined to use the chameleon: it has an inanimate appearance, and it has a power to exist for long periods without food. In fact, a century ago it was believed that the chameleon lived on air. But what attracts me the most about this small lizard, aside from its long tongue, is its talent to meld into the environment, to disguise itself so as to remain alive. Woody Allen, in his pseudodocumentary *Zelig*, paid tribute to the chameleon as a Jewish metaphor.

N. S.   Did you design *Hopscotch* to function as a democratic forum "where ideas can freely be exchanged"?

I. S.   It does, and constantly. The status quo is already represented in mainstream journalism. The goal of the magazine is to show the other side of things. And it has done so emphatically: the drug war in Colombia has been analyzed from the viewpoint of music and the infatuation with a culture of leisure; prostitution in Cuba, especially the *jineteras,* as the young girls who sell their body for a few dollars to voracious tourists are known as, have been approached from the feminist viewpoint. Then there's the issue of Spanglish: *Hopscotch* was the first periodical to run a piece of serious discussion on the subject, with a preliminary lexicon. It triggered an international debate that made room for a much larger examination—the pros and cons—of this crossbred vehicle of communication. And it also prompted me to compile a dictionary of Spanglish, made of some six thousand words and designed as an instrument of scholarship to legitimize this jargon in spite of the pompous intellectuals who have railed against it for years. *Hopscotch* also ran a piece by Mario Vargas Llosa on the treacherous diplomatic relationship between Haiti and the Dominican Republic. It served as a springboard for the Peruvian novelist's epic, *The Feast of the Goat.*

N. S.   In many ways, I perceive a spiritual and humanistic connection between *Hopscotch* and Martin Buber's publication *Der Jude.* Inspired by Ahad Ha'am, Buber initially envisioned a Jewish cultural renaissance in the pages of *Der Jude.* Illustrious contributors to the magazine included Max Brod, Gershom Scholem, S.Y. Agnon, Franz Werfel, and Franz Kafka. *Der Jude* also tackled thorny issues. For example, Buber used the magazine to advance the idea of a Jewish-Arab binational state in Palestine. Moreover, during his tenure as editor of *Der Jude,* Buber developed the beginnings of his famous philosophy of dialogue, a concept vital to his text, *I and Thou.* Is it reasonable to consider *Hopscotch* as a natural ally to the spirit of cultural dialogue embraced by *Der Jude*?

I. S.   Buber's *Der Jude* was an inspiration, as was *Partisan Review.* The word "renaissance" invokes the energy I sought to inject in *Hopscotch.* Through a new approach to education, Buber and Franz Rosenzweig attempted to reenergize the German Jewish community. And through high-minded intellectual discussion the so-called New York Jews (Howe, Kazin, Daniel Bell, even Trilling) approached Jewish culture anew. A magazine in these two cases was the open forum, the site of encounter and departure. *Hopscotch* too had this in mind. It emulated periodicals in the Hispanic world, such as José Ortega y Gasset's *Revista de Occidente* and Octavio Paz's *Vuelta,* each of which served as a catalyst of aesthetic and intellectual trends and tastes, thus opening new vistas for an entire generation of thinkers, writers, and artists. W. E. B. Du Bois and the folks involved in the Harlem Renaissance, especially those included in Alain Locke's anthology *The New Negro,* had a similar dream in mind. But *Hopscotch* for me was not only an artifact through which to reinterpret Hispanic culture; it also allowed me to recognize the Jewish component at its core. At the time I had also begun editing a series for University of New Mexico Press called "Jewish Latin America." The two projects are deeply linked in my mind: they nurtured each other.

N. S.   I've asked you to define an intellectual. How about an "internectual," a term I've heard you use occasionally?

I. S.   An "internectual" is an intellectual whose primary conduit is the Internet.

N. S.   A pejorative term?

I. S.   Not in the least. Each epoch poses its own challenges. In ours, the page has traded places with the screen.

N. S.   Let's talk a bit more about Wilson. He was of a rare breed. . . .

I. S.   A literary critic and anthologist who could speak in a popular vein, he read English, French, Greek, Hebrew, Hungarian, Italian, and Yiddish.

N. S.   Alfred Kazin said that Wilson wasn't interested in Spanish.

I. S.   He is no doubt right. I don't remember a single reference to Spanish is his oeuvre other than transient comments on Hemingway and George Orwell in reaction to the Spanish Civil War.

N. S.   Wilson was quoted once in the *New York Times* as saying: "I have been working, as a practicing critic, to break down the conventional frames, to get away from academic canons that always stand to keep literature provincial." Was Wilson, as they say, the "last" of the great public intellectuals?

I. S.   "Last" is a preposterous adjective: it announces a degree a finality that is obviously inaccurate. . . .

N. S.   Earlier you claimed that the Wilsonian "man of letters" is an "endangered species," "under siege," or "under serious threat of extinction" today. Your writings explore such grand polymaths and generalists as Walter Benjamin and Lionel Trilling, who you call "the paradigmatic public intellectual[s]." Indeed, in *The Inveterate Dreamer* you argue that in America "the role of thinkers and theologians in society has been be replaced by that of creative writers, who are elevated to the status of moral and intellectual gurus."

I. S.   The public intellectual as we know it is a product of the French Revolution. It is not a type or a character that we have in the Middle Ages or in the Renaissance, even though we have figures who are public and who are intellectual. But they don't sit, in society, at the crossroads where politics and literature meet in the way that Diderot and Rousseau and even prior to them, Montaigne, did. But it is really in the twentieth century that the intellectual, as a servant of power, becomes an embattled species. It is in the twentieth century when a dramatic change occurs. As mass culture becomes quantitative and diversified, there are many more people out there, many more readers, many more radio listeners, and many more TV viewers. There is also this sense that knowledge as such is at the core of our Western-civilized endeavor: the European person is the ultimate arbitrator, promoter, intermediary, and instructor of knowledge, a Virgil of sorts. Intellectuals have pulpits: the *TLS, Temps Modernes, Vuelta.* . . . In an introduction to a compilation of pieces from the now-defunct *Partisan Review,* Lionel Trilling states that the quarterly never had more than five to six thousand readers. And that was prior to 1950. On the other hand, you have magazines such as the *New Yorker* that become codifiers of taste. Wilson used the pages of *Vanity Fair,* the *New Republic,* and the *New Yorker* as his own pulpit.

N. S.   Is our age still conducive to such types?

I. S.   Ours, of course, is the age of the Internet, which makes its appearance in the last fourth of the twentieth century, announcing a revolution without borders. The Internet is the ultimate decentral-ized galaxy: its diameter nowhere and its heart everywhere. The word "web" is accurate: it ensnares you, it enchants you, making it impos-sible to depart. One jumps in and out . . . but does anyone care? That, precisely, is the attitude the Internet brings forth: an utter lack of relevance. An infinite bank of information is now at our disposal, but it lacks intellectual weight.

N. S.   What kind of debate matters once you have the Internet?

I. S.   *Partisan Review* became a forum on Stalinism, and a forum for the denunciation of the Gulag and musing on the division the Berlin Wall represented in Europe. Even though the *Partisan Review* pos-sessed a limited readership, its magnetic power was to be found in the names Clement Greenberg, Delmore Schwartz, Howe, et al. Times have changed: the reader's attention span has decreased dra-matically, intellectual debates are marginalized, interest in politics is at its lowest in decades. . . . Still, an artist must live in the present tense. Intellectuals need to feel the cultural beat in their heart; they need to communicate through the channels available. Each of us needs to dwell with the instruments of his own age. What good is it to feel nostalgia for the fifties?

N. S.   Society needs intellectuals more than ever today. . . .

I. S.   It absolutely does. They write rock criticism, draw comic strips, make movies, or a TV show. Perhaps the old-fashioned, outmoded model of Wilson as that figure no longer has merit. But there are others that are figuring out the way. Ours is a fractured, discom-bobulated society. In the United States—Blacks, Jews, Asians, Lati-nos, gays, and this and that. So everybody has their own little repre-sentative and nobody listens to anybody else. That isn't true, though. People read a lot, across ethnic, gender, and class lines. In fact, I have the impression that people read more than ever before. For one thing, more books are published today than at any time in the past.

In short, Wilson is a paradigm: he's the ultimate generalist: he didn't write about anything but about everything. Plus, his essays are always pleasure to read, which is more than one might say about scores of authors, especially in academia.

N. S.   Wilson's *The Wound and the Bow* explored the connection between pain and suffering and fine literature. And I've heard you say that tyranny is a generator of fine literature.

I. S.   I don't mean it like a formula, of course. But as a comprehensible global list of memorable novels, from *War and Peace* to the works of the so-called "Lost Generation" in the United States suggests dictatorship, devastation, and social upheaval give way to inspired reflections on the human condition. The printed word is used as a tool to leave notice.

N. S.   It also gives place to tragedy, personal and collective. The suffering spawned by Hitler was the common thread that pushed so many great writers to commit suicide. Primo Levi, Walter Benjamin, Stefan Zweig, Paul Celan, Romain Gary, Jean Améry, Piotr Rawicz, Ernst Toller, Ernst Weiss, Kurt Tucholsky, Carl Einstein, and Tadeusz Borowski come to mind. . . . Let's talk about critics who write fiction and vice versa.

I. S.   I don't think that creative writers have supplanted old-school intellectuals. Many of these public intellectuals have also been creative writers. Wilson wrote novels and plays, although they aren't good. The Middle Ages, Renaissance, and the Enlightenment gave us an extraordinary array of thinkers. Philosophy has lost its gravitas, though. Today, the job they did is performed by novelists and journalists. The novel and reportage have usurped the role of elucidators of the human spirit. Hermann Broch and Robert Musil have opened windows to our heart. Some of the authors are also critics and vice versa: George Steiner, for instance.

N. S.   In an essay included in *The Inveterate Dreamer* ["Harold Bloom: A Microprofile" *Contemporary Critics* (1999)] you say that high-profile academics such as Derrida and Bloom weren't public intellectuals but snobbish scholars.

I. S.   The work of public intellectual must generate pleasure in the reader. They should enlighten and entertain. Is this achieved by Jacques Derrida and Harold Bloom? I'm sure a myriad of colleagues would jump to say "yes," but I disagree. Literary theory, filled with secret codes and abstract categories, has done a disservice to literature: shamelessly, it has sucked the pleasure out of it. Bloom does struggle to be more open but his style is needlessly obtuse. Clarity, clarity, clarity. . . .

N. S.   Let's talk about the intellectual in the age of multiculturalism. Has multiculturalism contributed to the erosion of the stature of public intellectuals?

I. S.   "Balkanized" is the appropriate word. I think it has divided the audience, but is it all for the good? Prior to the age of the multiculturalist, it was a core of Europeanized white male intellectuals, with weeds of Latino or a bunch of African Americans, and so on. And today you have the African Americans, the Latinos, the white, quote, unquote, majority, who knows for how much longer, and each of them has a different readership. But is it true that they have a different readership? Perhaps it is. Perhaps people who read Cornel West, the majority, are black. And people who read John Updike, the majority are white. Is it for the better? I don't know. I don't have a clear answer. I surely do think the generalist, as a species, is dead. Maybe the species is simply undergoing a metamorphosis. The fact is that generalists are needed more as society becomes more global. Our graduate programs anesthetize students, they force them to specialize. The more they know about less, the better their grades and prospective jobs become. Indeed, our schools of specialization do considerable disservice to the intellect, stressing specialization at the expense of polymathic, encyclopedic knowledge.

N. S.   That is exactly what I want to ask you next: are we becoming increasingly specialized at the expense of broader understanding? Will specialization always be rewarded over generalization? And what effect does that have on literature? Does the commercial market more generously reward and encourage specialization?

I. S.   Specialization ought to be applauded. But generalists are essential. Stephen Jay Gould, for instance, illustrated to perfection F. Scott Fitzgerald's dictum that proof of a first-rate mind is the capacity to hold two opposing ideas at once. Gould juxtaposed biology and sports, genetics, anthropology, and popular culture. More akin to me is Isaiah Berlin: in my office, I have portraits of him, reproductions of some personal correspondence an editor at the *Atlantic Monthly* once gave me as a present, and an array of his books—his biography of Karl Marx, his collections *Against the Current* and *Personal Impressions,* his essays on liberty and the Enlightenment, the lectures he gave on Moses Hess and Chaim Weizmann, his volumes on the Russian thinkers and on Giambattista Vico and Johann Gottfried Herder. I also have a CD of Berlin's lectures for the BBC, which his son, a publisher in London, gave me in 1999. Berlin is somewhat of a polymath, too. Although he wasn't versed in popular culture and seldom spoke on technology, his scope was panoramic since his area of expertise was politics in the age of Emancipation and the modern history of ideas. When at the invitation of the *Jewish Quarterly* in England, a periodical to which Berlin contributed, I wrote a profile of Marcos Aguinis, my model was Berlin's astonishing essay on Anna Akhmatova and Boris Pasternak.

The market for specialized books is limited. Still, they flourish like mushrooms after the rain. Stephen Jay Gould's most accessible oeuvre was permanently on bestseller lists. Berlin, on the other hand, remains the property of an elite of initiated readers. Other examples are worth mention: Ruskin, Dámaso Alonso, John Livingston Lowes, Sainte-Beuve. . . . The case of Harold Bloom is paradigmatic. His books *The Western Cannon, How to Read and Why,* and *Genius* are quite popular. Nevertheless, they are poorly composed: careless in style, repetitive in content. How to explain their appeal? Perhaps it has to do with a certain inferiority complex by readers. Bloom fashions himself not only as a modern Falstaff but also—and mistakenly—as a reincarnation of Dr. Johnson. He is the erudite critic *par excellence*. The problem, though, is that his oeuvre doesn't develop arguments. It doesn't enlighten the reader. Instead, it is a fashion show in which the author emerges as invariably superior to the rest of us mortals. The evaporating nature of knowledge in our society might compel readers to seek Bloom as their all-purpose teacher.

I should add that this comment of mine on Bloom is not delivered out of envy. In my view, he isn't in dialogue with society but in a self-consuming monologue. He is also quite disdainful of ideology and of modern culture in general. This, I hasten to add, is the opposite of the stand taken by Isaiah Berlin.

N. S.   In America, do we lose interest in public intellectuals, such as a George Konrad or Václav Havel, because we eventually lose interest in a particular region of the globe where a stream of literary artifacts once flowed but suddenly runs dry?

I. S.   Taste is shaped by fashion, particularly in the United States. Milan Kundera, Havel, Konrad, and others from Eastern Europe were dissidents in the struggle with the Soviet regime. The moment Communism as a political system collapsed in Russia, our interest in these figures diminished. The same happened in Argentina, South Africa, and Afghanistan. . . . Why is Cuban art so important? Thanks to Fidel Castro. He, and no one else, is the first and foremost promoter of Cuban culture abroad. I discussed this, albeit briefly, earlier in our conversation. As unpleasant as it might seem, tyranny is a force of fine literature. In that sense, perhaps one ought to thank Joseph Stalin for an Isaac Babel, Augusto Pinochet for an Ariel Dorfman, Nicolae Ceausescu for a Norman Manea, etc.

N. S.   In "Autumn of the Matriarch," published in the *Nation* [9 March 1996; also in *The Riddle of Cantinflas*], you discuss the literature of Luisa Valenzuela, the Argentine author of *The Lizard's Tail,* in those terms. You argue that without a political power to oppose, her raison d'être has all but vanished. . . .

I. S.   There is something obscene in this view. It might even be taken as formulaic: "Give me a tyrant and I'll return to you a masterpiece!" It's absurd, of course. After all, the dictator used his power not to inspire but to destroy. Yet such are the twists of the human spirit.

N. S.   You've written that "the politics of the émigré intellectual are rarely scrutinized. They are turned into heroes largely because where they came from."

I. S.   By definition, the émigré has a double vision: that of the insider and the outsider. He knows other vistas and thus has points of comparison. This might make him a skeptic. In my own case, I value democracy because I've lived under a regime allergic to it. No doubt democracy is an imperfect system. It is also a form of dictatorship: not of a single individual, but of the many. Still, other options are even more flawed. . . .

N. S.   So can generalists still thrive in America, a place where, in your words, "talent is volatile and America specializes in spoiling it"? You have also stated that "the age in which ideas matter is long gone and with it the responsibility of the intellectual to verbalize, to ponder or to force upon people's consciousness, those ideas."

I. S.   Does it still matter? Yes, it does. This is a society that pays little attention to ideas. In fact, it is profoundly anti-intellectual. It hopes to make literature an endeavor for everybody. This, of course, enables it to measure success in terms of concrete numbers: a successful writer sells one hundred thousand copies of a book. In truth, literature is a most private, unpopular affair: it is not for the many but for the few. Borges once said that the difference between knowing that when he started as a writer his books had sold 200 copies or 217 copies and knowing that when he was in his old age they had sold 500,000 copies was dramatic. (I'm just using random numbers at this point). You can visualize 217 copies; 1,000,000 is an abstraction. The Talmud argues that to save a single soul is to save the world entire.

4

Translation and Its Discontents

N. S.   Where does language come from?

I. S.   If your question is figurative, my answer is that Language, with capital "L"—e.g., not the five thousand linguistic varieties one encounters around the world, but a single template that encompasses them all—is a Platonic archetype. . . .

N. S.   In "The Verbal Quest" [*The Essential Ilan Stavans*] you suggest that G-d is the receptacle of that Platonic archetype.

I. S.   Yes, G-d, according to the Kabbalah, communicated with himself through a system that is beyond our comprehension. But to relate to his creation, he uses a human language. And that language is Hebrew. In that sense, Hebrew, in my view, is simultaneously a vertical and a horizontal language. Let me explain what I mean: all human languages (Gaelic, Urdu, Latin, Piedmontese . . .) are *lashon b'nei adam,* i.e., horizontal vehicles that help us communicate at our own level; but Hebrew is *lashon b'nei adam* and also *lashon ha-kodesh,* that is, serves a double function: it enables us to communicate with each other, but it is also a vertical language in that it is a bridge between G-d and man.

But if you're asking me to ponder not abstract, mystical themes but issues of language formation and acquisition, then my answer is different. Where does our capacity to use language come from? It is ingrained in our metabolism before birth but it becomes activated as individuals go through a process of socialization. What we call verbal communication is the way in which, through a set of established symbols—the use of the word *chair* to refer to a four-legged piece of furniture on which we sit, for instance—we exchange ideas. Children learn to communicate through imitation.

N. S.   In what way are language and ideas related?

I. S.   They are deeply interconnected: symbolic language enables us to form ideas. In turn, ideas shape the structure of language. George Santayana once said: "I don't know what I mean until I see what I say." This often happens when I write an essay: in general, I know what I want to say, although before I've set ink to paper it is impossible to predict how the argument will develop. Only when the sentences begin to pile up am I able to figure the path my thought has taken. Still, not until I reach the end do I realize in full what I actually think about the topic I'm devoting the essay to.

N. S.   I've asked these questions because I'm interested in the topic of translation, about which you've reflected profusely. Susan Sontag argues, in an essay of hers in *Where the Stress Falls,* that there are three basic tactical approaches to handling translation: translation by explanation, translation by adoption, and translation by improvement. The last intrigues me the most. I wonder how often a translator improves the text beyond the ambitions of the original. Is it the translator's job to do so?

I. S.   Improvement is a volatile concept in literature. It is in the realms of science and technology where one might apply it. Still, I like the idea of "translation by improvement." I know a number of Italian, German, and Spanish authors whose fate in English has been the result of translators who have done that type of job. Literature is ruled by Darwinian laws, and the help of one of those translators is an asset in your favor.

I also like Sontag's idea of "translation by adoption." I'm not fully certain what she means (this often happens with Sontag), but what come to mind is the fate of the *Quitab alif laila ua laila,* known as *The Thousand Nights and One Night* in English: to us it is a doorway to the Arab world, even though the tales are from Persia, and the anthology has benefited enormously from its British, German, and French translators—Richard Francis Burton, Edward William Lane, Husain Haddawy, Enno Littmann, Antoine Galland, et al.—who even dared to introduce altogether new characters nowhere to be found in the original. Translation as recreation.

N. S.   Early on, we talked about your novella *Talia y el cielo*.

I. S.   A *novella,* really: it is barely one hundred pages long.

N. S.   It was published in Venezuela in 1979 and you later revised it for publication in Mexico. How did you emotionally approach and rework this text a decade later? Why did you want to revise it? Did you eliminate any story elements from the Venezuelan edition?

I. S.   I spent years on various drafts of *Talia y el cielo*. The manuscript was at one point many times what the final draft ended up being. It took me a long time, too, to find a publisher. When Plaza y Valdéz finally brought it out, I felt liberated. It was Alfonso Reyes, a Mexican polymath and a Hellenistic scholar, who said, in his book *Cuestiones Gongorinas:* "Esto es lo malo de no hacer imprimir las obras: que se va la vida en rehacerlas." Loose translation: therein the handicap in not sending a manuscript to the printer, that life is wasted in redoing it. A literary debut is like a Bar Mitzvah: you're called to present yourself in front of the community. But is there a "self" who is ready? Before *Talia y el cielo* I wrote another novel, *El Error,* about the experience my mother had teaching in a Jesuit university in Mexico City. It will never be published, though. If *Talia y el cielo* is my Bar Mitzvah, *El Error* is my circumcision, a ceremony that, compassionately, we have no recollection of.

N. S.   *Talia y el cielo* was translated by Amy Prince and included in your 1996 collection of short fiction, *The One-Handed Pianist and Other Stories*. How did *Talia y el cielo* evolve over the course of seventeen years? Are you tempted to retranslate it yourself?

I. S.   The English version that Amy Prince prepared was yet another opportunity to revise the novel. At that point, in the early nineties, I was incapable of translating it into English myself; my English was imprecise, ethereal.

N. S.   At least five translators contributed to *The One-Handed Pianist and Other Stories*. Could you talk about your experiences working with translators of your own work? How do the author and the translator collaborate?

I. S.   In most, though not all cases, it was the translator or an editor who approached me wanting to do the job of rendering a story from the Spanish into English. Different translators, in my experience, work in distinct ways: there are those who want the author out of the way as much as possible—in fact, many of them, I'm sure, wished the author was dead. Others send you a letter with queries. And yet another type wants to do the translation *with* the author: in close collaboration. I often try to be a passive collaborator: to let the translator do as he or she wishes. This, I guess, is because I'm convinced that translation is as important a creative endeavor as the one the author embarks on himself.

N. S.   Have you been dissatisfied with a translation?

I. S.   Every translation, the art of betrayal embedded in it, is problematic. So to be dissatisfied with a translation is an average reaction. But dissatisfaction makes room for curiosity. In other words, I believe that while translation is an ill-fated endeavor, we are all improved by it. Every communication is a form of misunderstanding, isn't it? And the act of translation only aggravates the situation.

N. S.   Do you still use translators to render your work?

I. S.   I have become my own translator—the mechanisms of translation are inside me at all times. I don't translate my work anymore. On occasion, others do it. But every time I sit to write, I'm conscious of the conundrum of languages in which I find myself.

N. S.   Your short story "Xerox Man" has as its protagonist one Reuben Staflovitch, a criminal photocopier who goes on a rampage to destroy Jewish classics. Is Staflovitch a translator?

I. S.   I don't think so. What he is is an editor. . . . Every passionate reader is one, don't you think? Before Staflovitch destroys the books, he xeroxes them. The xerox copy he leaves around, but not before extricating from it a single random page. He does this because he believes our universe is increasingly more imperfect. He simply wants to accelerate the process.

N. S.   In what way is the reader an editor, though?

I. S.   To read is to react to the world around us: the word of facts as well as the world of dreams. A novel, a travelogue, an argumentative nonfiction narrative, elicit in the reader a concrete set of responses. A week ago I reread V. S. Naipaul's *An Area of Darkness,* about his "sojourn" in India, released in 1964. As I browsed through it, I wished that he was less paternalistic, more evenhanded. Octavio Paz gave us a similar book: *In Light of India,* translated into English in 1997. Paz's style is melodic, but also verbose. His disquisition on religion and life are stiff. In my reader's mind, I've imagined a joint partnership, an impossible volume by Naipaul *and* Paz, one where the best in each might move center stage, and the worse might be dropped—an editor's choice, no doubt.

N. S.   What were your own experiences and impressions as translator of Felipe Alfau's *Sentimental Songs?* Did you have a chance to meet with Alfau?

I. S.   My relationship with Alfau is described in an essay in *Art and Anger.* I chanced upon his first novel, *Locos,* in a review by Mary McCarthy found in the *New York Review of Books.* Actually, it was an epilogue she wrote for a reprint by Dalkey Archive Press. As soon as I read the novel, I was hooked. I had a friend at Dalkey Archive, and he provided me with more of Alfau's oeuvre, as well as with some context. Soon I was writing a long essay in Spanish on him, which eventually became the introduction to the Mexican edition, released under the aegis of the publisher Planeta.

I tried to contact Alfau in New York City, but he was shy. I finally succeeded. Several months—perhaps even years—later my friend from Dalkey Archive and I went to visit him in a retirement home in Queens. For a while I toyed with the idea of producing an experimental biography of him. We began to meet at a regular basis. I taped many hours of interviews with him. I still dream of finishing my biography—maybe I will before I die.

Alfau gave my friend at Dalkey Archive Press the manuscript of a second novel, *Chromos.* Soon after it was published, in the early nineties, Alfau also took out of a drawer a volume of poems, *La poesía cursi.* Poetry wasn't his forte. Still, his talents as a novelist justified the effort of making it public, so it was agreed that I would translate it.

To translate poetry is to become a professional betrayer. It is harder to render than prose, at least to me. And yet, the endeavor was a worthwhile one. Since then I've also translated poetry by Rubén Darío and Gary Soto, respectively from Spanish to English and from English to Spanish. I have translated far more prose, of course: Yehudah Halevi, Cynthia Ozick, Milan Kundera, Alcina Lubitch Domecq,

Mario Vargas Llosa, even the composer Leonard Bernstein. I have often disguised my efforts as translator under pseudonyms. Over the years a couple of these pseudonyms have built a reputation.

N. S.   Why have you relied on the practice of using pseudonyms as a translator?

I. S.   So as to experiment with different stylistic strategies without the slightest appearance of inconsistency and anachronism.

N. S.   And what did you translate by Bernstein?

I. S.   When I was seventeen or eighteen years old, my brother used to frequently play Bernstein's symphony *Kaddish*. I was infatuated by it: an artist's delivery of his own "Kaddish." I translated it from English into Spanish. It is unpublished.

N. S.   In your essay "The Verbal Quest," you write that as readers of translated works, we might often be fooled into forgetting that we are in front of a translation. How invisible is the translator's presence? Do we only take notice of the translator's influence when we find the work achingly bad?

I. S.   We're always aware of his presence, even though, at times and for brief moments, we might forget about it. Benjamin liked to say that bad translations are those where the translator, a mere bureaucrat, is simply devoted to conveying information. These information artifacts are abundant in the market. Often they result from the frenzy of publishers and editors to rush a book to its audience. The rush, needless to say, invariably has catastrophic consequences. Some years ago a Barcelona publisher told me how the Spanish translation of the international thriller *The Little Drummer Girl* by John Le Carré came about. It appears that soon after the Spanish rights were acquired, news came that the Hollywood movie with Diane Keaton would soon be released. The thought of not having the rendition available in bookstores on time was unbearable, so the publisher rented a spacious office, put a dozen desks with an equal number of typewriters, and hired translators with a per-hour salary. Each of these translators was assigned a handful of pages. The translation was thus finished in record time and hurried to the printer without the merciful scrutiny of a copy editor's eye. The name of the Palestinian protagonist who has an affair with a female Israeli secret agent was spelled in at least three different ways: Nissim, Nachim, and Joaquim, if memory serves me. This allowed her the adjective of "promiscuous," a quality noted with perplexity by Spanish critics, and engaged her in a kind of feminist reversal of the harem Le Carré never intended.

N. S.   Conversely, though, a translation might also lull us into a gentle state of forgetfulness about the translator's job. Isn't this true?

I. S.   It is true, although, as I've said, this forgetfulness is not only temporary but artificial too. Ours is a universe infused with translations. From the conversation with a long-distance operator, a taxi driver, a tourist, and a newly-arrived immigrant, to the browsing of foreign channels on our cable network, the pleasure of a novel drafted in another language, to the debate on bilingual education and "English Only" and "English First". . ., ours is a universe inundated by translation. Increasingly, it is everywhere you go. Yet we are fixated on the fact that the degree of encounter in translation is dissatisfying, that something is always lost. It surely is, but, as far as I'm concerned, something is also won, so to speak. Who are we when we are translated? Has our self been adulterated, deformed, and reinvented? Might it have been improved, perhaps?

I discussed Sontag's dichotomy earlier. Let me suggest another binary system to approach literary translation with: the Flaubertian and the Nabokovian. Flaubert, as the author in control of his plot and characters, sought to disappear from his craft—to let his creation speak for itself. A similar approach is the one taken by a translation whose objective is to make the reader forget that the text isn't in the original language. In the end, though, the reader is aware of the effort, in much the same way the reader knows in *Madame Bovary* or "A Simple Heart" that even if the author has all but disappeared behind the curtains, he is always lurking behind. On the other hand, Nabokov, the king of novelistic self-consciousness, believed the author needed to be seen at all times in the act of manipulating his art. In translation, this means that the reader should never forget that what he is reading is an attempt to perceive the original through a lens.

The Flaubert/Nabokov equation isn't new, of course. It frequently pops up in the history of literature under different banners. Matthew Arnold, in his lecture "On Translating Homer," gave us a succinct appraisal of the role of the translator. He described the two sides: when the translator wants the reader to forget about him and "be lulled into the illusion that he is reading an original work" and when the translator seeks to retain every peculiarity of the original, making the translation as foreign as possible, so that the reader never forgets that he is in front of an imitation. This second approach justifies itself by claiming that the translator's first duty is to be faithful to history. But Arnold went beyond this equation. He described Homer's style and ideas as the embodiment of "perfect plainness and directness." In spite of this, the Greek poet for him has "a grand style," as grandiose as that of Dante. This contradiction might make translators despair. What to do? Arnold responds: "[Homer's] translator must not be tumid, must not be artificial, must not be literary; true: but also he must not be commonplace, must not be ignoble." I like the adjective "tumid": swollen, enlarged, puffy. In any case, for Arnold the translators of the *Iliad* fail because what they seek is simplicity and speed, even though these characteristics are to be found in Homer.

N. S.   Let me move you in the direction of literary translation again by calling attention to a controversial essay of yours, "Beyond Translation: Borges and Faulkner," published in *Michigan Quarterly Review* [40.4 (fall 2001)], in which you argue that an excellent translation of Borges into English might be as good as the original.

I. S.   When we read a work in translation without the original available to us, the translation becomes its Doppelgänger or vice versa: the translation *is* the original.

N. S.   But "as good as"?

I. S.   Sure, why not? How much longer will we nurture the complex that a translator is by definition inferior? Originals can be unfaithful to the translation.

N. S.   Does the commercial market create a natural rivalry between translations (advertised as newer, better, more faithful to the original) which critics sometimes comparatively review, analyze, pan, or praise? Is the commercial marketplace sensitive to translation quality?

I. S.   The market is only interested in profit. Profit in art and profit in business are different types, though. Does anyone—the artist, the translator, the agent, the publisher, the bookseller—profit from literature? By all means, and this is as it should be in a society ruled by the free market, not only of merchandise but of ideas too. Except that the artist himself profits in a way that only tangentially is material. His objective in drafting the work of art—but only if the work of art has been produced for its own sake—is to achieve a profit at the spiritual level.

The translator is also an artist, and, in a universe where the clone is as important as the source, his role is to shine by spotlighting the artist's talent. In that sense, the translator is a parasite of sorts: he lives off someone else. But he also allows the artist to flourish, to be freed from his own cultural and linguistic imprisonment, and in this sense he is a liberator.

N. S.   In the *Michigan Quarterly Review* essay, you've claimed that Borges writes in an Englishized Spanish. At what point in his career does this style emerge?

I. S.   He began to embrace an Englishized Spanish in his thirties. Borges adored British and American literature. His memorable pieces were drafted approximately between 1938 and 1955: "Pierre Menard, Author of the *Quixote*," "Funes the Memorious," "The Lottery of Babel," "Emma Zunz." It's in that period where the Englishized style becomes patent. The syntactical pattern of his Spanish is so similar to English, his oeuvre *almost* feels delivered in Shakespeare's tongue. Of course, there's the anecdote that he first read *Don Quixote* in English and when time came for him to read it in the Spanish original, he believed it to be a poor translation.

N. S.   You have written that translation is a "divine activity." Many serious studies of translation begin with the biblical tale of the Tower of Babel story (Genesis 11:1–9). Why has that story remained such a powerful example of the complexities of translation?

I. S.   It announces that, in a mythical beginning, the tension that tears us apart between unity and multiplicity wasn't present. The world at the start of the Tower of Babel is unified, but by the end it has been disjointed, torn to pieces, each of its parts moving at a different rhythm. The concept of a pristine human tongue is a dream every society nurtures, and eventually needs to reject. Again, I've explored this issue in some detail in my essay "The Verbal Quest."

N. S.   Indeed, the Tower of Babel is a tale about a rebellion against God. In a sense it is also a story about the uncloseable gap between language and understanding, though. Is translation likewise a utopian project seeking perfect yet impossible symmetry between languages?

86

I. S.   Translation is a quixotic endeavor: an impossible quest. Every translator seeks to create a "perfect" counterpart to the original, but perfection is not a human quality. And so the process itself is doomed from the start. This is not to say that the art of translation shouldn't be embraced. On the contrary, precisely because it is doomed it is so important to our civilized life. The tension between unity and multiplicity expresses itself today as the clash of nations, religions, ideologies, legal rights. . . .

N. S.   Ismar Schorsch, in his introduction to *Etz Hayim,* a progressive contemporary translation and commentary of the Torah issued by the Conservative movement, cites the Talmudic adage "each generation needs to bring forth its own interpreters." Proof of Schorsch's statement is the five hundred English translations of the Bible issued between 1611 and 1900. What inspires people to produce so many translations of religious liturgy? Is it because of rivalry?

I. S.   Language is in constant movement, and translation needs to keep up with it. If an original text, say, *Alice in Wonderland,* is forever fixed in the verbal choices Lewis Carroll made, the translation is never static. Instead, each generation must reclaim the classics by retranslating them, thus adapting the original to the linguistic usage of the day. The Bible is surely the most frequently translated work in the Western Hemisphere, followed by Shakespeare and Cervantes, Flaubert and Dostoevsky. I've counted nineteen different full-length translations of *Don Quixote* into English since the first part of the novel appeared in 1605 (roughly around the same time the King James version of the Bible was released in English): available in Shakespeare's tongue is the Elizabethan *Quixote,* the Victorian, the skeptic, the deconstructionist. . . .

N. S.   Is the translator in a sense a coauthor?

I. S.   If not the coauthor, at least the closest one ever gets to the perfect reader. After all, the translator is in contact with the original text to such a degree that he ends up learning of tricks and subterfuges the author himself might not even be conscious of.

N. S.   In *On Borrowed Words* you ponder another approach to translation: the one Martin Buber and Franz Rosenzweig opted for when they undertook a modern German translation of the Hebrew Bible. In that version, as you put it, "the musicality of the original could be heard and the strict syntactical nature of Goethe's tongue was adulterated." I quote from page 218, in which you allow Rosenzweig to talk for himself: "It is a gross misconception to believe that the translator, in order to fulfill his task, must adapt to German usage whatever is alien. If I were a merchant who had received an order from Turkey, I should send it to the translation bureau and expect that kind of translation. But if the communication from Turkey was a letter from a friend, the translation of such a bureau would no longer be adequate. And why? Because it would not be accurate? It would be just as accurate as the translation of the business letter. But that is not the point. It would be German enough; it would not, however, be sufficiently Turkish! I should not hear the man, his special tone, his cast of mind, his heartbeat. But ought this to be expected? Is it not demanding the impossible of a language to ask it to reproduce an alien tone in all its *alienness,* in other words, not to adapt the foreign tongue to German, but German to the foreign tongue?"

I. S.   A glorious quest, isn't it? To demand the impossible from a translator. . . .

N. S.   By the way, in your collection of essays *The Inveterate Dreamer,* I've come across a piece dated in 1994 where you depict a class of writers that lives "on borrowed words." That is also the title of your memoir. Why does the phrase resonate so strongly with you?

I. S.   The critic Morris Dickstein, also puzzled by the title, suggested that it is an image taken from real-estate jargon, as well as from business. "To borrow" is to be in debt, and also to obtain permission for the utilization of an item or property. It is exactly the feeling I have toward the various languages I have at my disposal. They are not my property; I simply have them on loan.

N. S.   *On Borrowed Words* dates your fascination with translation to your college years. In it, you wrote: "The issue . . . began to preoccupy me: How could Jews the world over write in so many different tongues? Why did they excel as translators?" Indeed, there is long and deep tradition of ancient Jewish biblical interpreters, commentators, and scribes translating to and from Hebrew, the divine tongue. Jews have translated Jewish writings from a long list of languages including Arabic, Greek, and Latin. The recently published *Norton Anthology of Jewish American Literature* contains a chapter exploring the American branch of this tradition, entitled "Jews translating Jews." Is the Jewish drive to translate simply necessitated by the Diaspora or are there other reasons for it? Do all cultures have the need to translate as an act of our common humanity?

I. S.   Jews have been shaped by polyglotism ever since the destruction of the First Temple. This has encouraged a need to navigate cultures by negotiating their various languages. Shmuel Ibn Tibbon' s school of translators in Toledo, to which we owe, among other highlights, the Hebrew version of *Moreh Nevukhim,* penned by Maimonides in Arabic under the title of *Dalālat al-hā'irīn* (the volume is known in Latin as *Doctor Perplexorum* and in English as *The Guide for the Perplexed*), is at the forefront of an exhaustive list of interpretative efforts. A number of major Jewish authors in the Jewish Diaspora have been involved, to some degree, with translation: Saul Bellow translated Isaac Bashevis Singer, and Singer in turn translated Rilke and Thomas Mann; Cythnia Ozick translated for Irving Howe and Eliezer Greenberg in *A Treasury of Yiddish Stories;* Isaac Babel translated Sholem Aleichem; Kafka studied Yiddish and Walter Benjamin Hebrew; Sh. Y. Agnon translated from Aramaic. . . . Indeed, Benjamin, in his introduction to Baudelaire's *Tableaux parisiens,* explores, albeit tangentially, this Jewish activity. He debates what he calls the "translatability" of a text. In his view, the lower the quality of the original, the less fertile a field it is for an engaging, inspired translation. Benjamin says that in a good translation "sense is touched by language in the way an Aeolian harp is touched by the wind." He ponders Hölderlin's translation of Sophocles, claiming that it extends the boundaries of the German language. Benjamin was a freedom fighter. He called for freedom in translation. He believed the task of the translator was to release in his own language that pure language, the essence behind the decayed barriers stuck in the words as a result of daily usage. This allows for a refreshing approach to the original, but, more than anything else, a recreation of it that is equally inspired, as valuable. And then he talks about texts that are injected by dogma. The Old Testament, for instance. Since its original is supposed to be the "true language," in the literal sense of the term, the Old Testament, for Benjamin, is essentially translatable. The task of the translator, in this case, is to bring that truth to his own language by unifying freedom and literalness.

N. S.   How does one evaluate a novel in translation? What criteria do you personally use? In *The Inveterate Dreamer,* you judged the oeuvre of Elias Canetti, Primo Levi, Isaac Babel, Moacyr Scliar, and Arthur Schnitzler, among others. In the *Nation,* you've also commented on Spanish-language authors such as Javier Marías, Alvaro Mutis, and Elena Poniatowska. When you review a book translated from the Spanish, do you read the book first in Spanish and then in English to compare the works?

I. S.   A translation ought to be judged on its own terms. While enjoying it, it is a disservice to have the original at one's side—unless one's objective is to scrutinize closely, in an academic mode, the translator's strategies.

N. S.   In a review in the *Times Literary Supplement* [12 January 2001] of Isabel Allende's novel *Portrait in Sepia* you describe her as "a global phenomenon." You report that she is translated into some "twenty-five languages, from Albanian to Icelandic." You further claim that, of all the Latin American writing stars, "none is more predictable" than she is. Have good translators helped to create the global phenomenon known as Isabel Allende? Is shrewd marketing a prime factor? Have you ever encountered a case of a skilled translator elevating a mediocre literary work? Is that true in her case?

I. S.   Allende is the queen of melodrama, a form of oversentimentalized art popular the world over. Bernard Shaw once cautioned never to underestimate what the public will buy. Her novels are derivative, uninspiring to me, but not to millions of people, whose emotions she massages in novel after novel. Allende has built her audience by means of a shrewd literary agent in Barcelona, first-rate—and well-paid—translators, and the undefeatable formula: *repeat, repeat, repeat.*

N. S.   Has she matured as an artist over the years, in your view?

I. S.   Your question deserves an essay in and of itself. "Maturity" is a word I've been ruminating over for quite some time. What does it mean? How might we measure a person's maturity? And how about an artist? As careers are scrutinized in a lineal fashion, might one read into them a process of deepening concern for a handful of obsessions? But this can only happen in retrospect, when the artistic path has been set. But the artist himself is unaware of that path until and unless he has gone through it, so for him maturity is something quite different from what it is for the historian.

Still, I suggest seeing "maturity" as the consolidation of one's own space in the universe. In artistic terms, this doesn't mean to me repetition. Instead, it means a shift of emphasis, an unhesitating stroke.

N. S.   In *Mutual Impressions* [1999], an anthology, you compiled the North-South divide's finest writers, your impressive roster included writers and poets who read their counterparts in translation. Do translations substantially influence a writer's perception of another writer?

I. S.   The translator mediates our approach to the author, the story, the style. . . . He is our telescope, one on which our perception of a newly found planet is based. Needless to say, this perception has an effect on our understanding of the milieu in which we live. John Updike one told me that it was a lecture delivered in Buenos Aires by Borges and eventually turned into an essay collected in *Other Inquisitions* that allowed him to discover Nathaniel Hawthorne.

N. S.   What does it mean to a writer in the so-called Third World to be translated into the English language? Are English translation and American recognition vital to a writer's career in the way that making it in Hollywood is for countless screenwriters, directors, and actors? Do writers from Latin America feel pressure to write for American literary tastes?

I. S.   As the lingua franca today, the English language is the ticket to universalism. No writer with aspirations of a global reach can afford to ignore it . . . and also, be ignored by it.

N. S.   Public demand in the United States has surged for translations of prominent Latin American writers. Has that demand finally eclipsed the public's desire for East Central European literature translations? Does an author's geographic location and language impact the author's success? How much affect do they have?

I. S.   Geography is fate. Think of Machado de Assis, the so-called "Henry James of Brazil"? You might ask: Why isn't Kafka "Prague's Felisberto Hernández"? Or Henry James "America's Machado de Assis"? I have sought to combat geography as a form of determinism in my own life. I have fought, with all my might, not to make my Hispanic birth a casualty of vision. Or to use my Jewishness as a jumping board to go beyond the milieu I was stuck to originally.

Hispanic letters are hot today the way Eastern European literature was attractive before the fall of the Berlin Wall. The *Zeitgeist* is on our side, but it will move on, as it always does. What matters in the end is not how fashionable you are but to what extent the literature that springs from you captures the palpitations of your era. The reception a book gets in the present marks its chances of survival, but posterity plays on us uneasy, surprising games, doesn't it?

N. S.   A publishing house might shackle readers to an inadequate or dated translation simply by holding exclusive translation rights. How much impact can an inadequate or dated translation have on writer's reputation? How often does a bad translation sabotage a writer's career?

I. S.   Often the choice isn't for the reader to make. Publishers are satisfied with second-rate translations, which they send out into the world with their blessing before going to the trouble of making them "at home."

N. S.   Prior to the rise of the copyright laws, translators and publishers could openly translate (some would say poach) any literary work without seeking permission. How do copyright laws affect what literature gets translated?

I. S.   The copyright law allows the translator the right to his intellectual work.

N. S.   Translators have slowly acquired stature and recognition among publishing houses. Indeed, an exceptional translation can reinvigorate a literary work's standing and bring new readers to the table. Translators like Gregory Rabassa, Joachim Neugroschel, and Michael Hofmann are given billing on the book's dust jacket. Why were translators underappreciated, unrecognized even, for so long? What caused their change in status?

I. S.   In the Middle Ages the concept of originality was dramatically different from ours. For Góngora to rewrite a sonnet by Petrarch was an illustrious endeavor. But the rise of capitalism made room for the idea of private property, and with it came along our romantic concept of artistic inspiration as a stroke of genius that is unique and, thus, unequivocally personal. For centuries the activities of the translator were perceived as derivative, secondary to the act of creation. But nowadays, in an age that has Andy Warhol as its idol, people have learned that the original and its copy are of equal importance. This has not only elevated the status of translation but has also opened up an entire area of intellectual curiosity. . . .

N. S.   Back to *On Borrowed Words*. In its pages you intertwine sentences in Spanish, Hebrew, Yiddish, and French. Some are then translated into English, while others are not. Why the discrepancy?

I. S.   My objective was to expose readers to the unfamiliarity of foreign tongues, an experience immigrants dwell upon without choice.

N. S.   Also, in the memoir you coined the word "translationality."

I. S.   It is a somewhat pompous term that people have found useful. By it I mean translation as more than a mere literary endeavor. Almost at every minute of the day I find myself cruising from one linguistic realm to another, becoming a mode of life, an I.D. card: in German, a *weltanschauung*.

N. S.   This results in your desire to make your memoir "illegitimate," and "somewhat bastardized." I cite from page 88: "To succeed," you state, "the original [of *On Borrowed Words*] ought to read as if written already *in* translation—a translation without an original."

I. S.   Yes, it is the way I experience life: as a facsimile, an imitation—a man without a shadow.

N. S.   And imitation of what?

I. S.   An imitation of a lost model

N. S.   Translation, then, pulsates through the heart of your identity. Does it make you feel scared to be a replica?

I. S.   Not at all, on the contrary, it's liberating. I don't have any duties toward genuineness. I've made peace with myself about my inauthenticity.

N. S.   You provide a remarkable portrait of your brother Darián, a musician and a stutterer, in *On Borrowed Words,* and show how his effortless mastery of English ultimately reduced his stuttering. This mastery inspired a bit of jealously in you, didn't it? To what do you credit your brother's outward transformation as a speaker?

I. S.   This is a difficult question. Eventually, Darián figured out the verbal strategies needed to "domesticate" his handicap. Today he hardly stutters in Spanish. In music—in songs, for instance—he never did, and in English one only reluctantly noticed it. Speech pathologists have explained this, but, I must confess, it nonetheless remains a mystery to me.

N. S.   What is the ethical responsibility of the translator?

I. S.   One and one alone: to be at once loyal and disloyal, respectful and disrespectful.

N. S.   As a counterpoint, what in your view is the ethical responsibility of the critic?

I. S.   To bear witness to the intellectual life of his time, to survey its terrain, to offer a map useful to navigate it. Let me invoke a code of honor I once memorized and hold dear to me. It is from a comment by Lionel Trilling on his idol Matthew Arnold: "No critic is ever right in the sense that he says all that may be said about an art," Trilling states, "or in the sense that what he does say about an art cannot, by one example or another, be shown to be incomplete. We properly judge a critic's virtue not by his freedom from error but by the nature of the mistakes he does make, for he makes them, if he is worth reading, because he has in mind something beside his perceptions about art in itself—he has in mind the demands he makes upon life; and those critics are most to be trusted who allow these demands, in all their particularity, to be detected by their readers. . . . To enjoy a critic doesn't mean that one agrees with his particular literary judgment, not with any of them. It is only necessary to be aware of the generosity and commitment of his enterprise."

N. S.   The task of translation has become riskier since the publication of Salman Rushdie's *The Satanic Verses*. As a result of Ayatollah Khomeini's *fatwa,* some of Rushdie's translators have been murdered or intentionally injured.

I. S.   But historically, translation has always been a perilous endeavor. To translate is to open up, to allow a text to travel. Think of the King James Bible. In 1604, a Puritan under the name of Dr. John Rainolds suggested to King James I of England that there were too many—and too loose and corrupt—versions of the Old Testament and the Gospels (including the John Wycliffe version and the so-called *Bishops' Bible* of 1568). King James liked the idea and invited the Dean of Westminster, as well as scholars at Oxford and Cambridge, to gather a group of specialists. The strategy was to be "translation by consensus": to solve the problem of individual interpretation, the group would establish the "correct" approach, standardize style, and offer a homogenized, "official" translation of the Holy Scripture. The effort, needless to say, has been replicated in other moments in history: the translation of Marx's *Das Kapital* by the Soviet regime, for instance. Conversely, in hermetic societies the effort *not* to translate foreign (that is, alien) material serves as a control mechanism against outside influences. In those cases, the translator is viewed as a spy.

Of course, the forty-nine individuals involved in creating the King James Bible in the end produced in 1611 an astonishingly multilayered translation that incorporated previous versions. The King James Bible serves as a model of perfection. That translation had myriad effects, among them the fact that it became a milestone in English for what was "proper" and "acceptable." Translations, thus, are more than interpretations. They might also serve as a normative mechanism.

N. S.   You've invoked Trilling. Not too long ago, I saw you compared to another critic: Dr. Johnson. He devoted himself to codifying, in scholarly editions, the English classics, produced novels, reviewed prodigiously, and compiled a dictionary of the English language. What is Dr. Johnson to you?

I. S.   An idol. . . . But the comparison is unfair: Dr. Johnson not only was at home in English but sought to purify Shakespeare's language of French mannerisms. I instead seek to ratify the degree to which it is a gluttonous tongue, supping at anything within its reach.

N. S.   Onward to Spain and its colonies across the Atlantic. In *On Borrowed Words* you recall historian Américo Castro's argument that "Spain came to find its soul in the Spanish language" in part because of Jewish translators in the court of Alfonso X. What effects, at the verbal level in particular, did the forced departure of the Jews in 1492 have in the Iberian peninsula?

I. S.   It is a complex question that begs for a far more detailed, patient answer than the one I'm able to provide you now. Américo Castro reinterpreted Spanish history though a kaleidoscope that stunned a wide sector of his readership. His interest in Jewishness is problematic, though. Still, it is unquestionable that by aborting the Jews, Spain paid a heavy price: its ticket to modernity. The expulsion left a vacuum, one impossible to fill. . . . Anti-Semitism became rampant as the age of toleration, personified by the *Siete Partidas* of Alfonso X, also known as *El Sabio,* was buried in an unspoken past. Ladino, the dialect spoken by Sephardic Jews, is a relic of that past. While it is useful for linguists to decode the Spanish of Gonzalo de Berceo, it is, as a result of the labyrinths of the Diaspora, part of Jewish heritage and not, in any significant way, a property of Spain per se.

N. S.   On the subject of Ladino, Elias Canetti spoke Ladino, but to my knowledge he never earned his keep with it. Are there any twentieth century authors that come to mind who famously paid their dues to Ladino as a language?

I. S.   Ladino lost whatever weight it had as a literary vehicle with the collapse of the Ottoman Empire. Although it remains a tongue for lullabies, maxims, jokes, domestic babble, and children's stories, it is hard to find in it expression of deep emotion. There are still journals, such as *Aki Yerushalayim,* a triquarterly published in Israel since 1979, but who reads them? Other tongues—including French, Turkish, Arabic, English, Portuguese, Hebrew, and Spanish—were embraced by the literati. Indeed, the roster of Sephardic authors is substantial: Albert Cohen, Edmond Jabès, Emma Lazarus, Carlo Levi and Primo Levi, Albert Memmi, Sami Michael, Edouard Roditi and A. B. Yehoshua. And aside from Elias Canetti, his first wife, Veza Canetti, wrote intriguing novellas and stories, among them *Yellow Street* and *The Tortoises.* But few of them, in your own words, "paid their dues." A history of Ladino literature is still unavailable. The departure from Spain, in my mind, resulted in a broken vessel whose multiple particles are disseminated the world over. In and of itself, the Ottoman Empire alone is an assortment of Diasporas. Not long ago, I read a biography of Kabbalist Isaac Luria, whose mystical fellowship in Sefad, an important center of intellectual and commercial activity for Jews in the sixteenth century, united people from various parts of the empire. Luria himself lived in Egypt before immigrating to Palestine. Pluralism and polyglotism were features of these Diasporas. Hebrew was a lingua franca, but Ladino, Arabic, French, Spanish, and other languages were also available. I dream of one day compiling an omnibus work of Sephardic letters.

N. S.   In a review in the *Nation* [15 October 2001] of the Mesoamerican literary anthology *In the Language of Kings,* edited by Miguel León-Portilla and Earl Shorris, you highlight scholars' attempts to unearth and preserve pre-Columbian literature from the ruins of History. You write that there is a scholarly tradition in Mexico "to open up the pre-Hispanic mind" and "give voice to a voiceless people." How successful have contemporary translators been in restoring the literature of Mesoamerica prior to the Spanish conquest?

I. S.   It is an ongoing project. Much survives in oral form, and thus the translation effort is filled with obstacles. But León-Portilla's oeuvre has opened the door to an awareness that reaches beyond Mexico. His monumental oeuvre is the tip of an iceberg built by scholars of various disciplines: history, anthropology, ethnography. . . .

N. S.   You compare León-Portilla to Gershom Scholem?

I. S.   León-Portilla also has a magisterial mind, and his lifelong quest has been, much like Scholem's, to open up an obscure—to some people esoteric—universe parallel to ours. I say "parallel" because León-Portilla shows the extent to which Mesoamerican letters are not a salvo from the past but a reality alive and well in the present.

N. S.   Your essay "Translation and Identity" [*The Essential Ilan Stavans*], where the topic is the role that translation played in the Spanish colonization of Mexico and Peru, made me wonder: how do translators and interpreters of Nahuatl, Quechua, Maya, and other pre-Columbian tongues, give, as you put it, a "voice back to a voiceless people"? How much of that voice is the voice of the translator?

I. S.   León-Portilla's most famous book is *The Broken Spears,* known in Spanish by the Faulknerian title of *La visión de los vencidos:* the vision of the vanquished. The title is symptomatic: in their quest to "civilize" the natives, the Spaniards, with the New Testament as weapon, sought to erase pre-Columbian civilization. They made people silent by tying their tongues, at times by cutting them out altogether. Through the effort of nineteenth-century and modern translators, the attempt to reinsert the tongue in its place is done—not without a hint of nostalgia, though. And nostalgia leads to distortion. The translator's voice is only a medium to bring back a lost voice, but it isn't the lost voice itself.

N. S.   How heavily did Hernán Cortés, Diego de Almagro, Francisco Pizarro, and Gonzalo Jiménez de Quesada rely on interpreters to subjugate indigenous Indian populations?

I. S.   Their success depended on their ability to convey their message to their enemy. In Mexico the mythical figure of La Malinche, an Aztec who became Cortés's mistress, is illustrative: she is perceived as the nation' s traitor, ready to use her sexuality to advance her own career without a kernel of remorse for the betrayal of her people. And there are others like her. The chronicler Bernal Díaz del Castillo talks of two Mayans, Melchorejo and Julianillo, who are equally emblematic. He is only one among many whose account is at our disposal. I hope one day we will have a full history of translation in the Americas, a much-needed compendium of loyalties and treason.

N. S.   Could translation projects serve as a form of restitution for vanishing or vanished cultures? For example, could a government accomplish restitution by means of a large-scale project financing the revival of lost cultural masterpieces?

I. S.   I wouldn't dare go in that direction. Whenever governments get involved in intellectual endeavors, the result is tragic. Think of Stalin's U.S.S.R, Senator McCarthy's America, Hitler's Germany, Fidel Castro's Cuba. . . . The list is too atrocious to compile.

N. S.   Is the written word the most resilient vehicle for preserving memory?

I. S.   In an evanescent universe like ours, I know of no more dignified, suitable format. How else might we survive death other than though memory? Memory is built on the remnants of forgetfulness. It is our most fragile, volatile venture. Each individual has its own bank, and so does each culture.

N. S.   Does preserving memory as literature require continuous marketing and distribution?

I. S.   Literature is a democratic, yet also an elitist endeavor. One is able to read, in a free society, anything one chooses. But how many people make those choices? Very few, really. And this is as it should be. I am interested in popular culture, in engagement with community, but the art of reading is for me a secluded, isolated, private one. I shy away from large, overinflated, bestselling books: if the masses embraced it, I tell myself, I probably won't, so I don't even try. An ancient Chinese proverb states that it is more dangerous to give a book to an uneducated person than a sword to a child. The Talmud suggests that books, like teachers, choose their pupils and not the other way around. [*Laughter.*]

5

Onto *la hispanidad*

I. S.　　The metaphor of the *hyphen* came about at the height of the so-called "culture wars." It was used to stress the dual—e.g., ambivalent—identity of ethnic Americans, whose self was split apart—a type immortalized in Stevenson's *The Strange Case of Dr. Jekyll and Mr. Hyde*. African-American, Jewish-American, Latino-American, Asian-American . . . the hyphen doesn't stress the conflict but the point of encounter: the bridge.

N. S.　　True, commentators have placed their attention on the early chapter of *The Hispanic Condition* [1995] called "Life in the Hyphen." But the metaphor is not empty of controversy. The *American Heritage Dictionary of the English Language,* in its fourth edition, states that hyphenated status may implicitly demean those whose identities are hyphenated: "Naturalized immigrants to the United States and their descendents have sometimes been termed hyphenated Americans in reference to the tendency to hyphenate such ethnic compounds as Irish-American or Polish-American. This term has come under strong criticism as suggesting that those so designated are not so fully American as 'un-hyphenated' citizens," and thus, "it [the term] is best avoided in all but historical contexts."

I. S.　　*E pluribus unum.* The United States, a sum of units, is a pluralistic society. Pluralism is not only a political category but a cultural one too. It succeeds not by imposition but by consensus. A society such

99

as ours, made up of numerous cultures, is invariably richer when those cultures are allowed to have their own space while, at the same time, communicating respectfully with the others. As the United States moves deeper into this millennium, the non-European component is likely to achieve power. There is reason to worry, some argue, because the nation might undergo a process of Balkanization. I doubt it, though. The *idea* of America is too ingrained, too widespread and deeply rooted, to divide people by ethnic turf. But it is clear that a monolithic, homogenized culture unready to offer space for minorities to affirm their distinctiveness is no longer feasible.

N. S. You are, according to the *New York Times* and other national newspapers, "one of the foremost critics of Hispanic culture," "the Skip Gates of Latino Studies," "the Balzac of contemporary critics," and "the Czar of Latino Literature." But you have also been referred to on the street as a "white Hispanic," "the Jew," *"el güero."* . . . In *The Essential Ilan Stavans* , you mention that once settled in the United States, you "suddenly began to be perceived as Hispanic (i.e., Latino), an identity totally alien to me before."

I. S. *Latino* is a mercurial term—nothing more than a convention. Nobody is really a Latino, the way nobody is European, Middle Eastern, and Asian. People might be Chinese, Greek, Salvadoran. . . . Until I was twenty-five years of age, the main feature of my identity was my Jewishness. I often come across Mexicans, of course, but mine was an ethnic—or rather, a cultural—enclave. The fact that I was Mexican mattered less than the fact that I was *un judío*. Conversely, the moment I arrived in New York my Jewishness ceased to matter and, ironic as it might be in New York, I suddenly became a *mexicano*—a Mexican among other Hispanics: Colombians, Argentines, Dominicans, and Puerto Ricans. I had inadvertently inserted myself in the current—the *pluribus*—of Latino identity north of the Rio Grande, where nobody knows what a Latino is but everyone recognizes it instantaneously. . . .

N. S. This reminds me of Walter Mosley. He acknowledges his indebtedness to his Jewish and African American heritage in shaping his daily experiences. But in *USA Today* Mosley stated: "A lot of people would say to me, 'Well you're multiracial.' And I am. But in this society, I'm black. That's not my color, but that's how I'm seen by others." Instead, you have a triple self: Jewish, Mexican, and American.

I. S.　　No, I have a single self forked into three. . . . No society is free of stereotypes. They are the oil that makes the engine work. . . . Latinos are a diverse bunch. This diversity makes it challenging for other Americans—also for Hispanics outside the United States—to understand them in full. The easy solution is to simplify: Latinos, every single one of them, are brown, Catholic immigrants with a limited knowledge of the English language. That, at least, is the image exposed at the level of pop culture on TV and in Hollywood. But the educated elite isn't better off, I'm afraid. There's a longstanding, acute disdain for *la hispanidad* north of the Rio Grande. It goes back to the Spanish-American War of 1898 and maybe beyond to the Mexican War of 1848. The term *barbarism* is often applied to Hispanics.

N. S.　　On the NPR program *Talk of the Nation* [30 September 2002] that profiled Hispanic identity, you said that Latino immigrants have "become something we were not in our country of origin, and we are called to represent that particular culture, constantly being asked, 'Is this typical or authentic Mexican food, or is the way all Mexicans feel or think or dance or act or dream?'" You further go on to assert: "This is a wonderful country, the United States, a country that uses stereotypes in order to define itself, define its individuals. We all struggle to debunk those stereotypes." And here I paraphrase: A political leader who starts as a liberal and ends a conservative, a Catholic individual who converts to Islam, an immigrant who jumps from a remote village in Honduras to the gardens of Bel Air—each of us is the protagonist of a journey. Everything changes and so do we, constantly, especially in America. But are immigrants in the United States forced to betray their roots, pushed to transform themselves into impersonators?

I. S.　　Yes, of course. They become reluctant ambassadors of their primary culture, a culture they know only partially and about which they have ambivalent emotions. I, for one, became *Mexican* the moment I left Mexico: a representative, in people's eyes, of the people south of the border. So was I considered Mexican in Mexico? Not quite, not to the same degree. . . . In *The Decline and Fall of the Roman Empire,* Edward Gibbons states that in the *al-Qu'rān* there are no camels. The fact astonishes him. How to explain a total absence of camels in the supreme book of the Muslim people? But think about it: why should Arabs emphasize camels when the animals are so common in the region? Tourists need to find camels for their Kodak moment, but not the natives. This anecdote, about which I talk in *On Borrowed Words,* is useful to ponder issues of authenticity: the immigrant is forced to represent for others the exotic stereotype of his indigenous culture. And so, as I arrived in Manhattan in the mid-eighties, others asked about tequila, sombreros, and piñatas.

N. S.   The tension between civilization and barbarism is at the core of the Americas. You explore at length these themes in the introduction to *Facundo, or Civilization and Barbarism* [1998].

I. S.   It's a mysterious book. Domingo Faustino Sarmiento, a journalist, activist, diplomat, and president of Argentina from 1868–1874, used Juan Facundo Quiroga, a nineteenth-century outlaw and opponent of the Juan Manuel de Rosas regime, to explore the contradiction between order and chaos, civilization and barbarism, in his native Argentina. How is barbarism understood in particular? Toward the end of *Vida de Quiroga,* as *Facundo* was known when first published in 1845, the protagonist returns in his carriage. A plot to assassinate him is about to unfold. The depiction Sarmiento makes of the murder is stunning: the reader feels the bravery, the cowardice, the blood spilt. . . . Sarmiento, in the early passages of his volume and elsewhere in his oeuvre, advocated the decimation of the Gaucho population in the region. To compensate for the destruction, he advocated immigration to Argentina from Italy and other points of departure on the Old Continent. For Argentina to become *civilized,* for the European model to be fully digested, any remnant of the native culture must be erased. The urban centers such as Buenos Aires were for him bastions of order and education, whereas the countryside was primitive, animalistic, and dangerous. In our modern eyes, this is an atrocious theory. Fortunately, as president he backed away from implementing it as policy.

N. S.   Borges believed that Argentina's fortunes would have been better off if Facundo, and not Martín Fierro, was the nation's number one hero.

I. S.   The book *Martín Fierro,* by José Hernández, also about Gauchos, was, in Borges's eyes, not only too romantic, but too adulterated to pass as "authentic Argentine literature." He used to make a distinction between *literatura gaucha* and *literatura gauchesca:* the former, though less refined, emerged from the landscape in which these provincial types thrived; the latter, on the other hand, is a theft performed by urban dwellers—a depiction of Gaucho life by non-Gauchos. Still, as with all prima facie comments by the author of "Funes the Memorious," this one should also be taken with a grain of salt. Borges also said that Facundo is "the most memorable character of Argentine letters."

Anyway, the equation Sarmiento used is an ancient one. It dates back not to the Crusades, but to the expansion of Roman culture in its satellite colonies. It is made patent in Shakespeare's *The Tempest,* where Caliban is made to represent the instinctual forces of nature. It is also in the essays by Michel de Montaigne, the opinions of the French Encyclopedists, and in the historical views modeled by Georg Wilhelm Friedrich Hegel and Oswald Spengler. At the dawn of the twenty-first century, it is ubiquitous. It is inferred from the theories laid out by Arnold Toynbee and also in *The Clash of Civilizations and the Remaking of the World Order,* a study by Samuel Huntington that, perilously, permeates our understanding of contemporary life. For instance, the division between North and South in the American continent is seen through this prism: culture vs. savageness. Likewise, the tension between Western civilization and the Arab world has also been tinted this way.

N. S.   Why are Huntington's ideas "perilous"?

I. S.   Huntington presents a schematic diagram of the collision of civilizations. He suggests that Latin America, for instance, is to be understood today as a civilization that is somewhat different from what he names *Western* (that is, Europe and the United States). The point is well taken: since 1492, as the region halfheartedly entered modern times, the goal has been to integrate it to the European model. The problem, though, is that around 35.3 million Latinos live north of the Rio Grande. Where should we place them? Are they an integral part of Western civilization? The answer, it strikes me, is that the concept of civilization as defined by the Harvard University professor is too rigid. Do we really exist in a world divided by such polarities as North and South, and East and West? Isn't the South *inside* the North and vice versa?

N. S.   The dichotomy, then, is an illusion.

I. S.   Of course. Miscegenation has been a feature of the human race since the Pharaohs in Egypt: black and white, North and South—where are the boundaries? The processes of migration, assimilation, and miscegenation result in a form of alienation from within culture—in *imposture*. In fact, since 9/11, the concept of the impostor has acquired a different implication. Muhammed Atta and his ringleaders pretended to be part of Western civilization: they went to the gym, used ATMs, enrolled in aviation schools. . . . For a period of time, their identities melded into the environment. They kept their secret mission to themselves until the moment of truth forced them to uncover their faces.

Ever since the Inquisition was established in the Iberian Peninsula in 1481, the Hispanic world has been used to these twists of identity: *marranos, moriscos, conversos,* crypto-Jews, and crypto-Muslims are all types forced to be something they refuse to embrace. The Americas were colonized by them: their fingerprints are part of our culture of deceit.

N. S.   Why isn't Sarmiento read in the United States?

I. S.   He is, to the degree that a foreign author born in 1811 and dead by 1888, might be: among students, primarily.

N. S.   My own question leads me to a book review you penned in *World Literature Today* [70. 4 (fall 1996)], where, you state, "a writer can be born into the wrong language and geography."

I. S.   I believe that to be the case. Felisberto Hernández, an Uruguayan born in 1902 and who died at the age of sixty-two, whose stories and novellas are mesmerizing, is, in style and manner, utterly *Kafkaesque.* Or better, Kafka might be described as *Hernándezesque.* But the Czech is the recipient of international fame. Why? He was a Jew from Central Europe, a culture and an area at the core of Western civilization. Hernández, on the other hand, used Spanish as his tongue and he was from a remote part of the world, from which highbrow art isn't supposed to emanate. The relationship between languages and cultures is colored by the way the empire approaches its colonies. The New York publishing industry today pays attention to artistic items from Berlin, London, Paris, and Rome, and to a lesser extent Barcelona and Athens. Often, a work by a Chinese, Romanian, or a Sudanese author might even be translated into English not from the original but from French—that is, when the work is already available in

France. Otherwise, it is likely to remain ignored. This explains why, from World War II onwards, the number of literati who switch languages, from a colonial tongue to the language of empire, has increased dramatically.

N. S.   You've used the term "fake" to describe Sarmiento.

I. S.   His books emulated European models. He perverted those models, he revamped them. For instance, *Facundo* opens with a quote in French: "On ne tue point les idées." In Spanish: "Las ideas no pueden ser decapitadas"; and in English translation: "Ideas cannot be beheaded." An exquisite statement, except that, as I've stated in the introduction to the Penguin Classics edition, it's a misquotation attributed to Hippolyte Fortoul. It actually belongs to Diderot, who said it somewhat differently: "On ne tue pas de coups de fusil aux idées."

N. S.   A deliberate misquotation. . . .

I. S.   Yes. In that sense Sarmiento is an impostor: he falsifies or "fakes" culture.

N. S.   Another "explorer" of the Hispanic psyche is Alvar Núñez Cabeza de Vaca, one of the earliest Spanish adventurers to Florida and the Southwest. About whom you wrote in *Chronicle of the Narváez Expedition* [2002].

I. S.   Cabeza de Vaca was a charlatan, a consummate liar who, after being shipwrecked, lost touch with most of the expedition he was part of, led by Pánfilo de Narváez. He wandered across the continent, convincing the Indians he stumbled upon that he was a magical healer. I'm deeply attracted to the explorer as liar.

N. S.   Why?

I. S.   Explorers have a unique turn at history. Their chronicles are the first reports audiences get of life on the fringes. The conquest of the Americas is filled with liars and self-aggrandizers. Cabeza de Vaca simply happened to be a considerably talented one.

N. S.   You describe Cabeza de Vaca as an "imperfect explorer."

I. S.   Perhaps I should have said "the perfect imperfect explorer," for he is representative of the Spanish colonial enterprise in the Americas: a dunce in search of . . . what? As part of the doomed expedition of Pánfilo de Narváez, he sought power and earthy possessions but his ship capsized, he lost his sense of direction, and ended up naked and hungry among the Indian tribes, to whom he presented himself as a messiah of sorts. Isn't that what the *conquistadores* were about? The difference between Cabeza de Vaca and the others is that he was a bit more honest—or more foolish. He got fame and fortune alright, and then he lost them. . . .

N. S.   Borges, too, plays with themes of deception and illusion. . . .

I. S.   Yes, Borges might be the ultimate faker in a culture of deceit.

N. S.   What was the price they paid for their deceit?

I. S.   Sor Juana Inés de La Cruz, for one, paid a heavy price. She lost her library, she lost her tongue, she lost her pen, and then she proceeded to die. Reinaldo Arenas also paid dearly. He was imprisoned, he was forced into a silence he refused to embrace in Cuba. Finally, he was released by the Castro regime. But he went in the opposite direction and he became promiscuous in New York in the age of AIDS and ultimately paid for it, too. From absence to presence, from silence to outburst, the journey had been asymmetrical. That is also the result of repression. Arenas is a homosexual, he doesn't become an imposter the way others would become, meaning hiding who they are, being quiescent. . . . I remember in the case of Manuel Puig that he would describe himself in his own words as *un maricón hecho y derecho*—"a flaming fag." Puig frequently trotted out the names of Hollywood stars to describe authors, kind of to tease them: Borges was Joan Crawford, Mario Vargas Llosa was Esther Williams, José Lezama Lima was Lana Turner, Carlos Fuentes was Ava Gardner. . . . Also, I remember when journalist Ricardo Rocha asked: "Manuel Puig, ¿es Ud. homosexual?" Are you gay? He became nervous, and then replied: "One doesn't ask such questions in public, Señor Rocha." Likewise with the pop singer Ricky Martin. When interviewed by Barbara Walters and she asked, "Are you gay?," he answered: "Let us move to the next question."

N. S.   Your essay "The Latin Phallus" [*The Essential Ilan Stavans*] ignited some controversy when you subtly explored the possibility of Borges's homosexuality and Cortázar's bisexuality and the mysterious circumstances of his death. Could you talk about the controversy surrounding the essay's publication?

I. S.   Homosexuality in the Hispanic world is a silenced topic. Years ago, when I questioned Borges's sexual preferences, I became the target of accusations by his widow and literary agent. They complained that such realms ought not to be discussed in public. Their [Borges's and Cortázar's] respective estates were unhappy with my insinuation that either of them could have been homosexuals. It was as if you were touching a sacred cow. And both estates wrote letters, there was discussion, there was polemic. In and of itself, the controversy is revealing: in a culture where sexualities are sharply delineated (macho male, submissive female), the intelligentsia becomes not the instrument to diagnose the symptom, but the symptom itself. Someone said to me at one point, "Ilan, you're married with children. What if someone accused you being gay?" *Accuse?* Are gays criminals? Are they depraved? Is there shame in it? Why use the term "accuse"? Obviously, I speak from a north-of-the-border viewpoint. The answer to these questions in Latin America is a rotund "yes."

N. S.　　But has there been a loosening of these repressive reins on homosexuality in Latin America?

I. S.　　To this day, homosexuals are still segregated. But Cuba is a case unto itself. Elsewhere in the hemisphere, minor changes have taken place. Not too long ago in Mexico, a soap opera featured a gay character as its protagonist. It was a milestone, although collectively, deep down, machismo remains pervasive and homosexuals are seen as satanic figures. Other minorities also suffer segregation.

N. S.　　The comedian John Leguizamo produced and was slated to star in Leon Ichaso's film on Nuyorican playwright Miguel Piñero. Apparently, he dropped the part because of his reservations about the portrayal of the playwright's relationship with teenage boys. Leguizamo stated once that "I didn't want to portray him as a child molester, because we have so few Latino heroes. Before I knew that, he was a huge inspiration to me, but when I found out about it, his image was tarnished." What do you make of Leguizamo's uneasiness?

I. S.　　Although I understand Leguizamo's claim, I'm in disagreement. The abundance of negative images in the media is astonishing. On the other hand, we cannot flee away from the reality that surrounds us.

N. S.　　In *The Hispanic Condition* you write that "homosexuality is another repressed ghost in the closet [in Latin America], also to be understood in the light of the schism dividing our collective soul. Since ours is a galaxy of brute macho types and virginal and devoted women, gays, although fatally crushed in the battles between the sexes, represent another facet of what I refer to as 'translated identities.'" You've explored the topic of homosexuality in your controversial essay the "The Latin Phallus." Can you explain the idea of homosexuality as a translated identity? And are gay writers forced to behave as *de facto* imposters in the context of Latin American politics?

I. S.   The tension between the sexes in that context is intense. A number of gay authors are quite important: Manuel Puig, Virgilio Piñera, Reinaldo Arenas, José Lezama Lima, and scores of others. They have paid a price as a result of their sexuality. . . . As victims of a repressive environment, these literati, in order to communicate with their *authentic* readers, encode their texts with secret messages. That, in a nutshell, is what I mean by "translated identities." In *Respuesta a Sor Filotea,* an apology that abounds in Latinate quotations, Sor Juana asks for forgiveness for her unpardonable sin: her womanhood. But what is her atonement about? She uses the devices at the disposal of the translator: she hides behind a mask, she falsifies her humbleness.

Hers is an extreme case, but the other authors I've listed engage in a somewhat similar practice. This attitude toward codes is typical in the crypto-Jewish tradition: one states one viewpoint, although in truth one embraced its polar opposite. You know, in 1982, when President José López Portillo nationalized the bank industry in Mexico, an atmosphere of fear was felt everywhere. People were afraid to be open about their financial transactions. The Yiddish term *"lokshn"* and its Spanish equivalent *"tallarines"* were synonyms for "dollars." These synonyms were often used in telephone conversations. As a dialogue began, these themes would be an invitation for conversants to engage in a fiesta of possibilities: a *sopa de tallarines* meant a bank account in dollars, a *pasta con verduras* referred to stock options, etc. Repression is the mother of metaphor.

The art of encoded messages reminds me of an argument made by Leo Strauss, an esteemed philosopher at the University of Chicago and teacher of Allan Bloom (author of *The Closing of the American Mind*). Strauss wrote a seminal essay on *The Guide for the Perplexed* in which he argues that a reader interested at once in philosophy and in theology might read the book by Maimonides in various directions: as a argument in favor of creationism, but also against it, as an invective against Aristotle but also as an attack on Platonism, as a panegyric of the Bible but also as a dissertation on the possibility of G-d having a limited power on earth. No matter how we approach it, there's always another possible reading of *The Guide for the Perplexed*—at least one more, if not many. But how can it be that a book can be read in both directions? Is Maimonides in favor of or against Aristotelianism? The key term, of course, is "perplexed." Who, according to Maimonides, is a *perplexed* person? What might that individual be perplexed about?

The Rambam was a genius. In large part, our modern Jewish identity, eight centuries later, is modeled on his legal, philosophical and moral lessons. His objective was virtuous: to simplify the Talmud, which, for the average dweller, was a Rubik's Cube of judicial opinions. Aside from the *Moreh Nevukhim,* he authored the *Mishneh Torah* and the *Commentary on the Mishna*—a towering contribution, by all accounts. He was equally versed in rabbinical Responsa, ethics, philosophy, and medicine. These texts were produced strictly for believers, though. But what about Jewish skeptics? Those, exactly, are the targeted readers of *The Guide for the Perplexed,* the ones that understand that faith is not prescription for existential doubt.

Superficially, the theory behind Maimonides is that readers might be grouped at different levels: there is the desultory one that approaches a text superficially; and then there are the agile, penetrating ones, able to decipher encoded messages behind the words and sentences. On a deeper level, though, Maimonides suggests a more interesting idea: he announces that a certain author might actually deliver a book whose true significance is only available, not to everyone, but to a small bastion of readers. An undemocratic idea? Perhaps, but literature, at its core, is undemocratic. Furthermore, literature—the literature that matters, at least—is always a game of mirrors in which what you get isn't what you see. Something exquisite is lost in translation. Or is it not? [*Laughter*]

N. S.   Your friend Richard Rodríguez is a controversial figure with Latinos in the United States. The last passages of *On Borrowed Words* reproduce a conversation the two of you had in a café in San Francisco. What has he expressed to you about the reception he faced from the Hispanic world, as an openly gay writer?

I. S.   It took Richard decades to come out of the closet. One of the reasons—the substantial reason—*Hunger of Memory* is so tortured, so disliked by a portion of its readership, is, I believe, because of the unconfessed nature of the author's sexual orientation. Overtly, the autobiography is about being a scholarship boy, about being Mexican-American in the age of affirmative action, about bilingual education. . . . At its core, though, it is about gender, although Rodríguez doesn't seem to have this aspect of the narrative conscious in his mind.

When I sit with Richard to converse—and I've indulged in these types of conversations with him several times—the topic is seldom his homosexual identity. Instead, we talk about politics and memory, about language and silence, about the sorrowful state of world affairs. Often we disagree, which for me is crucial. Why have friends with whom you regularly agree? I'm against scores of points in *Hunger of Memory*. Likewise, I've expressed my opinion in public on *Days of Obligation* and *Brown,* the two volumes that complete Rodríguez's trilogy about American life at the end of the twentieth century.

N. S.   Do you see the similarities between the outrage that Rodríguez generated and the one generated by Octavio Paz in his assessment of the Mexican-American community?

I. S.   Paz's odyssey is one that delineates a journey from the edges of power to the center. Eventually, he himself became the status quo in Mexico. Rodríguez too has traveled far: from a low-income household as the child of immigrants to a middle-class life in the Bay Area. His regular contributions to the *News Hour with Jim Lehrer,* his op-ed pages in the *Los Angeles Times,* place him at the core of the ethnic debate in the United States today. He used to write in *Harper's*—not so much anymore. Nevertheless, he remains a marginal figure. Somehow, in spite of the regularity with which his oeuvre is anthologized, he doesn't sit in the U.S. literary canon in a place that is roughly the equivalent of where Octavio Paz sits in Mexican letters. Whenever Paz would get himself involved in a controversy, its effects would be felt widely in various levels of the cultural hierarchy. Rodríguez's controversies, instead, pass by unattended. Take the case of the polemic surrounding "The Pachucos and Other Extremes," which is the starting chapter of *The Labyrinth of Solitude.* Ever since its original release, before 1950, it has been the subject of a heated debate. In

Mexico the volume as a whole is a robust machine of secondhand opinions. Chicanos, in particular, dislike that segment thoroughly. *Hunger of Memory* also is contentious, but it is the subject of debate only among a limited number of people: those interested in ethnicity. In fact, this number could be circumscribed even more to those concerned with *lo hispánico*.

Curiously, *Hunger of Memory* isn't available in Spanish for Mexicans to read. It was published in a regrettable translation by a university press on the Iberian Peninsula, which never pushed its circulation. It pains me because the volume is canonical in Latino literature in this country. It tells much about being Mexican in the United States. The fact that it isn't available in Mexico amounts to censorship, as far as I'm concerned—censorship and nearsightedness.

N. S.   Was censorship based on his political views?

I. S.   No, it was based on ignorance. Mexicans don't want to know what Mexican-Americans think. They don't think that Mexican-Americans think. They think that Mexican-Americans are migrant workers, mindless, going from one place to another, incapable of producing anything of value. Not that someone is sitting in a bureaucrat's office saying "we're not going to translate Richard Rodríguez." But the thought doesn't come to anybody, which is distressing, don't you think? [*Laughter.*]

N. S.   In *The Riddle of Cantinflas,* there is an essay entitled "How Hispanics Became Brown." What do you think of Richard Rodríguez's memoir simply called *Brown*?

I. S.   It is richly textured. . . . It is also evasive, unspecific, exuding metaphors. For him "brownness" is a synonym for "miscegenation"—that is, *mestizaje*. America in the dawn of the twenty-first century is brown, he argues.

N. S.   At a literary evening at the City University of New York in early 2002, you called Rodríguez "a Jewish writer." . . .

I. S.   Because of his obsession with memory and words, I guess. He is regretful but also tenacious, intrigued by a present that is a result of an intricate past. In *Days of Obligation* he holds an allegorical conversation with his father that, at its core, strikes me as a biblical dialogue.

N. S.   Oscar "Zeta" Acosta, a Chicano lawyer and outlaw of the Civil Rights movement, is the subject of your book *Bandido* [1996].

I. S.   An individual in whose honor the word "excess" appears to have been coined. . . . He left us a couple of autobiographical volumes: *The Autobiography of a Brown Buffalo* and *The Revolt of the Cockroach People*. "Zeta" inhabited impossible contradictions: a self-loathing Chicano, focused on the destruction of his own life. My biographical rumination was disliked by the Chicano establishment, which resented the fact that it wasn't the byproduct of an insider.

The same criticism came as a response to my essay "Sandra Cisneros: Form over Content" in *Academic Questions* [4.9 (fall 1996); also in *The Essential Ilan Stavans*].

N. S.   What made Acosta so fanatical?

I. S.   "Zeta" belongs to the age of Jack Kerouac, Allen Ginsberg, Hunter S. Thompson, and Henry Miller, a time in which, as Truman Capote illustriously put it, people didn't write, they simply typed. That is, their style was automatic, not in the Surrealist sense of the term: it was mechanical, automatic, and spontaneous. That spontaneity, that resistance to delineation, to the act of being circumscribed, is what makes him so compelling.

N. S.   Was the main criticism of *Bandido* the absence of bona fide Chicano credentials?

I. S.   It is a criticism that runs through our multiracial culture. . . . When filming *Malcom X,* Spike Lee put it this way: "No one who isn't black should be allowed to touch the story of the leader of the Nation of Islam." The argument, of course, is frightening. It suggests that only what pertains to our ethnicity should be addressed in art. Could you imagine how limited we would be if as a society we were to endorse such doctrinaire approach? Art is nothing but an invitation to break boundaries, to go beyond ourselves, to experience life through another set of eyes. In Shakespeare's age, the part of Othello, as a result of the requirements of the culture, was interpreted by a white actor. Blacks didn't have a place on the theatrical stage. Still, the fact that a nonblack plays the role is an extraordinary proposition. Knowledge in general pushes us out of our skin. If we only limited ourselves to what we've experienced, nobody would study the Middle Ages because, obviously, nobody today went through them. The approach can be extraordinarily confining: our own family, school, religion. . . . Why do we read books? Why do we go to the movies? To reach out, to escape our own condition. Should we not perform *West Side Story,* a musical retelling of the tragedy of *Romeo and Juliet* that to some people is offensive in its representation of Puerto Ricans in New York? Should we not stage *The Merchant of Venice* because of its anti-Semitic ingredients? Of course we should, time and again. Each performance should be an opportunity to understand the context in which Shakespeare composed his dramas, the ideas that inspired him, the social, intellectual, and theological texture of his time.

The criticism label thrown at me after *Bandido* appears to be ongoing. A student whose undergraduate education was done at the University of California in Santa Barbara once told me that a teacher of his often repeated: "Never criticize a Chicano in public. You'll immediately become the enemy." It is a troublesome state of affairs to understand criticism as a destructive endeavor. The critic serves an invaluable function in democracy, reflecting on who we are, where we've been, and where we're going—attempting to understand the relationship between our daily lives and the dreams we dream. By definition, the critic is at once an insider and an outsider: he is simultaneously a member of society and also a visitor.

N. S.   You've often expressed dismay with the lack of serious criticism in Latin America. Could this be attributed to the influence of the Catholic Church?

I. S.   It is proof of the Iberian heritage. The age of Reformation never really took hold in the Iberian Peninsula. This is because Spain nurtured a strong Counter Reformation that cancelled any possibility of a free-flowing, open dialogue of ideas. Just as the rest of Europe was being swept away in the eighteenth century by a growing bourgeoisie that fashioned itself as a conduit of a fresh, reinvigorated mentality, one impatient with the Ancient Regime, the Spaniards allowed themselves to be swallowed—*devorados*—by dogmatism. In 1776 and 1789, as the American Revolution and the French Revolution are unfolding, France was already submerged in its Romantic movement. But Spain had a second-rate Romanticism in the nineteenth century. Only Mariano José de Larra is a thinker who, although stretching it somewhat, might be worthy of our attention. We owe to him sentences such as "aquí yace media España, murió de la otra media" [herein lies the dead half of Spain, seceded from its other half]. The entire peninsula got itself lost in the philosophy known as *Krausismo,* a reaction against the Enlightenment modeled after the mediocre German thinker Karl Christian Friedrich Krause. Aside from Larra, one needs to search patiently to find figures who represent the embrace of reason against fanaticism. Gaspar Melchor de Jovellanos, active in Madrid, is among the most progressive. And who else? The Spanish and Portuguese Americas inherited an inflexible, fastidious, orthodox approach to ideas. This, too, is the legacy of the baroque style: dogmatism. Whereas in the United States, revolutionary figures—those Joseph Ellis called "the Founding Brothers"—were capable not only of subverting British rule, but of establishing a Declaration of Independence and a Constitution that offered a set of republican reforms affecting the participating states of the newly formed Union, in the Spanish and Portuguese Americas the *revolucionarios* didn't quite know what to do once the ties to the empire across the Atlantic were cut. Their solution: to assassinate one another until a single surviving figure became the ultimate ruler. That pattern, I'm afraid, has been followed from one revolutionary movement to another in our hemisphere: from Cuba to Nicaragua, the corollary of a revolution is tyranny. And tyranny is a form of feudalism. Alfonso Reyes and Octavio Paz often decried the state of criticism in Mexico, ruled by *compadrasgo,* friendship and nepotism. Not too different is the situation in Argentina and Cuba. To criticize, it is understood, is to either celebrate or to attack. But the function of criticism is quite different: to enlighten, to ponder large political and intellectual issues, to place ourselves in history.

N. S.   Could I ask you to illustrate the idea of the baroque in the Hispanic world?

I. S.   In Mexico and Peru, the baroque, grotesque, and monstrous are evident in colonial times. It is featured in architecture, music, religious art, and folklore. Keep in mind that, at the time of the conquest and colonization, Spain was amidst a period of baroque aesthetics: Diego Velázquez, Quevedo, and Góngora are a handful of representatives. Calderón de la Barca is responsible for the play *Life Is a Dream,* in which Segismundo, the imprisoned successor to the throne, wonders: am I trapped in a reverie? The Iberian psyche was infused with ornate, self-referential imagery. Cuba was equally baroque, though on the island the style has perpetuated itself to the present in ways unseen in the rest of the Americas. The explanation might have to do with the density of Cuban culture: not only do Afro-Cuban and European artifacts interact constantly, but the island, as a result of its geographical location, has been, since the sixteenth century, a port of entry and departure of products and people the globe over.

From 1523 to 1810, art and letters in the Americas abound in baroque examples. Sor Juana Inés de La Cruz left us with plays and an epistemological meditation entitled *First Dream*. The first lines are superb: "Piramidal, funesta, de la tierra / nacida sombra, al Cielo encaminaba"; in English: "Pyramidal, doleful, mournful shadow / born of the earth. . . . " Her superb sonnets are immortal:

> Este, que ves, engaño colorido,
> que del arte ostentando los primores,
> con falsos silogismos de colores,
> es cauteloso engaño del sentido;

In Margaret Sayers Peden's translation:

> This that you gaze on, colorful deceit,
> that so immodestly displays art's favors,
> with its fallacious arguments of colors
> is to the senses cunning counterfeit.

Sor Juana is also a protofeminist of immense power:

Hombres necios que acusáis	Misguided men, who will chastise
a la mujer sin razón,	a woman when no blame is due,
sin ver que sois la ocasión	oblivious that it is you
de lo mismo que culpáis:	who prompted what you criticize.

Likewise her contemporary, Carlos de Sigüenza y Góngora, although his lyricism is of a different kind.

In Quevedo, Sor Juana, and Sigüenza one has characters that look at themselves and reflect on the act of looking at themselves. In many ways it's very close to the postmodern, or what we have come to call postmodern, in which we are all actors of a larger play. An attribute of *la mentalidad barroca,* the baroque mind, is that it is hierarchical, much like the Catholic Church and the map of the universe it supported during the Renaissance.

N. S.   Let's move to popular culture—in particular, to comic books. You've frequented comic strips since adolescence. Eventually, you published a tribute of sorts: *Latino USA* [2000], an irreverent cartoon history illustrated by Lalo López Alcaráz. How did the project come about?

I. S.   My passion for comic strips dates back to the seventies, when, growing up in Mexico City, I religiously stopped at the neighborhood kiosk to acquire the latest installments of *Los Agachados, Kalimán,* and other lowlife Mexican superheroes. I learned much about the nation's past, about its quest for identity. My passion didn't diminish as I became an avid reader of novels. In fact, the art of juxtaposing Madame Bovary with Cantinflas, Raskolnikov and Mafalda, was rewarding; each spoke to another part of me, and sometimes to each other. So the telephone call from a New York editor to invite me to produce a cartoon history of Latinos was nothing but thrilling. It allowed me to pay tribute to the pop culture of my youth, through translation: in English and for a readership light-years away from my native culture.

In shaping it, my dream was to be at once responsible and irreverent. I wanted to prove that a scholar need not be imprisoned in the squared formats of strict intellectual prose; that risks ought to be taken to explore different means of communication. Fine history should be fun too, shouldn't it? The idea once suggested by Thomas Aquinas that only the future is malleable is untrue. The future, actually, is rather immovable; people are incapable of touching it, until they become part of it. It is the past, instead, that changes constantly: each of us, alone and as part of a generation, constantly redefine it so as to map out our own roots, to define who we are and why. Latinos, the nation's fastest growing minority, are a sum of heterogeneous parts. In this volume I attempted to reflect that multiplicity of selves and multiplicity of pasts.

My literary influences—Cervantes and Pirandello, in particular—are overt. A history of Latinos is also a history of their present circumstances and a history of the historians that take upon themselves the task of delineating the past. My characters, at one point, enter my own library, read my books, and criticize my own oeuvre. This is to show that a critic's eye—or better, a critic's "I"—should be even-handed. Nothing should be left untouched, not even his own status as storyteller.

N. S.   In your collection of essays *The Riddle of Cantinflas* you say that political cartoons and murals in turn-of-the-century Mexico functioned as snapshots of contemporary affairs for the popular masses. You further claim that José Guadalupe Posada is "the founding father of genre." Do you also consider Posada the Abraham or Patriarch of the modern comics industry in Mexico? If so, why?

I. S.   No doubt Posada was a liberating figure. He refused to see art as a quest of the individual. His lampoons were for the masses. He didn't even sign his engravings. After he died, he was buried in an unnamed grave. But Posada's ubiquitous *calaveras* belong to Mexican folklore. The Mesoamerican imagery is alive in his oeuvre. That's why, I trust, Diego Rivera and the other muralists embraced him wholeheartedly: in him, the nation's history came alive in a nonelitist fashion. The ideology of Muralism is a twist of Posada's mandate: to bring art to the people.

N. S.   In the United States, the much heralded explosion of the comic industry was built on the innovations of such legends as Will Eisner (The Spirit), Joe Shuster and Jerry Siegel (Superman), Stan Lee (Spiderman, Silver Surfer, Fantastic Four), Jack Kirby aka Jacob Kurtzberg (Spiderman, Captain America, Silver Surfer, The Hulk, Fantastic Four), and Bob Kane (Batman). All were Jewish artists. Michael Chabon's *The Amazing Adventures of Kavalier and Klay* is a paean to these Jewish pioneers. Did any of these Jewish artists, staples of the U.S. industry, influence the comic book industry in Mexico?

I. S.   I'm sure they did, but their influence was empty of any Jewish content. Shuster and Siegel were instrumental in the shaping of heroes like *Kalimán,* and so were Lee and Kane. But even in the United States the Jewishness of these artists was a secret. How many people knew around World War II that *Superman* was a *"yeshiva bokher"*? *El Payo, Chanoc, Rocambole, Memín,* and *Detective Fisgón* are very diverse characters. A few trace their roots to nineteenth-century feuilleton literature, where the Mexican peasant is portrayed as ingrained with preternatural forces. But there are also characters—I'm thinking of *Los Agachados,* by the anti-Semite Eduardo del Rio (aka Rius)—who nurtured their talents in Soviet strips and, later, in the popular images of the Cuban Revolution.

N. S.   Do you agree with Ariel Dorfman and Armand Mattelart's assessment in their book *How to Read Donald Duck* that the United States' comic industry is an agent for American imperialism?

I. S.   That unfortunate book was popular at the height of the Cold War. A foolish, nearsighted Latin American left wholeheartedly embraced it. But the masses were far more intelligent: they ignored it altogether. Proof of the foolishness of its authors is their refusal—in the volume itself—to be comprehensive and evenhanded. They neglected to reflect, for instance, on native-made comic strips. Why didn't Dorfman and Mattelart "scrutinize" the ideological message of a *Kalimán*? The answer, I think, is a rather simple one: in their eyes an artist's origin is also his fate. Thus, to draw strips in Chicago is to be a CIA agent. They also believed that the societies north and south of the Rio Grande would always antagonize each other.

N. S.   How often did clearly Jewish characters make an appearance in Mexican comic books? Were the featured Jewish characters complex or merely flimsy stereotypes? Take for example, the conflicted impulses of heroism and villainy that mark Magneto in the Marvel comic book *X-Men.* In a daring move of character, Magneto, the leader of the Brotherhood of Evil Mutants, has been portrayed by the creators of the comic book over the years as a Holocaust survivor of either Jewish or Gypsy origins (the multimillion dollar blockbuster movie opts to paint him as a Jewish Holocaust survivor). I must admit that despite the character's complexity, I have not grown comfortable with the idea of the Holocaust survivor as major comic book villain. Does Magneto have a counterpart in the Mexican comic industry?

I. S.   Magneto as a strip hero could only emerge in the United States, where the Holocaust is a fundamental compass in the shaping of modern Jewish identity and where Nazism and the Arabs in popular culture are quintessential evil forces. Europe and Russia have modeled a different type of comic-strip enemy, and so has Latin America. Thus, an in-depth exploration of the Holocaust such as Art Spiegelman's *Maus* is American to the core: it strikes right at the heart of

America in the last third of the twentieth century: through anthropomorphic animal strips, it reflects on the Jewish quest for survival during World War II.

The only appearances of Jewish characters in Mexican strips that I remember, and they are scattered, are of the anti-Semitic stereotype of the capitalist moneylender. Often these appearances were insinuated, rather than overt: an avaricious patron would have a Jewish last name, for instance. As far as I recollect, never did the local superheroes have Semitic ancestry. The only occasion in which a more open discussion of Jews and their origin appeared in strips was in a nasty issue by Rius fully dedicated to the Jews. I mentioned it to you, as I did in the foreword to *Latino USA,* because I was thoroughly shocked when I came across it, to the point that my overall endearment to the genre changed forever. In it Rius praised Hitler and supported the thesis of the *Protocols of the Elders of Zion.* But Rius only articulated what other comic strip artists also thought: that Jews were conspirators in a campaign to conquer the globe.

N. S.   It fascinating to observe the recent rediscovery of Theodore Seuss Geisel's political bite and savvy vintage editorial cartoons. In the New Press's *Dr. Seuss Goes to War,* Geisel is in top form, skewering the isolationism and anti-Semitism that made up World War II America. I am curious to know if and how the Mexican comic book industry grapples with complex political themes?

I. S.   Sustained studies of Hispanic comic strips have yet to be written, but it is clear even without them that popular culture south the Rio Grande—and comic strips, in particular—as in other places, has served a therapeutic function when digesting complex political themes. In the last dictatorial years of the P.R.I., as the Institutional Revolutionary Party—Mexico's governing party from 1929 until the late 1990s—was called, the satirical strip *El Chamuco* ridiculed the political establishment, thus smoothing the democratic transition. Likewise, major characters have tackled major issues such as the sexual revolution, the fall of Communism in Russia, the drug trade from Colombia to the U.S.–Mexican border, etc. And national themes of inescapable relevance are also scrutinized: corruption and the excesses of political authority, race, gender, and geographical differences. . . . The moral divide that cuts across Mexican society is obvious in these strips. For instance, semipornographic strips like *La Pervertidora* tend to portray urban people as sexually insatiable whereas the rural population is seen as purer and more controlled.

N. S. While it appears readership of comics is quite robust in Mexico, U.S. readership has plummeted in recent years. Comic giant Marvel was in fact teetering on the brink of bankruptcy. Nonetheless, Art Spiegelman's *Maus* beat the system, proving that history and comics are not unusual bedfellows and that historical themes can be a commercial hit with the reading public. Likewise, Icon Books in London (publisher of *Walter Benjamin for Beginners*) has undoubtedly placed a stamp on the marketplace for illustrated works focusing on this past century's deepest thinkers. Does the format of the comic inherently lend itself to a more digestible reading of the complex themes of history? Is there any danger to presenting history through comics?

I. S. I don't see any danger. *Maus* and *Freud for Beginners* are baby-boomer artifacts; they speak to an audience that not only grew up with comic strips but that never outgrew them—a post–World War II audience that ventured into entertainment in unforeseen ways. The marriage between history and popular culture is a fruitful one: the same Steven Spielberg that brought *E. T.* to a theater near us gave us *Schindler's List* and is seen today as a cornerstone in the effort to preserve the memory of the Holocaust for the future.

Economic hardship aside, today the comic strip is alive and well. I'm convinced we have not yet seen even a fraction of its endless permutations. Last year I got as a gift a wonderful French strip version of Proust's *A la recherche du temps perdu*. Its existence makes me confident that as our society gravitates more emphatically from words to graphs, even metaphysical inquiry and nuclear physics might be articulated, even disseminated, through comics.

N. S. Some of the press reviews for *Latino USA* are calling for the text to be distributed in the classroom. What do you see as the "pedagogic possibilities" of *Latino USA?*

I. S. It is a volume that hopes to instill a "critical eye"—that is, a critical "I"—in the reader. History in it isn't sacred: the reader is invited to be displeased, and to suggest different alternatives. I don' t want the study of history at the basic level to be tedious, or to shy away from multiple interpretations, to be allergic to exploring alternative ways of reconstructing the past.

N. S.   I want to return to this idea of "fakers" we've talked about before. Fakers are also Doppelgängers.

I. S.   Yes.

N. S.   Is the concept of *hyphenated identities* another manifestation of the Doppelgänger? Is it possible for someone to find himself or herself inadvertently trapped on one side of the hyphen? Could one half of the hyphen be an imposter's ruse? For example, a Cuban-American might find one side of the identity coin outweighs the other.

I. S.   At different periods of life, an individual with multiple identities might oscillate more toward one than the others.

N. S.   Your essays and stories abound with this type of personality. Mark Twain's literature—and his life, for that matter—was also populated with Doppelgängers, twins, doubles, imposters, and impersonators. Twain used this literary device less as a gimmick, and more as an insightful commentary on the reasons for and psychological consequences of imposture. *The Prince and the Pauper* and *The Tragedy of Pudd'nhead Wilson* are stories about identities that are imposed, swapped and orphaned. Oscar Wilde, Julio Cortázar and Ernesto Sábato also steered this course. You've made a reference earlier in this conversation to *The Strange Case of Dr. Jekyll and Mr. Hyde,* a novella that, judging by the disquisitions on it in your oeuvre, appears to fascinate you. Where does your attraction to Doppelgängers come from?

I. S.   Doppelgängers are a reminder of the myriad selves that inhabit us.

6

Lexicomania

N. S.   I've been told that you own a large collection of dictionaries. . . .

I. S.   It is the portion of my personal library that is truly organized. The rest sits in a state of utter disarray. Alison always complains about the mess my books are in. But she never complains about the dictionaries. In *After Babel,* George Steiner states that "serious readers are dictionary addicts." Personally I'm in awe of the sheer idea behind a dictionary, which strikes me as romantic: the attempt to fix language between covers, to free it from its volatility.

N. S.   Is yours an addiction?

I. S.   No doubt. I'm obsessed with dictionaries. Over the years, my relationship to them has changed. I used to go to dictionaries in order to find out definitions, to expand my vocabulary. The dictionaries I frequented then were, for the most part, intralingual. As an adolescent, I used to walk around with a notepad in which I listed any word I might encounter whose meaning evaded me. For instance, around 1982, when I read for the first time *Hopscotch,* I composed a large lexicographic catalogue. Parts of it are still inside my copy of Julio Cortázar's novel. I did the same with Alejo Carpentier's *Ecue-Yamba-O* and Mario Vargas Llosa's *The War of the End of the World,* among scores of other books.

N. S.   On average, how many words do you think humans use per diem?

I. S.   I once read that an average English-language speaker uses about two thousand different ones. Mass media is responsible for standardizing our vocabulary. Still, it varies and changes from region to region. And among authors, lexicographic quality is a stamp of their personality. If one made a comparative study of the language used by Ernest Hemingway and William Faulkner, the results, I suspect, would be startling: although the two communicated in English, not only their grammar and syntax, but their choice of words is dramatically different. After all, they come from different geographical regions, different classes, different educational systems, different cultural traditions.

N. S.　　How different are the dictionaries you use today from the ones you used as an adolescent?

I. S.　　Since I moved to the United States, my dictionaries have been comparative: Spanish/English, Spanish/French, Hebrew/English. I've also acquired multivolume sets of the *Oxford English Dictionary* and princeps editions of classics such as the *Tesoro de la lengua española o castellana* by Sebastián de Covarrubias.

N. S.　　You've called the one by Covarrubias an "urtext of Iberian lexicography."

I. S.　　Released between 1611 and 1613, under the auspices of the Holy Office of the Inquisition, it was the most serious attempt at codification of the Spanish language. Subsequent efforts, such as the *Diccionario de autoridades,* published in 1719, which became the official organ of the Real Academia Española de la Lengua Castellana, are based on the foundations laid out by Covarrubias. In recent years, researchers have gone back to Covarrubias to investigate the entries that, for a variety of cultural reasons, either he or his printers decided to leave out. I, in turn, often spend nights of insomnia studying his definitions of words such as *judío.* I have in my library a single-volume princeps edition of *Tesoro,* as well as a three-volume set of *Autoridades.*

N. S.　　The power of language is at the heart of my next question. I'm impressed by Marguerite Feitlowitz's devastating work, *A Lexicon of Terror: Argentina and the Legacies of Torture.* Feitlowitz graphically explores the Argentine government's "perversion of language" during its Dirty War. According to Feitlowitz, the regime was "intensely verbal," spurring on "deformations in the Argentine language" (words such as *"desaparecido"*). To understand this "lexicon of terror" she asked her interview subjects: "What words can you no longer tolerate? What words do you no longer say?" Does each government author its own lexicon of terror? Or is the Argentine case unique?

I. S.   Each regime authors its own lexicon. This is not only a lexicon of terror but also of happiness. After 9/11, for instance, the word "America" tasted different. I, for one, felt uncomfortable with it. This is a democratic nation that uses propaganda—through radio, TV, movies, books—to align its forces against adversity. An entire lexicon of hope was poured out by the George W. Bush administration. The same occurred after Pearl Harbor. In Cuba, China, Korea, and Angola, the Communist regimes disseminated a lexicon that enabled them to achieve their goals internally and externally. This often results in deliberate lexicographic saturation generated by a certain term, such as the use of the word "imperialist," for instance.

N. S.   Do you think for subsequent generations that the bitterness of these words will fade or will it be revived with the next new despotic regime?

I. S.   Each generation appropriates and refurbishes language. It revamps eclipsed terms and invents new ones. Language is never static—it is in constant change.

N. S.   You often use the dictionary as rhetorical device in your essays. Over time, I've kept a compendium. You've already mentioned a handful: *Webster's Dictionary,* the *OED,* and the *Diccionario de la lengua española,* for instance. But you've also drawn definitions from the *Dictionary of Imaginary Places.* And you've used Ambrose Bierce's *The Devil's Dictionary* to define the word "egoist" as "a person more interested in himself than in me." Why use dictionaries to draft your essays?

I. S.   What is an essay if not a personalized diagram of ideas, built through words? That pattern becomes meaningful only as a reader connects one word to the next. In and of itself, each of these words is a symbol: a conventional sound and series of graphs to refer to an object in the universe. As I craft my pieces, I invariably wander about a specific term: how did the word "mask" come to be, for instance? What etymology lies behind it? My reaction is to open a dictionary, to let the various meanings the word has acquired over time to stream out in front of the reader's eyes.

N. S.   Do words or labels create the people? Take as an example the political controversy over the terms "Hispanic" and "people of color."

I. S.   There is a dialectic between the name and the thing. What is the connection between an actual rose and the word "r-o-s-e"? Is the name an essential component of the item? Language is arbitrary: it describes the universe through randomness. Why use the word "table" for a horizontal object with four legs and a flat surface? Why isn't a table a "chair"? In the first chapters of Genesis, Adam names his surroundings. He doesn't have a preconceived approach to the naming and we are not told in that chapter more than the fact that he has named things. Names hide the attribute of objects. In Biblical times, it was thought that the name of G-d contained G-d's power and that it should be kept away from the majority of people and only be known to a small—very small minority—sometimes a minority of one who would repeat it on the most sacred of days, and in the most sacred of places, so that it wouldn't be forgotten, like when the temple was destroyed, we forgot the name of G-d. Different synonyms—*"Elohim," "Adonai," "Yahweh"*—are used to refer to the omniscient.

One might also extrapolate from words and connect them to senses. That is, go beyond the mere randomness that has been defined by Saussure in his studies of language, the mere randomness of words connected to objects. At one point, the essence of that object appears or is contained in the word that we use. Take for instance, the word "yellow." Depending on the language you use, the sense of yellowness comes closer or farther from us. *"Amarillo"* in Spanish, "yellow" in English, *"amarelo"* in Portuguese, *"flavus"* in Latin. *"Amarillo"* to me is the closest to the essence. At times my intuition tells me that an object has the wrong word. I will feel that they aren't deeply connected. At times one has a strange reaction to people's names. "Oh, he is called Joshua, although he doesn't look like one." The question, of course, is: *who* does look like a Joshua? In our mind, all Joshuas, in Platonic fashion, have fused into one: they have become an archetype. The moment someone deviates from that archetype, a fracture in knowledge occurs. That's what language is about, isn't it? A conventional means of communication that is born in randomness.

N. S.   Or the term "concentration camp": some have found its historical origins in South Africa's Boer War; others point to Spain's involvement in late nineteenth-century Cuba. Then there is the hackneyed

African-American rap group "Concentration Camp," with an album called *Da Holocaust Too*. And speaking of destructive words, you've written on the concept of *la pureza de sangre*.

I. S.   "Purity of blood" is at the heart of Hispanic civilization, inspiring the *Reconquista,* drawing Jews and Moslems out from the Iberian Peninsula, articulating the mandate for religious and ethnic cleansing for the Inquisition as a policing institution. . . . The Catholic Church was the supreme ruler, the synagogue and the mosque its servants. In an atmosphere in which difference was threatening, a theory of hierarchical superiority was devised, one that was a precursor to the racist views of Adolf Hitler and the Nazis. Not skin color but faith— therein the key to otherness. Justified by *la limpieza de sangre,* people were persuaded to either convert or disappear. Thus, the birth of the New Christian, as well as the appearance of crypto-Jewish and *marrano* cultures. Indians, *mestizos,* mulattos, and *zambos* in the Americas also suffered categorization. Activists such as Fray Bartolomé de Las Casas used the so-called *leyenda negra,* the Black Legend as a weapon to undermine the practices of the Spanish Empire. He too was a racist, though: to liberate the Indians from the misery they were subjected to, he suggested importing African slaves to this hemisphere. To this day, purity of blood, somewhat attenuated as a theory, but still pervasive as a definition of turf, underlies domestic and social relations in the Spanish-speaking orbit.

N. S.   What is *rascauchismo*? It appears in your essay "The Riddle of Cantinflas" [*The Essential Ilan Stavans*] and in *Bandido*.

I. S.   It is slang for "cheap quality." The term is popular in Mexico. Nevertheless, *"rascuache"* has become a favorite term among Chicanos. It denotes a culture that, by choice, uses kitsch to rebel against the Anglo establishment.

N. S.   How about the term "Third World"?

I. S.   It came around in the seventies. Legend has it that the Mexican president Luis Echeverría Alvarez introduced the term in a speech at United Nations. Also, it has been related to Frantz Fanon and his book *The Wretched of the Earth,* which appeared in English in 1963 with a preface by Jean-Paul Sartre. Fanon died young: at the age of thirty-six. He didn't live to see the connection. Anyway, the term has a Dantesque quality to it, don't you think? But truth is that "Third

World" as a term came about in the fifties, coined by a French demographer Alfred Sauvy. To me, it recalls the nine Circles of Hell in the *Divine Comedy*. The premise is that, in terms of industrialization, there are three worlds: the first one is the most advanced (Europe, the United States), the second includes nations like Portugal and Greece, and the third is a junkyard that includes Africa and Latin America.

N. S.   What about *"mestizo"*?

I. S.   It made its first appearance in the oeuvre of "El Inca" Garcilaso de la Vega, author of the *Comentarios Reales* and himself a product of miscegenation. "El Inca" died in 1616. He used it to describe a person of mixed Spanish and Indian heritage. *Mestizaje,* coined by him, has become an ever-popular, and also controversial, racial process, especially in Mexico and Central America, reflected upon, among many others, by José Vasconcelos in the chapter *"Mestizaje"* that is at the outset of his 1927 book, *The Cosmic Race*. Octavio Paz also explores it in *The Labyrinth of Solitude*.

N. S.   And the term "labyrinth"?

I. S.   It probably has a Hellenistic root. The Minotaur was trapped in one such structure made of interdependent passages deliberately built in a bewildering fashion. It has become a favorite image to describe the Hispanic psyche, although, as you know, it was ubiquitous too in Central Europe under the Soviet regime.

N. S.   In *On Borrowed Words* you claim that "As a language, [Spanish] is somewhat undeserving of the literature it has created. This might explain why I enjoy rereading *One Hundred Years of Solitude* far more in English than in the original, as well as *Don Quixote*." In what way is the Spanish language "undeserving?"

I. S.   It is too amorphous, too malleable, too imprecise.

N. S.   And what about the definition for "Latino"?

I. S.   It is an open-ended term. Its source, of course, is Latin, that is, Roman. But is there something Roman among Latinos? In certain parts of Hispanic America, it is used to denote a Creole individual. It was also used to describe the south-of-the-border population in the United States. The term came in vogue in the eighties, and was meant to replace Hispanic. It was Richard Nixon who had systematized the use of "Hispanic" in government documents. Thus, the community felt it came from above. Latino, instead, was homemade.

Of course, "Hispanic" is gender-neutral, whereas "Latino" isn't; hence, "Latin*a*" and "Latin*o*." As far as I'm concerned, it is too loose, to abstract a term. I still prefer "Hispanic," although I recognize its ideological baggage.

N. S.   Since you've brought up the topic, let's talk about shifting meanings in lexicography. For example, the way Borges used the word "gringo" in his fiction differs from the way "gringo" is used in the United States nowadays.

I. S.   Up until the early part of the twentieth century—and still in some regions on South America—a gringo was a foreigner. That is the meaning Paul Groussac, Borges, Ezequiel Martínez Estrada, and others gave to it. In Mexico, Central America, and north of the Rio Grande, it is used to describe an Anglo person.

N. S.   From reading your essays, it is obvious that you love etymology. In fact, you could be described as a *lexicomaniac.* The mutability and the infinite variation of words enchant you. In *Latino USA,* for instance, there are eighteen different names showcased for the river dividing Mexico and the United States. And in your essay "The Latin Phallus" you list the various Spanish language terms for "penis" and "homosexual."

I. S.   In Ecuador alone, there are 108 ways to describe the penis and 72 to refer to homosexual-related usages. [*Laughter.*]

N. S.   Are there certain words that have changed our world, like the Christian concept of salvation?

I. S.   These terms are injected with so much meaning, it makes them twirl around. They ought to be spelled in capitals: MARXISM. Just like "History," in whose name massacres are justified. Other overcharged terms are "G-d," "progress," "creation," "revelation," and "redemption." . . . (The last three, of course, form the triptych modeled by Franz Rosenzweig in *The Star of Redemption.*)

N. S.   These concepts can also generate controversy. Unquestionably, it's healthy and positive that people are discussing word usage and definitions. You have focused a good part of your scholarship on these issues. In "The Sounds of Spanglish" [*The Essential Ilan Stavans*] you reflect on the explosion of this new, powerful, hybrid language. You also teach a course titled "The Sounds of Spanglish" to your Amherst College students (profiled on NPR's *All Things Considered*) and have compiled a Spanglish dictionary. Perhaps until recently we couldn't have conceived of a Spanglish dictionary, simply because the term was not in the literary conscience yet. Although the term has had street credibility for quite some time now, the praise goes to you, to a large extent, for the respectability is has acquired.

I. S.   Your suggestion reminds me of Ludwig Wittgenstein's dictum: "Only what might be described through language has a place in the universe." Of course, if an item, an event, a circumstance might be described, the question is: how so? This Wittgenstein doesn't address. Spanglish has been around for at least one hundred and fifty years, since the Treaty of Guadalupe Hidalgo was signed between Mexico and the United States in 1848, de facto ceding two thirds of Mexican territory to the Americans. But it wasn't recognized as a form of communication until it acquired more widespread, recognizable attributes. This delay makes me think of an argument put forth by Edmundo O'Gorman about Christopher Columbus and the so-called "discovery" of America in his book *The Invention of America*, in which he makes an inquiry into the historical meaning of the concept of the New World. O'Gorman suggests that one is capable of finding only what one seeks. At first sight, this statement might appear to be a commonsensical statement, yet it underlines the complex issue of "epistemological identification." If you didn't know what gold was and suddenly stumbled upon a gold chip in the middle of the road, you wouldn't pick it up, would you? Columbus encountered the New World because in the European imagination from Plato to Thomas Moore the seed of a land across the ocean was already ingrained. Likewise with Spanglish: as one looks into the past knowing exactly what one is looking for, numerous signs of it are likely to be found, primarily in the Southwest. And the inquiry will quickly let us know that names such as *"caló," "pachuco," "pocho,"* and the like have been used since the forties.

N. S.   How would you define the word "Spanglish"?

I. S.   Spanglish is a cultural phenomenon in urgent need of study. A version of *Romeo and Juliet* in Spanglish was staged in the Bronx in 2003. Hallmark greeting cards are available in Spanglish. And the presence of this mongrel tongue on TV shows such as *¡Mucha Lucha!* is on the ascent. Spanglish, I believe, resembles Yiddish and Ebonics, but it has much that is different from these mongrel tongues too. It springs out of code switching; thus, it is, as its core, an act of translation: immediate, instantaneous.

N. S.   Will we one day need translators for texts in Spanglish? Where will translators and readers find their lexicon for unlocking this verbal code?

I. S.   I do believe there will one day be translations of Spanglish into other tongues—perhaps even into Spanish and English. Yiddish in the thirteenth century was perceived as a jargon of the illiterate, yet six centuries later it became the source for Sholem Aleichem's masterpiece, *Tevye the Dairyman*. Something similar might occur among Spanglish artists, for there are already a myriad of them—poets, essayists, folklorists, storytellers—hard at work in their bilingual, bicultural craft.

N. S.   Returning briefly to government-mandated language, I understand the Mexican government also has a policy of limiting the kinds of English words that are incorporated into the Spanish language?

I. S.   The reaction by the people is "ha, ha, ha." . . . Languages need institutions to support them, but those institutions cannot turn those languages into static objects of display. By definition, our tongue is the freest, most democratic organ in our body. It cannot be legislated. Max Weinreich, the Yiddish lexicographer, once said that the difference between a language and a dialect is that a language brings an army behind it. The Nazis attempted to annihilate Yiddish. In the Zionist battle for the language of the Jewish homeland, Hebrew emerged triumphant. The reason people speak Spanish and Portuguese in the Americas is because the colonists, missionaries, and explorers arrived with the Bible on one hand and a weapon in the other.

N. S.   I'm interested in the critical debates surrounding Spanglish. How would you compare Spanglish to Ebonics? Do you think these hybrid languages legitimate a worldview excluded by the dominant language?

I. S.   Ebonics, its roots in the slave culture, is a product of the inner city today. It is primarily spoken by young African-Americans; thus, race and class define it. Spanglish breaks race and class boundaries: it is spoken by lower-, middle-, and upper-class individuals of different national and economic backgrounds. Plus, it is not solely a phenomenon of the United States. It is alive in Spain, in the Caribbean—Puerto Rico might be its laboratory—and all the Americas.

I've seen Spanglish described as "an invented language." But aren't all languages invented? A handful are the specific byproduct of scientists: Esperanto, for instance. The majority, however, are the result of a slow process of accommodation: social, educational, political, and syntactical. This reminds me, on the subject of individually devised languages, in the twenties in the River Plate, of the movement known as *Ultraísmo,* which established the appropriate circumstances for the invention of an artificial, utopian tongue.

N. S.   What, specifically, is *Ultraísmo?*

I. S.   Around 1918–19 Borges and a group of avant-garde artists and intellectuals published a periodical under the name *Ultra.* The title drew inspiration from the term *"Ultraísmo,"* invented by one of Borges's idols, the Sephardic Jew Rafael Cansinos-Assens, who was also part of this group. Art at the time already experienced an inferiority complex vis-à-vis science. The credo of the Ultraístas was to renew literature, to insert it into the twentieth century, to reinvent it altogether. Cansinos-Assens wanted language "to reach its ultra today exactly as our scientific and political thought hopes to."

N. S.   Is *Ultraísmo* still in vogue today?

I. S.   Oh no. *Ultraísmo* attempted to replace *Modernismo,* which in turn was replaced by *Creacionismo* and by the countless other -isms we've become accustomed to.

The invention of artificial languages is due to the Uruguayan painter and *wunderkind* Xul Solar (his true name was Oscar Augustín Alejandro Schulz Solari), whose symbolist art is hypnotizing. Part Italian and part Lithuanian, Xul Solar died in the sixties. As far as I know, he doesn't have a school of followers. But his legacy is crucial. The mind is treated as an engine of signifiers whose vision could be expressed in a number of different manners. The language of watercolors, architecture, music and literature, and the individualized languages of the world (Mandarin, Turkish, Mayan . . .) are only a limited variety. Others lay hidden in our unconscious. Xul Solar, a friend of Borges, by the way, sought to uncover some of these concealed alternatives. To some, those alternatives belong to schizophrenia, but not to him. Indeed, there's a hilarious anecdote about Xul Solar included in Borges's "Autobiographical Essay" that explains the kind of intellectual energy he exuded. Apparently, one afternoon Borges stumbled upon his friend. "What have you been doing?" Borges asked. Xul Solar answered: "Nothing whatsoever, except for founding twelve religions after lunch."

By the way, this makes me think of an effort of mine. Years ago I sent a review of a nonexistent book to a Mexican literary supplement. Purportedly, this extraordinary volume had been published in a computer-generated language devised by scientists at Caltech. I quoted several lines, which, I suggested, were at once significant and representative: "Yzpf.xland ig shpofftjkk auff siend im die," for instance. And "Uf khhjgfs if wef an gantshifte lkgjhfilkj ogq lkhj ghljhg im dish jastche." In 1927, the physicist Arthur Eddington, in his book *The Nature of the Physical World,* is credited with the notion that an army of monkeys typing interminably could produce all of the works at the British Museum. [*Laughter.*]

N. S.   There is a cartoon panel in *Latino USA* with an incensed, stuffy, bow-tied Yale University bureaucrat shouting "Spanglish. Did you say a Spanglish dictionary? That impure mixture of English and Spanish. No, no, no. We should teach our children to speak proper languages, not dialects."

I. S.   It is time for intellectuals to change their approach to Spanglish. Believe me: by ignoring it, it won't go away! The debate is still about what is correct and what isn't. As measured by the standards of Spanish and English, Spanglish is obviously incorrect. But so what? In their process of formation, dialects and jargons are often defined as improper, uncultivated, and incorrect. Still, they exist because there is a need for them: people use them to communicate a portion of their life which cannot be communicated otherwise.

My passion for Spanglish—what I've described elsewhere as "my love affair"—is the result of concrete circumstances. I describe the process in my essay *Spanglish para millones* [2000]: at one point in the mid-nineties, I had a student from East L.A. at Amherst College. He came to my office and said, "Professor Stavans . . ." but then he stopped. He started again: "Ilan, I'm givin' up *mis estudios* in this colegio. I can't handle it, vato. I'm out, *de regreso* in my *casa*." The language he used was gorgeous: broken, polluted, imperfect. . . . Do you know what I felt? Sheer envy. He was able to be freer in his tongue than I was in my snobby, artificial English. That day I promised myself I would study *his* language, so as to feel at ease in his home.

My opinion is that English is crucial for immigrants to advance in America. Also, that we should teach proper Spanish in the classroom. But these attitudes should not stop us from analyzing the patterns and context of Spanglish: where does it come from? Who speaks it? Is it only a vehicle of communication or might one also describe it as a state of mind? And what kind of future does it have? I'm not in the business of prophecy, so I don't dare answer the last question. But why not answer the other ones with the tools we have at our disposal? Maybe one day a *Don Quixote* and *Tevye the Dairyman* will be delivered in Spanglish. Meanwhile, it is already a widespread way for Latinos to explain and express their existential dilemma.

N. S.   Yiddish unlike Spanglish is now primarily spoken by the ultrareligious. I can't imagine this transformation ever taking place where Spanglish becomes the language of the ultrareligious. But do you believe that Spanglish could take up the overt political overtones that Yiddish-inflected socialism and communism espoused?

I. S.   It is already infused with ideology. To speak Spanglish is to emphasize a type of *mestizo* identity that is part Anglo, part Hispanic. Spanglish, no doubt, announces a fresh approach to *mestizaje:* a juxtaposition of tongues, ethnicities, worldviews.

N. S.   Let's talk about *Spanglish: The Making of a New American Language* [2003].

I. S.   It was a decade-long project. After my encounter with the student from East L.A., I began to collect every Spanglish term I came across in classified ads, magazines, on TV and radio, on the street and in the classroom. The lexicon grew rapidly. At the time, a friend in New York organized a luncheon with an editor in the reference division at Random House. During the meal, I described the accumulated material and the editor suggested a minidictionary. I thought it to be a challenging idea but didn't imagine it would involve so much of my energy.

As my research evolved, I realized there wasn't a single Spanglish but many: Chicano, Nuyorrican, Cubonics, Dominicanish, etc. In and of themselves, these varieties aren't homogeneous: the Spanglish spoken by Chicanos in San Antonio is different from the one used in Chicago; similarly, Puerto Rican Spanglish in the Caribbean is not the same as its Nuyorrican counterpart. Hence, my list became more sophisticated, defining words by national and geographic origin, by chronological usage, etc. Also, there's the variety of Spanglish used on the Internet, known as Cyber-Spanglish.

The quest to organize the material has its own dynamic. Scores of Spanglish terms are to this day limited to oral exchanges. The act of pinning them down requires scrupulous syntactical analysis. Also, spelling is unstable. Take the case of the frequent word "e-mail." I've seen it spelled *"imeil"* and I've also seen it transformed to *"emailito," "meilito," "mailito,"* and *"manuelito."* The majority of words fluctuate with equal ease. Three examples: *"liquiar," "liquear," "likiar"* = "to leak"; *"marketa," "marqueta"* = "market"; and *"hangeo," "jangueo," "hangueo"* = "to hang out."

N. S.   Have Spanglish terms already forced their way into contemporary Spanish dictionaries?

I. S.   Some dictionaries are obviously more liberal than others. There are some like *clave* that include an astonishing amount of Anglicisms, and even Spanglishisms. It always depends on the ideological approach taken by the editors. The same goes for English: the *Random House Dictionary of American Slang* is generous in examples that have African, Asian-Pacific, and Hispanic semantic roots.

N. S.   Is there an establishment hostility toward Spanglish?

I. S.   For some purists in Spain, the spread of Spanglish is the last episode in the Spanish-American War of 1898. In the United States, conservatives see Spanglish as a sign of laziness on the part of Latinos. For them it is proof that English is not being adopted quickly enough. In my view, Latin America is the most patient, warmhearted region in its response. This is explainable, of course: for over five hundred years, the region has undergone a process of acculturation to the Spanish model. People south of the Rio Grande know perfectly well what it means to be subjugated by an imperial force, to learn a foreign language in order to adapt to the colonial reality.

According to some linguists, Spanglish is the transition state in the acquisition of English by Latinos: Spanish is in the background,

English in the foreground . . . and Spanglish in between. This theory suggests that, in the process of assimilation, Spanglish is doomed to disappear the moment the immigrant becomes *fully* American. I believe there is some truth in this argument, but it needs to be approached with caution. Unlike other immigrant languages (Italian, German, Yiddish, Mandarin . . .), Spanish has been around in the United States for at least a century and a half. Why hasn't it disappeared already? Other immigrant groups have all but given up their native language with the second generation. The Jews who came from Russia and Eastern Europe arrived to the Lower East Side with the *mama loshn:* Yiddish. Their children understood Yiddish, but didn't speak it fluently and for their grandchildren it is an object of nostalgia. For the latter only a handful of semantic relics prevail: *shmuck, schmooze, kosher,* and so on. In the case of Latinos, Spanish remains a strong force for the grandchildren of the immigrants who crossed the border. In fact, no other minority has ever achieved the same linguistic success—or defeat, however one sees it. Proof of it is Univisión and Telemundo, the two full-fledged TV networks in the United States, which, according to the *New York Times,* are the fastest growing in the nation. Proof too is the scores of radio stations in California and Texas. And the popularity of Latin music *en español.* . . .

N. S.   In *World Literature Today* [74.3 (summer 2000)] you wrote that you responded to a cynical BBC reporter by stating that "Spain, in the galaxy of the European Community, has the lowest birthrate. There are 34 million Spaniards, less than the overall total of Latinos. So who is in the position to establish the rules?" In your opinion, will the sheer numerical strength of Latinos turn the tables on the Real Academia in Spain? Will Latinos in the United States dictate the rules of the Spanish language one day?

I. S.   To some degree, yes.

N. S.   The linguist John McWhorter points out in the *Power of Babel* that if we were to speak an English purely derived from Anglo-Saxon words we'd have the verbal capacity of a three-year-old.

I. S.   No such thing as a pure language exists, simply because languages are in constant flux. Or better, a pure language is a dead language, a language incapable of movement.

N. S.   Hebrew is the only true example of the successful revival of a language that was considered for all intents and purposes extinct or nearly on its last legs. There have been attempts to revive other languages and dialects, but they fall way short of success Hebrew has achieved.

I. S.   Even the Academy of the Hebrew Language in Israel put forth not too long ago a strategy to combat the penetration of Anglicisms in daily usage. That strategy is also mimicked in France, Italy, and Germany. . . .

N. S.   Sa'adia Gaon was the first to write comprehensive treatises on the Hebrew language. He wrote a dictionary and a book of Hebrew grammar rules. Antonio de Nebrija was the first codifier and grammarian of the Spanish language. Does the Academy in Spain romantically believe in a pristine connection between today's Spanish and Nebrija's?

I. S.   On the Iberian Peninsula there's a hypernationalistic embrace of Nebrija, the first grammarian of the Spanish language, as a messianic figure of sorts. In the same *annus mirabilis* in which the edict delivered by the Catholic Kings Ferdinand and Isabella expelled the Jews, and that was simultaneous with Columbus's navigation across the Atlantic, Nebrija, at the University of Salamanca, published his grammar. The events of his age made him conceive of *la lengua castellana* as "the language of empire." His, thus, wasn't only a semantic but also a colonialist effort.

Interestingly, Nebrija registered in 1492 the word *"balsa"* to describe a boat. Four years later, he exchanged it for *"canoa,"* an Americanism imported through the help of explorers and missionaries. The replacement is essential: it announces that not only had Spain arrived in the Americas but the Americas had also arrived in Spain. In other words, Spanish from then on would need to be sensitive to the coinage of words across the ocean. It no longer was the sole property of the population of the peninsula. From 1496 on, it was also the property of the colonials under the tutelage of the Spanish crown.

N. S.   How many words from Latin America were ultimately imported back to Spain?

I. S.   Thousands. . . . I don't know if anyone has offered an approximate total. Anyway, the Real Academia Española de la Lengua is the one in charge of their acceptance. Its house is next to the Museo del Prado in Madrid. To this day, it has the same motto it's had since its founding in the eighteenth century: "Limpia, fija y da esplendor"; in English: "Clean, fix, and grant splendor." As a Jew, obviously, the word "clean" frightens me. How might a language be cleansed? Of what and by whom? What do you need to clean? It is a xenophobic term that invokes the Spanish approach to Jews and Muslims prior to and during the fifteenth century. And the term *"da esplendor"* is equally troublesome: splendor at the expense of what?

N. S.   Talk to me more about Cyber-Spanglish?

I. S.   Regularly we decry the death of another language in the globe. Why don't we also celebrate the birth and development of new ones? Whatever ideological disposition one has toward Spanglish, the phenomenon offers an extraordinary opportunity to witness the birth and development of a dialect. In its infancy, Spanish, as it separated itself from vulgar Latin a millennium ago, underwent a transformation not unlike that of Spanglish. By this I don't necessarily mean to suggest that Spanglish will evolve into a fully grown language. Maybe it will, but I'm not concerned with that result. What attracts me is the opportunity to see its current status, the way it changes every day in front of our eyes.

About 10 percent to 15 percent of the lexicon I've compiled is made of Cyber-Spanglish terms, such as *"forwardear," "downlodear,"* and *"el mouse."* In the past, the coinage of a fresh word could take a decade. Thanks to the Internet and mass media, the speed is faster nowadays. For example, every time the word *"parquear"* and *"parkear"* ("to park") is used on Univisión in *Sábado Gigante* and *El show de Cristina,* it is heard by more people than the readers of *One Hundred Years of Solitude* in Spanish since its publication in 1967. The effect, one can imagine, is stunning: the repetition of the word has pushed it toward some sort of standardization. I've talked to Jorge Ramos of *Noticiero Univisión,* the equivalent of Peter Jennings on ABC News. On camera, in his Spanish-language speech, he never says *"carta verde";* instead, he says *"grincar"* for "green card." Otherwise, his viewers wouldn't understand him. So the term becomes ubiquitous.

The Internet has a less profound effect. Still, it disseminates terms widely and rapidly regardless of age, race, class, and nationality.

N. S.   How exactly does the Real Academia go about including fresh terms?

I. S.   It is done behind closed doors. A debate ensues. Once the erudites settle their differences, the results are announced to the world. I visualize the erudites as long-bearded, with magnifying glasses. . . . Suddenly, a messenger comes from the outside with a newly coined term from Quito, Ecuador: *"pinga."* The erudites discuss it, browse various reference sources, then conclude with a resounding *"no."* One tells the messenger: "Please return to the infidels. Tell them their term is unacceptable."

Obviously, my portrait is mythical. The Royal Academy of the Spanish Language in Madrid includes young, cosmopolitan, Jeffersonian voices: Mario Vargas Llosa, Antonio Muñoz Molina, Juan Luis Cebrián. . . . Some are in favor of Spanglish. Unfortunately, these voices appear to be outnumbered today by these strange dictatorial figures that believe Spanglish is a degeneration of the language. But change is the only constant of our universe, isn't it? Everything changes, even change itself.

N. S.   Has Vargas Llosa himself commented on Spanglish?

I. S.   As far as I know, not openly. Octavio Paz, on the other hand, once said. "Spanglish is neither good nor bad. It is simply atrocious." Again, he was a product of his age. Today the veteran generation is by definition antagonistic. They describe it as a McLanguage. I, too, am the subject of ridicule: among other epithets, I've been called the Cheech and Chong Professor of Spanglish at Amherst College. But people approaching fifty years of age, whose education was permeated by American pop culture, are more flexible. For them it isn't an *either/or* issue but an *and/and* one: Spanish *and* English *and* Spanglish.

N. S.   And if Borges was alive today?

I. S.   He probably would look down at Spanglish. He died in the late eighties, when Spanglish was already widespread. Although advanced in age, at least he might have been acquainted with the phenomenon. As a young man, in his *Ultraísta* days, the reaction, I'm confident, would have been different. After all, there is something exquisite about the innovative, improvised nature of a tongue born out of requisiteness. Perhaps it would have reminded him of Joyce's English and of Xul Solar's invented lexicons.

N. S.   In July 2002, you published in *La Vanguardia,* a newspaper in Barcelona, a translation into Spanglish of Part I, Chapter 1 of *Don Quixote.* I understand the translation was also released in the Americas. I've heard you recite the first lines on the radio. It is quite compelling, especially when read aloud. Could you repeat them for me?

I. S.   "In un placete de La Mancha of which nombre no quiero remembrearme, vivía, not so long ago, uno de esos gentlemen who always tienen una lanza in the rack, una buckler antigua, a skinny caballo y un grayhound para el chase. A cazuela with más beef than mutón, carne choppeada para la dinner, un omelet pa' los Sábados, lentil pa' los Viernes, y algún pigeon como delicacy especial pa' los Domingos, consumían tres cuarers de su income. El resto lo employaba en una coat de broadcloth y en soketes de velvetín pa' los holidays, with sus slippers pa' combinar, while los otros días de la semana él cut a figura de los más finos cloths."

N. S.   What has been the reaction?

I. S.   Controversial, as one might have expected. As far as I'm able to judge, there are three groups: those that dislike it in full; those that embrace it with equal candor; and those that applaud the effort but dislike the translation.

N. S.   Why did you do it? Also, why *Don Quixote?*

I. S.   In a debate on Spanish radio, a purist told me: "Spanglish should not be taken seriously until it produces a masterpiece of the caliber of *Don Quixote.*" I responded by suggesting that, before that happens, one could try to adapt Cervante's novel into this *mestizo* tongue. Before the evening, Sergio Vila-Sanjuan of *La Vanguardia* and I had already talked about turning the idea into a concrete excerpt. This I accomplished upon my return to Amherst a few days later.

   Confessedly, my challenge is to recognize—to find—a middle ground between the various Spanglishes I'm acquainted with: Chicano, Nuyorrican, Cubonics, etc. My choices are defined by this challenge: some terms belong to one group, others to another. In a way, the Spanglish I used is nonexistent—it is a composite, an invention. And then comes the translator's spontaneity. The best compliment I've received is that the translation is Joycean.

N. S.   To return to the topic of dictionaries in general, what is your favorite definition in the dictionaries you've collected?

I. S.   A difficult question. Perhaps the definition of *"día"* ["day"] offered until quite recently by the *Diccionario de la lengua española,* which, as you know, is the official dictionary of the Spanish language. Gabriel García Márquez once wrote an entire essay on the preposterousness of this definition. The dictionary declared that *día* is, roughly, the time it takes the sun to rotate around the earth. Incredible, isn't it? It tells tons about Iberian culture. It is clear that in the land of the Inquisition, Galileo's revolution took centuries to be fully recognized. The definitions that attract me the most aren't those of obtuse terms. I'm more interested in how dictionaries define what's most common to us: "water," the color "green," the number "zero." . . .

N. S.   Do dictionaries speak to us or do we speak to them?

I. S.   Some years ago I delivered a lecture at the University of Michigan at Ann Arbor entitled "Ink, Inc." It addressed that question you've asked: What is the dialectical movement between society and dictionaries? Are these volumes descriptive or normative? It is a crucial difference and dictionaries satisfy the two functions: there are those that have an aura of "officialdom," which turns them into instruments of verbal control; but there are also dictionaries—such as a lexicon of slang, for instance—whose function is to describe verbal patterns alive in the world. But the difference between these functions is less clear-cut than what purists would want you to believe. To remain useful, normative dictionaries need to be updated constantly, which means they absorb the changes that occur in society—ergo, they are also descriptive. Likewise, a descriptive dictionary is often used as a source people go to to standardize their own speech. In any case, this is a rich area of thought. I'm eager to explore it in detail. Happily, soon after the lecture in Ann Arbor, a publisher asked me to ruminate on the topic in a slim volume, which she wants to release as *Dictionary Days.*

The role of dictionaries, by the way, goes hand-in-hand with that of academies. Spain, Italy, and France each have a so-called royal academy of language, sponsored by either the monarchy or the federal government. These institutions are often perceived as policing our speech: at least in the popular imagination, they're not about how we talk, but about how we *should* talk. Why doesn't England have a similar legislative entity? The equivalent is the Oxford University

Press, but it's a private institution whose mandate isn't to offer linguistic decrees but to educate. In the United States, the equivalent of the *OED* is *Webster's Dictionary,* followed by a vast array of editions released by different publishers, like Random House and Houghton Mifflin. Again, none of these has a legislative function. This, to my mind, is an interesting question. In the nineteenth century, Matthew Arnold wrote intelligently about the need to establish in England a sort of Academie Française. His argument was ignored, though. The reason is simple: the Britons, and by extension the Americans, are too individualistic a people to let the government meddle in their speech. Dr. Johnson's *A Dictionary of the English Language,* published in 1755, was produced over a period of almost a decade in London in an effort to cleanse the tongue of the day, as Johnson himself put it, of "excessive Galicisms." It was, strictly speaking, an independent affair, the way the English do things: a scholar's quest, devised by his own accord, funded through donations, and released by a private publisher.

N. S.   So you believe the average dictionary maker to be a chronicler of usage. . . .

I. S.   But is there an *average* maker of dictionaries? Show me where, please? Dr. Johnson famously defined a "lexicographer" as "a harmless drudge."

7

A Biographer
in Macondo

N. S.   I want to return to an earlier topic in our conversations: the boundaries between fact and fiction in Hispanic civilization. My interest in this conversation is to discuss your views on biography as a genre, and in particular, to talk about your quest to produce a biography of Gabriel García Márquez, the author of *One Hundred Years of Solitude* and the recipient of the Nobel Prize for Literature in 1982. But let me do so by asking: Is biography a form of fiction and vice versa?

I. S.   By all means. Biography and fiction are impossible to divorce.

N. S.   Yet in the United States people acknowledge that divide.

I. S.   North of the Rio Grande, people go out of their way to mark a straight, uncompromising difference between the two. Enter any bookstore and you find a section of fiction, one of nonfiction, and a third of biography. Wouldn't it be better to dump them all into a single category, literature? Is it really possible to distinguish between fact and fantasy?

N. S.   It is the lesson learned from *Don Quixote*.

I. S.   Miguel de Cervantes understood that between sanity and lunacy there is but a thin line, and likewise between fact and fiction.

N. S.   In *Imagining Columbus* [1993], you state that, "as a nonfiction genre, biographies are dangerous in that they enlarge or shrink the natural size, talents, and defects of their object of study."

I. S.   Biographies should be shelved in the fiction section. For one to be successful, the biographer must be at once present and absent in every page: too much ego is terrible, too little is absurd. In that sense, every biography is also a veiled autobiography. You mentioned Heinrich Heine the other day. Once, on a crowded subway ride in New York City during rush hour, a homeless man jumped into the train I was in and began singing in an atrocious fashion. People were squeezed like sardines: elbows and hands and mouths and chins sprung from everywhere. The collective disgust could not be contained. "Be quiet, please," someone shouted. "Not here, not now," another person said. The homeless man wouldn't stop, though. He knew he was generating discomfort, but that, precisely, was his objective. He also knew that no one would hand him a penny. Then, after a few minutes, he screamed: "If you pay me, I'll stop."

Often we come across characters in fiction who are used there as revenge by the author for an injury suffered. In some cases, the fiction comes across as wonderful; in spite of the revenge, it is first-rate and in others it's just pure revenge, venom, acid. What a sibling remembers of life is so different from what his other siblings remember. So in the end, what is memory? How should we define it? To me, memory is an incredibly evasive function. For years I've searched for a satisfying definition, but I only come across stilted versions hammered out by one lexicon after another. In his *History of Western Philosophy,* Bertrand Russell argues that there is no way to prove that the world was not created five minutes ago with a memory of two thousand years. Memory is a treacherous data bank: every time we make either a deposit or withdrawal, the currency in our hands looks different.

N. S.   You've written that "to be outstanding, a biographer ought to have the heart of a novelist and the punctiliousness of a historian."

I. S.   It is important to see the biographee in perspective. You have to understand the motivations that make each of these characters tick. And, at the same time, you have to have the idea that you are learning history, getting the facts, grasping the past. And if those ingredients are not there, you don't read the second chapter.

N. S.   I remember once reading an interview with Jacobo Timerman. It was conducted right around the time he was composing his memoirs in Uruguay just prior to his death. He complained that he was flooded with requests by would-be biographers. He was upset that biographers acted as if his life started when he went to prison.

I. S.   Media-driven publishers often have something concrete in mind: they are hungry to know what happened in a particular moment to a certain individual. They forget that our lives are a series of accidents, each of which is crucial for those before and after in the sequence. A fine biography finds a balance between the beginning, the middle and the end. Still, it is natural to be more attracted to one period than to another.

N. S.   In your essay on Alberto Gerchunoff that serves as the introduction to *The Jewish Gauchos of the Pampas* [1997; also in *The Inveterate Dreamer*], while you're hunting for his biographical data, you announce that you're more interested in the beginnings of the Argentine *homme de lettres'* career rather than its end.

I. S.   It happens to all of us. Of Dostoevsky's oeuvre, I'm more interested in *Crime and Punishment* and *The Brothers Karamazov* than in *The Double*. Likewise, there are certain elements in his biography—his Christianity, his literary technique, his mental illness—which might attract the biographer more than other facets of Dostoevsky's life. In short, why does one write biography and for whom? Does one write for the reader in the present or for the reader in the future? The answer isn't complicated: a sharp, important biographer doesn't have his contemporaries, but his precursors and successors, as his competitors. Literature always travels in time, backwards and forwards.

N. S.   You've claimed in the past that biography as a genre is under-appreciated in the Third World.

I. S.   It surely is. Dr. Johnson wrote on biography in an essay in the *Rambler* that "no species of writing is more worthy of cultivation." The author of *Lives of the English Poets* believed that biography offered the power of example. In other words, my chronicling another person's life might result in one being able to learn to live one's own life better. Biography is a by-product of capitalism, with its emphasis on individuality and privacy. I'm in awe of the nineteenth-century approach to the genre: the individual as a mere excuse for a wide-ranging disquisition on human nature in general. Anthropology, biology, philosophy, psychology . . .—these disciplines were essential ingredients. Instead, the trendy approach that permeates our present is that of exposé: gossip, gossip, gossip. Of course, there are outstanding exceptions: Leon Edel's multivolume biography of Henry James, for instance. A curious example is *Sor Juana, or, the Traps of Faith,* by Octavio Paz. In spirit, it is close to models like *Facundo* by Sarmiento. Paz explored the life and times of colonial Mexico, mixing erudition with a desire to compare the pulse of the seventeeth and twentieth centuries.

And then, of course, there is Boswell's *Life of Samuel Johnson,* published in 1791. Its sheer voluminousness is a feast for the intellect. Does one need a personal friend to chronicle your life? What about impartiality? And what about the biographer as the obnoxious stenographer, endlessly transcribing your conversations, as trivial as they might be? These are questions that arise from Boswell's minute style. Furthermore, to what extent is the biographer, and not the biographee, the actual protagonist of the endeavor?

N. S. Geoffrey Hartman, a literary critic at Yale University, once observed the recent acceleration of case examples of "false witness syndrome." For him, "false witness syndrome" is sometimes the byproduct of "memory envy." This often happens in a culture such as ours where the retrieval of memory is critical for identity formation. In that sense, he argued that social precedent has been set where strong painful memories that are questionable are valued over none at all. Do you agree with Hartman's concept of "memory envy"?

I. S. Memory is such a fragile human endeavor. What is it, really? To what extent is the past—my past, our past—retrievable? Is it worth spending a single day, let alone a lifetime, retrieving the past? Does that not become an obstacle in the embrace of the present? On the other hand, the reduction of memory to fiction is dangerous. It leads us to the type of universe envisioned by David Hume and Bishop Berkeley. In legal cases, memory is the stuff on which a man's fate might depend. But it is more: the identity we have as individuals, as nations, as civilizations, depends on its formation and manipulation.

N. S. Manipulation. . . .

I. S. There are scores of suitable examples. Take the academic debate that surrounds Yiga'l Yadin, the Israeli archeologist who uncovered the secrets of Masada, in the Dead Sea, during the sixties, using as a road map the historian Flavius Josephus. The discoveries of the remnants of those involved in the revolt against the Roman Empire, and the collective suicide that ensued shortly after the death of Herod in AD 73, coincided with a period of intense nationalism in Israel. Zionism was successful in the formation of a Jewish state. But the state needed a pantheon of heroes that could inspire a generation of soldiers in the war against the Arabs. Was Yadin an iconoclast? Did he doctor facts in his book *Masada: Herod's Fortress and the Zealot's Last Stand*? A nation's memory might also suffer from envy. Theodor Herzl used envy as an excuse for the movement of masses from Eastern Europe to Palestine: he asked, "Why can't we, the Jewish people, have a state like everyone else?" Memory ought to be truthful to facts. But imagination plays a large role in it, whether we want it or not.

N. S.   Henry James was so leery of the popularity of biography as a literary genre that he burned many of his papers to dodge the biographer's gaze. Not long ago, I came across a passage translated by Ritchie Robertson from Arthur Schnitzler's *Buch der Sprüche und Bedenken* that haunts me. The following passage details a writer's tendency to aggrandize their ordinary faults in their memoirs: "It is quite easy to talk in all honesty about one's weaknesses, one's vices, even about one's crimes. But to avoid talking about them as though these weaknesses were extremely charming, these vices unusually interesting or even, at bottom, disguised virtues—and as though these crimes were the boldest and most grandiose ever committed— that takes art, and this is where real truthfulness would have to begin. It is seldom to be found in autobiographies."

I. S.   Each of us perceives the universe through a single lens, and that lens becomes the center of gravity. Schnitzler is right: it is easy to improve on our weaknesses by portraying them as enchanting. We are trapped in ourselves because of these weaknesses.

N. S.   And are honesty and interest at odds in literature? After all, it's easier to elevate an ordinary man into a hero than to extraordinarily describe the ordinary man.

I. S.   What makes biography tick is the opportunity it grants to calibrate the pulse not only of an individual, but of an entire epoch. The genre itself is a house of mirrors. What do you think it takes to be a reliable biographer? The curiosity to find out to what extent the individual and his context are intertwined and the patience to scrutinize in detail another person's odyssey. Biographers go through cyclical periods of attraction and repulsion toward their subjects: from infatuation to reservation to anger to empathy. . . . A fine biography, I think, is a *rara avis*. The author should never lose his identity, becoming but a shadow of the biographee. He should never upstage his subject but he must recognize he is the one in full control.

N. S.   Readers are challenged when a writer's moral judgment is called into question. Such as when he abuses his celebrity, reputation, or public stature. Countless examples leap to mind. Philosophers Martin Heidegger (a registered Nazi party member) and Paul De Man (a journalist for the pro-Nazi Belgian newspaper *Le Soir*), and Nobel Prize–winning novelist Knut Hamsun (an endorser of Quisling's Nazi puppet state) were all swept up in or submitted to the prejudicial reign of Nazi terror. In Heidegger and De Man's cases, their dignity was defended by their former protégés Hannah Arendt and Jacques Derrida (both Jewish). Despite winning the Nobel Prize, Hamsun fared much worse: his literature is relatively obscure to the larger reading public here in America (though that is not entirely a result of his political choices). Nevertheless, Isaac Bashevis Singer wrote respectfully of him in the afterword of the 1967 English edition of Hamsun's novel *Mysteries*. He claimed "the whole modern school of fiction in the twentieth century stems from Hamsun." Singer's generosity notwithstanding, a writer's actions are not always immune from criticism. How do the biographical details of a writer's life color or prejudice the way we read or think about their work?

I. S.   For years deconstructionists have tried to persuade us that a work of literature is divorced from the author who produced it. It seems to me that nothing is further from the truth. A writer is in full view in his oeuvre: his qualities and limitations, his aspirations and perversities. We are citizens of our time. As such, we are tested by the forces that constantly shape us. Ultimately, we are tested by how we responded to those forces. Were we cowards choosing the easy way in political and moral conundrums? How did we handle our personal life? Did we put our egos ahead of everything else? Were we capable of seeing beyond our very noses?

N. S.   I want to focus more on Singer. You edited a four-volume edition of stories by Isaac Bashevis Singer [July 2004] for the Library of

America. What kind of unpublished material from the Singer corpus did you unearth while researching his papers at the Harry Ransom Humanities Research Center in Austin, Texas?

I. S.   A treasure trove: unfinished stories and novels and even a memoir, a plethora of correspondence, countless photographs.

N. S.   Having peered at many of Singer's private papers, in your estimation how much does the *shtetl* haunt him?

I. S.   Less than most people think. Although he was often portrayed, especially in 1978 at the time of the Nobel Prize, as the connection between American Jews and the *shtetl,* the fact is that Singer is a quintessential urban creature. The majority of his stories and long narratives take place in New York, Warsaw, Miami, and other metropolises. Instead, the connection to the *shtetl* was at the core of Sholem Aleichem and David Bergelson, authors Singer despised as impossibly melodramatic. And by melodramatic, obviously, he meant sentimental.

N. S.   You talked about Singer's forays into translation. What was his reputation as a translator?

I. S.   He did it for money. Translation interested him only as a money venture—and in his own case, as a bridge to reach America readers.

N. S.   Singer serialized his novels in the pages of *Das Forverts* starting with *Der Sotn in Goray,* known in English as *Satan in Goray.* Indeed, weekly episodes of Singer's treasured stories were also broadcast on WEVD radio. Why has the format of weekly serialization been scratched from most publications today?

I. S.   In the age of Dickens, people sought not only news but also entertainment in dailies and weeklies. But entertainment today is ubiquitous. TV, movies, and the Internet have kidnapped our attention. Short fiction is still published in magazines like the *New Yorker* and *Playboy,* but even there the genre is embattled.

N. S.   How much of a role did Singer's son, Israel Zamir, play in his life? What about the boy's mother, Ronye Shapira?

I. S.   He parted ways with them when he immigrated to America. They left for Russia and eventually for British-ruled Palestine. In the U.S., Singer met Alma Haimann Wasserman, whom he married in 1940. The theme of bigamist Jewish males in the New York of the early twentieth century is, to a large extent, an autobiographical source.

Although he periodically sent them money for a while, he kept them at a distance. Zamir chronicles his difficult relationship with Singer in his memoir *Journey to My Father, Isaac Bashevis Singer*. In it he described the way in which, once he approached him to reestablish connection, Singer, the ultimate utilitarian, was only interested in his son as a potential translator of his novels into Hebrew. And indeed, Zamir, in order to remain close to him, translated a number of his father's books into the sacred tongue. By the way, Alma also translated Singer's work, and so did several of his mistresses. Plus, his nephew, Joseph Singer, the son of his older brother Israel Joshua, was also his translator. A series of incestuous affairs, no doubt.

N. S.   *The Family Moskat* was the first of his novels to be translated for an English-language audience. But, as you said before, Singer's fame didn't spread until a few years later, when "Gimpel the Fool" appeared in *Partisan Review*. I wonder why. . . .

I. S.   Probably because American Jews, especially the intellectual elite, were ready to see Eastern Europe in a more nostalgic ways. The emulation of the *shtetl* as a Paradise Lost of sorts had begun. . . . He ended up the ultimate American Jewish *zeyde,* i.e., grandfather. But the correspondence and other paraphernalia at the Ransom Center shows a much darker, less benign self lurking near us. [*Laughter.*]

N. S.   In your essay "Language and Tradition" you've suggested that Singer is "the transitional figure that cuts literature into pre- and post-Holocaust." Is that what you meant by his legacy?

I. S.   He helped American Jews handle the difficult period of the Holocaust in an oblique fashion. Think of it: how many tales by Singer are set inside a concentration camp? In direct terms, none actually. No concentration camp serves as a prominent setting in his stories. Some of his characters return from the ashes. Others are possessed by nightmares of World War II. Surprisingly, though, Singer is uncommitted to the topic, in spite of the fact that in 1939 his mother and younger brother Moishe were deported from Dzikow in a cattle car, where they are reported to have frozen to death. Other authors, among them Elie Wiesel, Primo Levi, and of course Anne Frank, addressed the destruction of European Jewry far more unswervingly for American readers. Still, Singer was the official link with "the world that was no more." He knew this and exploited the fact as much as possible. In an interview in *Commentary* in 1963, the interviewers asked him if it would be fair to say that he was writing in a somewhat artificial or illusory context, as if none of the terrible things that had happened to the Jewish people during the last two decades really did occur? Singer replied that yes, it was fair to say that. "Every man assumed he will go on living," he added. "He behaves *as if* he will never die. So I wouldn't call my attitude artificial. It's very natural and healthy. We have to go on living and writing."

N. S.   You've described Singer's writing as having "a salute to sensuality, carnality, and heresy." Do you think this what made him such an appealing personality to the readers of the *New Yorker* and *Playboy*?

I. S.   I do. He injected demonology and sexuality into Yiddish literature. And the American reader, since colonial times, has been interested in evil and eroticism. For him Yiddish was "the tongue of martyrs and saints, of dreamers and Kabbalists—rich in humor and in memories that mankind may never forget." In a figurative way, Singer said, "Yiddish is the wise and humble language of us all, the idiom of frightened and hopeful Humanity."

N. S.   Singer was sixty-two years old when he branched out into writing books for children, including the award-winning *Zlateh the Goat and Other Stories*. Was the shift in genres easy for Singer?

I. S.   It came late in his career, at the insistence of one of his editors. Singer didn't really trust his talent as an author for young readers. But his success was immediate and far-reaching. When he received the Nobel Prize, he said that there were five hundred reasons why he began to write for children: "[1] children read books, not reviews. They don't give a hoot about the critics. [2] Children don't read to find their identity. [3] They don't read to free themselves of guilt, to quench the thirst for rebellion, or to get rid of alienation. [4] They have no use for psychology. [5] They detest sociology. [6] They don't try to understand Kafka or *Finnegans Wake*. [7] They still believe in God, the family, angels, devils, witches, goblins, logic, clarity, punctuation, and other such obsolete stuff. [8] They love interesting stories, not commentary, guides, or footnotes. [9] When a book is boring, they yawn openly, without any shame or fear of authority. And [10] They don't expect their beloved writer to redeem humanity. Young as they are, they know that it is not in his power. Only the adults have such childish illusions."

N. S.   What are the challenges in instructing students about controversial works?

I. S.   It is our duty to offer to our students works of literature that highlight the way an intellectual responds to the test of his era. We must present the text in context, explaining the forces that shaped it in its origin.

N. S.   From the pages of the *Guardian* and the *Independent* in London, a polemical biography of Arthur Koestler by David Cesarani disclosed episodes of sexual misconduct, abusiveness towards women, and allegations of rape. Cesarani's work has provoked much public debate that involved Julian Barnes and Koestler's official biographer, Michael Scammel. Edinburgh University removed a bronze bust of Koestler as result of student reaction to Cesarani's claims. Should one separate the merits of a work from the tarnished stature of the subject? When does private life completely overwhelm public accomplishment? And along the same line, how do authors with a questionable record of violence towards women fare with female readers? For instance, Norman Mailer stabbed his wife, Louis Althusser strangled his, and William Burroughs accidentally shot his second one in a drunken game of William Tell.

I. S.   The private and public realms can never be fully separated. Writers are often ugly people: selfish, abrasive, even necrophiliac. Koestler was a bastard, George Orwell was a saint—both, it strikes me, are essential to our understanding of the anti-Communist age among Western intellectuals. The two ought to be read. For my own taste, Orwell is a far better writer. Fortunately, he also happens to be less of a scoundrel, but that is no reason to read him. In fact, when a writer is "perfect"—e.g., perfectly balanced—he probably will have little that is insightful to say about his environment. Koestler was an idol of mine in my adolescent years. I read everything of his I could put my hands on: his autobiography, *Darkness at Noon,* his essays on science, his novel on Palestine before 1948, his book on the Khazars *(The Thirteenth Tribe),* etc. I remember perfectly the day he committed suicide with his wife: I was flabbergasted. Time has not been kind to him, though. Not long ago I tried to reread him. This happened when David Cesarani's biography appeared. I met Cesarani briefly, actually. I was then in London and in large measure my attempt was due to the interest the biography awakened in me. I started with

Darkness at Noon and then moved onwards to the essays on episte-mology. I was disappointed. My adolescent passion, my naiveté per-haps, had evaporated. Koestler wanted to be a polymath, but his prose is flat, light, and unremarkable. Worse even, it is terribly un-inspiring. It was at that time that I came to Orwell too: I read *Bur-mese Days,* his novel about Paris, his extraordinary essays. The style is crystalline, the élan behind the words commanding. . . .

N. S.   How about the impact of government on an author's life? Frances Stonor Saunders' book *The Cultural Cold War: The CIA and the World of Arts and Letters* is a blistering (and perhaps overstated) pro-file of a CIA-bankrolled organization known as the Congress for Cultural Freedom. During the fifties and sixties, the Congress and its affiliates (such as the American Committee for Cultural Freedom) sponsored traveling art exhibitions by abstract expressionists such as Jackson Pollack and magazines, including *Encounter, Public Interest, Transition,* the *Partisan Review* and the *Kenyon Review.* Projects funded by the Congress had a notable roster of writers such as André Malraux, Stephen Spender, Robert Lowell, Mary McCarthy, Albert Camus, Lionel Trilling, Czesław Miłosz, and Isaiah Berlin. Many but not all of the intellectuals whose lives were somehow touched by the Congress were unaware of its direct connection to the CIA. Saun-der's book raises questions about the moral rectitude of those who handled or benefited from CIA money. As witting or unwitting bene-ficiaries of a CIA-funded cultural agenda, did these publications and authors compromise their status as independent thinkers?

I. S.   Not in my view.

N. S.   In the end what are the limits of public forgiveness? If a work is in-spirational, do we tend to be more forgiving of its author? Should we be? How difficult is it to rehabilitate the stature of a public intellec-tual haunted by damaging biographical details? Take National Book Award winner and Holocaust survivor Jerzy Kosinski for example. The *Village Voice* questioned the authenticity of his work (citing pla-giarism and a heavy reliance on ghostwriters). Assuming these allega-tions are true, how do you approach Kosinski's work?

I. S.   I'm acquainted with a number of authors and books, from Danny Santiago to Forrest Carter, the latter the author of *The Edu-cation of Little Tree,* whose true identity has been "unmasked" in public, resulting in shame. Add to the list the names of Binjamin Wilkomirski and Rigoberta Menchú, about whom we've already conversed. What to do with them? Are these authors unworthy of our attention? On the contrary, the moment we find out who they really are, we should study their legacy—its labyrinthine paths— more closely. Kosinski is in the same category. The genre of the Holocaust memoir becomes stronger as a result of his plagiarism and charlatanry, for it allows us to see the limits of truth and honesty and the travesty that literature at times becomes.

N. S. As a practical matter, many people continue to read these works without knowledge of the author's background. The latest edition of *The Education of Little Tree* makes no mention of Forrest Carter's intimate ties to the Klu Klux Klan and George Wallace. Moreover, it's a children's book. You've edited books for children. Should children still read this book?

I. S. If no biographical knowledge is involved, then the matter is settled. Borges received a medal from Pinochet. Should we stop reading him in response? Edmund Wilson and Ingmar Bergman failed to pay their taxes. Dante aligned himself with corrupt political friends. Is this reason enough to disqualify their talent?

N. S. What about more serious offenses, like racism and bigotry? If we include writers in literary canons based in part on extraliterary criteria, such as their ethnicity or culture, shouldn't their other extra-literary particulars be a basis for including or omitting them from the canon too? At some point don't a writer's acts color our understanding of the work?

I. S. Acts and words go together: one should not push aside an author whose oeuvre is extraordinary because of mistakes made in life. Take the case of Pablo Neruda's Stalinism. A wrong choice, no doubt, but Neruda didn't conspire to kill anyone—even though he wrote a book on *el nixonicidio,* that is, a call for the extermination of Richard Nixon. Should his work be eclipsed because of some poor ideological choices? Not at all, I say. Readers are free to do with one's page as they wish. The moment a work is released into the world, it is no longer the author's property. It has become part of tradition.

To break out of the academic cocoon, to seek public forums, is to allow oneself to be exposed to an open season of criticism. In spite of this, I, for one, have sought this path. I have done so as an alternative to the intellectual stagnation that takes places in universities and colleges nationwide. Of course, once one does something like this, all sorts of adjectives are invoked: for instance, "interloper" and "inauthentic voice." I've become the subject of curiosity, even intrigue. I disregard these side effects, though.

N. S.   It seems to me that sometimes the reading public is more concerned with a writer's deeds than a writer's words. Would you say that the "tell-all" biography—or autobiography—is the most popular American cultural literary phenomenon?

I. S.   It surely is popular: Americans are obsessed with erasing the boundary between the personal and the communal. No public figure is left unscrutinized. Americans not only love but also identify with imperfections—the more imperfect the public figure, the more compelling the odyssey becomes. The "tell-all" tale functions as a mirror of sorts: we use it to measure our own shortcomings as individuals against those people whose life is in full display.

N. S.   You've talked about the state of biography in America. Let's focus on Latin America. You've claimed that because of "the long-standing resistance to the public confessional mode, to the communication of inner fears, the literary genre of autobiography is not well-regarded in the Hispanic world." Latin Americans, you argue, "go to the grave with their personal secrets intact." What is the root of this resistance?

I. S.   The pride that results from sharply separating the public and private realms. The Spanish word "hogar" is emblematic: more than a house, it is a home—a home that is simultaneously trench and refuge. The term is infused with a spirit of seclusion. Octavio Paz reflects on it in *The Labyrinth of Solitude:* he claims that Americans spell out their troubles in public, whereas Mexicans keep everything inside. The dichotomy might appear to be Manichean but I think it is truthful. In the United States people forget the difference between the street and the bedroom. Through tabloids such as *Star* and *National Enquirer,* the line is offensively, aggressively eliminated. No comparable artifacts exist in Mexico. The closest is the newspaper *¡Alarma!,* fully devoted to yellow journalism, though not to celebrities. The culture is attuned to the eerie, but never to the openly confessional.

N. S.   Why is that?

I. S.   The answer is to be found in institutionalized religion. Catholicism offers a concrete, personalized space for confession. It is a space made for the priest's ear only, not for his eyes. Supposedly, what is confessed is quickly forgotten. Psychoanalysis, practiced for decades by the upper class in Mexico, is also about confession: secular, targeting another type of redemption. Its appearance in the fifties was a symptom of modernization: the Hispanic upper-middle class, as is the pattern, wanted to be *like* Europe, to be *like* the United States. The confessional mode entered the intellectual realm as well. The marketing of literati at the world level persuaded many to target their products to a global market. This resulted in authors of the Americas producing landmark memoirs: *Itinerary* by Octavio Paz and *A Fish in the Water* by Mario Vargas Llosa are examples. The "Autobiographical Essay," written by Borges in collaboration with Norman Thomas di Giovanni, appeared in 1973 in the *New Yorker*. Pablo Neruda published his book *Confieso que he vivido: Memorias,* known simply as *Memoirs* in English, in the last years of his life. Gabriel García Márquez released the first volume of his autobiography in 2002: *Vivir para contarla,* gloriously translated into English by Edith Grossman as *Living to Tell the Tale.* And in the same year, Carlos Fuentes published *En esto creo.* Don't get me wrong. . . . Autobiography has never been entirely absent in the region: Sor Juana Inés de la Cruz, Domingo Faustino Sarmiento, Rubén Darío all published memoirs. Still, Latin America unquestionably opened up to the West in the twentieth century. Proof of it, I believe, is the centrality of the genre today. The question is to what degree that slow change is essential. Will it transform the culture altogether, or is it only superficial?

N. S.   Vargas Llosa's early fiction has autobiographical overtones, for instance. His scandalous marriage to his aunt made its way into *Aunt Julia and the Scriptwriter*. However, his fiction is not outright autobiography.

I. S.   Obviously, his fiction also contains autobiographical elements: *The Storyteller,* for instance. Even *Conversation in the Cathedral* and the pseudoerotic novels *In Praise of the Stepmother* and *The Notebooks of Don Rigoberto* display an autobiographical element, although it is obviously less apparent. Julio Cortázar is equally personal in

Hopscotch, and Borges placed himself as the protagonist of stories such as "The Aleph" and "Funes the Memorious."

N. S. Literature travels and so does the immigrant. In *The Hispanic Condition,* you argue that "autobiography is a favorite genre of immigrants." Do you mean all immigrants or just immigrants to the United States?

I. S. Everywhere. . . . Having gone through the dark tunnel, the immigrant emerges ready to tell the tale.

N. S. That tunnel leads to "the cult of testimony" that scholar Robert Alter talks about. He thus explains the contemporary fascination with the Marquis de Sade: readers want to get a firsthand account of his misadventures. . . .

I. S. Instead of "testimony," I suggest the word "*text*imony." As we narrate our own lives and those of others, we turn events into texts. By doing so, we elevate anecdote to the category of truth. Is that what Alter is after? Testimony is physical "proof" but the border between that proof and fiction is mercurial. This is because memory itself is intangible: we are who we want to be . . . and autobiography is the opportunity to narrate our odyssey in *our* own terms.

In 1998, as part of the research for *On Borrowed Words,* I returned to the *Yidishe Shule* in Mexico, the institution I had gone to from kindergarten until high school. The last time I had been in the premise was some fifteen years before. The building had been sold to the Ministry of Marine Affairs. I had heard it was dilapidated. Still, I wanted to visit it because I needed to reencounter the site where some crucial scenes of my childhood and adolescence had taken place.

It was a mistake, though. A policeman allowed me in. I wandered around the hallways for about half an hour. Piles of government containers were stored in the yards, windows were broken, doors were closed. . . . As I walked, I was overwhelmed by sadness. I asked myself: is this what the past ultimately becomes—a ruin? I left the place in a state of shock.

I committed the same mistake in Israel. With my friend Hillel Halkin, I traveled to the Kinneret in order to visit Kibbutz Tel-Katzir, where I had lived in the early eighties. Again, the place was in a state of disrepair. It was no longer a kibbutz; it had become a commuting suburb of Tveria. In what way does it pay off to revisit the chambers of memory? Those chambers are invaded by mirrors reflecting mirrors . . . onward *ad infinitum.*

As I look back at the visits to the *Yidishe Shule* and to Tel-Katzir, I'm convinced that only the present exists. The past and the future are sheer inventions.

N. S.   It is just as you wrote: "Invariably, memoirs and *testimonios* are subjective accounts, they falsify through enchantment and persuasion." In the story "The Invention of Memory" [*The One-Handed Pianist and Other Stories*] the protagonist, Zdenek Stavchansky, a Czech émigré to Mexico, revisits his past, time and again, every night through a clever device: he takes out from a treasure box a set of costumes. They all belong to different periods of his own life. By dressing himself in them, he activates long-lost recollections. Do you think memory is a burden?

I. S.   No, memory is responsibility.

N. S.   Let me return now to my original question. In the past five years, you've devoted energy to an intellectual biography on the Columbian Nobel Laureate, Gabriel García Márquez. You wrote in *Art and Anger* that Gabo, as he's known among his peers, "remains a literary subject in search of a biographer." You began your work on the subject with a profile originally published in the *Michigan Quarterly Review* [34.2 (spring 1995); also in *The Essential Ilan Stavans*].

I. S.   It is my dream is to produce a biography that is not a standard, gossipy life story. My model is Octavio Paz's biography *Sor Juana Inés de la Cruz: or, the Traps of Faith,* published in 1982. He took Sor Juana, her life and her work, as an excuse to explore the colonial period in Mexico: the crossroads where religion and politics and male and female viewpoints collide. Gabo is a participant in crucial twentieth-century moments. His life and oeuvre highlight the tension between politics and literature in the Hispanic world: the banana boom in South America; *el bogotazo,* as the riot that occurred in Bogotá after the assassination of popular liberal leader Jorge Eliécer Gaitán in 1948 is known; the Cuban revolution; the Padilla Affair; the neoliberal movement of the eighties. My objective is to consider through him not only an entire generation but a whole continent. The biography should be written in English, for, confessedly, the readers I have as targets are north of the Rio Grande and in Europe.

N. S.   In *On Borrowed Words* you acknowledge *One Hundred Years of Solitude* as a masterpiece, and suggest that everything else in his oeuvre is secondary. . . .

I. S.   That novel alone justifies him. In spite of its success, though, the Colombian has sustained his talent quite well.

N. S.   Do you consider García Márquez the apex of the Latin American literary boom of the sixties?

I. S.   No doubt. That movement was always an amorphous mass. Critics insert Isabel Allende, Laura Esquivel, Manuel Puig, Juan Rulfo, and Borges in it . . .—anybody and everybody. *The House of the Spirits,* for instance, wasn't published until 1982. *Pedro Páramo* appeared in 1955, but Rulfo wasn't represented by Carmen Balcells in Barcelona. Esquivel is a product of the nineties. Puig also came late into the game. And Borges . . . well, Borges is the source. Anyway, Gabo is the consummate leader: an icon, an emblem, a paradigm.

N. S.   How does Mario Vargas Llosa fit into this picture?

I. S.   Depending on the source, Gabo was born in 1927 or 1928; Vargas Llosa in 1936. In other words, there is nearly a decade in between them. The Colombian is a Mediterranean type, whereas the Peruvian is a Europeanized dandy.

N. S.   Vargas Llosa may be a Europeanized "man of letters," but he doesn't look at America with Europeanized biases. What is your impression of him?

I. S.   I admire him wholeheartedly, although as a follower I felt betrayed when, after he lost the presidential election to Alberto Fujimori in 1990, he immediately moved to the Iberian Peninsula and became a Spanish citizen. Still, his odyssey is astonishing and his style hypnotizing. He started as a portentous novelist. In his mature years, though, his qualities as an essayist have superseded his talents as a fabulist.

N. S.   Didn't Vargas Llosa write his PhD dissertation on García Márquez?

I. S.   Indeed. The title of the dissertation is *García Márquez: historia de un deicidio*. Its thesis develops fully the Peruvian's concept of *la novela total*—"the total novel." The book was published by Barral in Spain. But after their rift, Vargas Llosa never allowed for it to be reprinted again.

N. S.   As for García Márquez, he bloomed early as an artist. . . .

I. S.   By the age of forty he had already given us superb stories and a handful of first-rate novellas, including *No One Writes to the Colonel* and *Innocent Eréndira*. But *One Hundred Years of Solitude* is his magnum opus. It isn't only a milestone in his career but a benchmark in Latin American letters.

N. S.   How should one compare the original Spanish-language edition of *One Hundred Year of Solitude* to the English version translated by Gregory Rabassa?

I. S.   Gabo once said that Rabassa's version was better than the original. I personally love the English version: it is a masterful recreation of a puzzling novel.

N. S.   How will you arrange the different sections in the biography you're planning: strictly chronological?

I. S.   It should be a chronological book that will follow Gabo's life, from birth to maturity and to the moment in which the biography finds him. Through all of these moments, his travels through Eastern Europe, his encounter with Fidel Castro, his sympathies for the Zapatistas and his commitment toward open press, free press in Colombia.

N. S.   Will it be a traditional biography that involves fieldwork and interviews with all the relevant players?

I. S.   I've done numerous interviews already. Gabo is quite ill with cancer somewhere in California, in seclusion, trying to finish the different volumes of his memoirs that he's doing in mathematic format. He only talks to a handful of people: Alvaro Mutis, Fuentes, his wife Mercedes, his children, his doctor. If I saw myself as a reincarnation of James Boswell, I would devote my entire existence to Gabo. But mine won't be an official biography. Instead, it will be open-minded, critical, though admiring too.

N. S.   And what elements of his literature will you place under critical scrutiny? What elements of his work stand out to you as praiseworthy?

I. S.   My job is to place his life and career in the larger context: historical, political, artistic, personal.

N. S.   Some literary giants never make a completely successful transition to screenwriting. The old Hollywood studio system exploited writers like Dorothy Parker, Dashiell Hammett, F. Scott Fitzgerald, Nathaneal West, and Faulkner. It's fascinating to see the work they produced in Hollywood's golden age. However, their screenwriting projects often fail to stand out among their greatest literary works.

I. S.   Right. You have cases like Steinbeck, who authored and collaborated on screenplays. Think of Elia Kazan's *Viva Zapata,* Emilio "El Indio" Fernández's *La perla,* and the pseudodocumentary *The Forgotten Village.* . . . But I agree: the allure of the cinema—the drive to find a wider audience, to seek fame and fortune—vanishes like smoke in the wind.

N. S.   García Márquez has written original screenplays. He has also collaborated with other authors on adaptations. Why hasn't he allowed *One Hundred Years of Solitude* to become a movie?

I. S.   Imagine if one could see the face of Ursula Iguarán, Colonel Aureliano Buendía, or even the gypsy Melquiades? For such a graphic novel with so unconfined a style, the process of adaptation onto the screen would inevitably impoverish it. It always happens: once the movie appears, it serves as a counterpoint and is contrasted to the text. Gabo received offers from Anthony Quinn and Francis Ford Coppola. A considerable pile of money was involved. Happily, he declined. One ought to appreciate his dignity and steadfastness, don't you think?

N. S.   In this day and age, many writers draft a novel, but they also have their eye on the silver screen. Michael Chabon, for instance, has a working relationship with the producer Scott Rudin. Rudin is actually credited in the acknowledgments of *The Amazing Adventures of Kavalier and Clay.* Beyond that, Chabon's *The Wonder Boys* was made into a film with Michael Douglas and his other works have been snapped up and optioned as screenplays. Do you know if García Márquez ever starts out writing looking to make the leap to the silver screen?

I. S.   He is an avid moviegoer. Plus, his imagination manifests itself in scene-by-scene sequences. But I don't think he keeps an eye on the silver screen. His respect for literature is too deep and uncompromising.

N. S.   How have his numerous screenplays critically fared?

I. S.   Poorly. . . . Gabo was instrumental in the foundation of the Cuban Film School. He's also been a close collaborator with Robert Redford on the Sundance Film Festival. In the eighties he did a handful of screenplays under the general title *Amores difíciles* that were produced by Televisión Española. Each is based on a plot and is directed by a filmmaker from another part of Latin America. Tomás Gutiérrez Alea from Cuba made *Cartas del parque* [*Letters from the Park*], for instance. *Milagro en Roma* [*Miracle in Rome*] was in the hands of Lisandro Duque. Years later, Arturo Ripstein from Mexico adapted *No One Writes to the Colonel*. And there is a version of *Eréndira* with the Greek actress Irene Papas and an Italian film based on *Chronicle of a Death Foretold*. All in all, the reaction of critics has been dismal. Gabo is invariably celebrated as a storyteller, but his imagination overwhelms the medium of film. By the way, one of his sons, Rodrigo, is in the film industry. He directed *Things You Can Tell Just by Looking at Her*.

N. S.   Are these films popular, though?

I. S.   None of them has become a success.

N. S.   Edmund Wilson's *The Boys in the Back Room* took to task Hollywood for its negative impact on creativity. Has film culture by now ruined the novelist's craft?

I. S.   No, it hasn't. Films need stories and they often find them in literature. From World War II onward, literature and film have coexisted on a stage of promiscuity, influencing each other at every turn.

N. S.   To his credit, Borges wrote film scripts with Bioy Casares. Carlos Fuentes also has several writing credits under his belt. For instance, *The Buried Mirror* was made into a PBS documentary and *Gringo Viejo* was made into a movie with Jane Fonda. Several of Mario Vargas Llosa's novels were turned into movies. *Aunt Julia and the Scriptwriter* was recast in an American film version as *Tune in Tomorrow* with Keanu Reeves. I suppose García Márquez's heavy involvement with his films prevents an American remake with a box-office draw.

I. S.   In spite of its cinematic qualities, Macondo, the village in *One Hundred Years of Solitude,* remains intangible.

N. S.   Can you compare and contrast García Márquez's critical reception in Latin America vis-à-vis Europe and the United States?

I. S.   At one point in *No One Writes to the Colonel,* Gabo comments that in Latin America, newspapers talk about news in Europe and that the newspapers in Europe talk about Latin America. This he describes as a sign of parallel censorship. Wouldn't the citizens of this side of the Atlantic be better off reading European newspapers and vice versa? It's an insightful suggestion. Gabo also mentions in the *Paris Review* interview that for a Latin American writer to be accepted in his own nation, his own hemisphere, culture, he first needs to be accepted in New York City, or by the United States or in Europe. That's Gabo's case, too. Before *One Hundred Years of Solitude* was released, it started to circulate in small chapters in different magazines. Cortázar, Fuentes, and others read portions and commented on them, sometimes in print. When the novel was finally published in 1967, in Buenos Aires, it became an astonishing success. It sold thousands of copies within weeks.

Needless to say, this wasn't his debut by any means. By then he had published with small- and medium-size houses. But not until he was adopted as a client by Carmen Balcells did he strike gold. To a large extent, it was thanks to Balcells that Gabo found his audience. In the United States, when Rabassa's translation appeared in 1970, published by Harper and Row under the editorship of Cass Canfield Jr., in-house opinion was lukewarm. Then John Leonard wrote a magnificent review in the *New York Times* and the novel became an immediate success. It sold approximately thirty thousand hardcover copies. In paperback it has sold millions, though.

Interestingly, the French edition includes changes to the dedication in Spanish, as well as a number of different elements—certain names, flora, etc. In some cases, these might be the fault of the translator. But Gabo initiated some of them also.

N. S.   You raise a fascinating point concerning editorial and stylistic changes in foreign-language editions of García Márquez's work. In "The Gringo's Tongue," your interview with Ariel Dorfman (in *Michigan Quarterly Review* [34.3 (spring 1995); also in *The Inveterate Dreamer*]), the Chilean author of *Death and the Maiden,* claims "that there are very few editors in Latin America: your book undergoes little change between the time you submit it and the finished text." Could you explain the editorial process in Latin America in general? And specifically with regards to García Márquez, do you know whether or not, when publishing houses translate his writings, they actually edit them?

I. S.   In Latin America the career of editor per se doesn't exist. I'm talking, of course, about the intermediary who gets down-and-dirty with the manuscript. By "dirty" I mean a voice ready to suggest changes. . . . In general, though, Gabo never allows anyone to mingle with his oeuvre. His is the opposite approach to Borges, at least on some occasions. It is well-known that at the request of—or perhaps, subjugated by—his translator Norman Thomas di Giovanni, Borges made significant changes in the English versions of his essays and stories, and then went back and altered the original versions to reflect these changes.

At any rate, in the United States, the role of the editor is crucial. But the role of the editor is crucial with translations in a different way. Both the translator and the editor toy with the translation. Then there are the cases of Ariel Dorfman, Rosario Ferré, and Manuel Puig: these three authors write in Spanish *and* in English. In other words, they are their own translators.

N. S.   You too are in this category.

I. S.   I am. But out of sanity, I've stopped translating myself. [*Laughter.*]

N. S.   Why?

I. S.   Because the translations I do of my own work end up becoming altogether different pieces: I introduce another set of characters, I expand the argument in a different direction, etc. I prefer others to do a straightforward job.

N. S.   What is your own experience with editors in Latin America and in the United States?

I. S.   Nothing much has changed in Latin America in this matter. The editors I've worked with south of the border and in Spain never get involved in the text. They look at the volume, sign a few in-house orders, and move on to the next project. On the other hand, in the United States the traditional role of the editor is dying quickly. My first editor at HarperCollins was also Cass Canfield Jr. He was in charge of *The Hispanic Condition*. (In fact, the volume is dedicated to him.) We spent a lot of time together, reworking parts, adapting the structure to different ideas. The experience was astonishingly rewarding. Exactly the same happened when I worked with Jonathan Galassi at Farrar, Straus and Giroux on my book *The Poetry of Pablo Neruda*. Nevertheless, the majority of editors I've come across are on the opposite side of the spectrum. In fact, I would go as far as to describe them as almost illiterate. Some of them never bother to read the manuscripts that arrive on their desk. They quickly assign them to freelancers, thus putting them out their vision. The tradition is in better shape at small presses: Fiona McRae at Graywolf in Minnesota, for instance, is an example of discerning eye and unswerving support.

N. S. You've mentioned García Márquez's resistance to editorial changes. Can one actually date the moment in his career when he begins to reject wholesale editorial changes in his work?

I. S. He works endlessly. He not only has the same computer, but the exact same office—same room, same color painting, same desks, same amulets—in the different houses he has in Mexico, Colombia, and Cuba. He reworks until he is fully satisfied. At that point the manuscript goes to the press: no obstructions, no interference.

N. S. So do his books suffer from a lack of editing?

I. S. Not in the least. I've heard time and again, particularly from American readers, that *One Hundred Years of Solitude* might have benefited from some cutting. . . . I disagree wholeheartedly: it is compact, its cast parades through the pages with an exact sense of purpose.

N. S. Your interview with the Romanian author Norman Manea [*Salmagundi* 113 (winter 1997); also in *The Inveterate Dreamer*] raises an intriguing issue involving translation and the writer's craft. When considering a translation of his own work Manea claims the "bargaining has affected me emotionally and intellectually. I discover myself making simplifications, easy choices in the text so that translators will not have a difficult time." In García Márquez's case, do you think, that he, like Manea, changes the way he writes for the sake of his translators or his European and American audiences?

I. S. At some point in his career, the artist becomes conscious of his own reputation. Thomas Pynchon and J. D. Salinger are prime examples: they hide like ostriches in order to avoid the ocean of fame. Others might overindulge in that ocean of fame and applause. But those are extremes. In the middle, you have a writer who knows that his or her reader is no longer the person who is sitting across the table in his local restaurant, a place where he was born and where he will die. These people he knows by heart. There's a moment in which reputation comes in the form of recognition, not only by those around you immediately, but by those beyond you in space and time, and that impacts the way you write. And there is a moment in which one feels—I think that after *One Hundred Years of Solitude,* I as a reader sense this—that García Márquez is writing more for the outside world about Latin America than ever before. And at the level of translation, that might have to do with certain choices, although I don't think he's a writer that has simplified his prose or the baroque style and imagery that he uses. Take the stories in *Strange Pilgrims:* all are set in Europe. In Gabo's earlier period, the Old Continent was too remote, too unconquerable a landscape.

N. S.   Some writers claim that the only audience they're driven to write for is themselves. . . .

I. S.   Writers find all sorts of subterfuges to do their job. Or else, they don't. . . .

N. S.   You mentioned earlier that García Márquez embraced the Cuban Revolution. What way has the Cuban revolution influenced his writings?

I. S.   Many of his readers are outside Cuba. Many Cuban exiles detest García Márquez because of his, I think I would put it, servile friendship with Castro. Others would be less critical, but equally troubled. They would say that García Márquez has become stagnant in his ideological maturity, that he fails to see the dark side of Fidel Castro, that he can criticize General Augusto Pinochet, but how come he doesn't criticize the Cuban regime and all its excesses, civil rights abuses, lack of freedom, and so on. In his literature, everything affects literature and literature affects everything. He never has written fiction about Fidel Castro. In fact, the term "dictador" doesn't apply to the Cuban leader, as far as Gabo is concerned. In his essays, though, he has directly discussed current affairs in Cuba. He also talked about the Elián González and Padilla affairs, prostitution in Havana, etc. So he has not been mute as an essayist on these events. But in his fiction, these aspects aren't an integral part, at least not in so far as they relate to Cuba. For instance, *News of a Kidnapping* is a wrenching account of the urban violence perpetrated by the Colombian cartel. Could Gabo produce a similar account on a pervasive facet of Cuban society? I doubt it: after all, he is guest on the island.

N. S.   In your essay "The Master of Aracataca" [*Art and Anger*], you raise the question of whether García Márquez's "material circumstances contradict his ideological beliefs."

I. S.   It is an ancient contradiction. Should the speaker of the oppressed live like them too?

N. S.   How does *el otro,* "the "other," fare in García Márquez's literature: homosexuals, lesbians, Jews, and Africans?

I. S.   His towns are small and the presence of foreigners is even smaller. In *Chronicle of a Death Foretold,* Santiago Nasser, the protagonist, is Lebanese. There are other Arabs in his town.

N. S.   Jews?

I. S.   I've found no Jews in the work. Nor have I come across Asians and gays. Africans are an altogether different story, of course. Macondo is a coastal town in the Caribbean Basin, a region where the African slave trade was significant.

N. S.   Let me return to where this conversation started: morality in literature. Does our culture have a tendency to sanitize or lionize authors without considering their full complexity and contradictions? More generally, do we readers oversimplify people and their times?

I. S.   It is the other way around, at least in literature. Readers, I never fail to conclude, are far savvier, far more astute than publishers and media people would want to us to think. I'm invariably amazed at how readers disregard reviews, for instance, and embrace a book for what it says to them directly, not for what the reviewer, whose opinions are summarized in a blurb, thought that it said. The objective of a fine novel or essay is to show us that what we see is never as simple as it appears at first sight.

N. S.   Edmund Wilson once said: "There is one thing the essayist cannot do—he cannot indulge himself in deceit or concealment, for he will be found out in time." Philip Lopate shared this view: "The personal essayist must above all be a reliable narrator." How often do biographies get it wrong, only to be found out later?

I. S.   Quite often, I'm afraid. Sometimes a bad biography is invaluable, though. In any case, literature is a most elitist activity. It isn't for the masses but for the few. Public speeches and sermons are for the masses, and so are TV and radio shows. Having said that, let me say something about the personal essay: I find it the most attractive genre of all; it fits my temperament to a "T." I agree with Wilson: a good personal essayist can't hide behind words; on the contrary, the essay is the most honest and humbling of all literary formats: an invitation to show your train of thought without subterfuges.

The same, no doubt, ought to be said about biography. As James Boswell proved, this is a genre in which not only the biographee, but also the biographer, is tested. Even if one might select an individual who is honest and dignified, it is our quality as chroniclers—as interpreters and enablers—that will make the biography rise or fall. Transparency is crucial: after all, we are what we write. . . .

8

Of Rabbis, Books, and Mirrors

N. S.   Do you believe in G-d?

I. S.   Yes, I believe in a godhead, capricious and unconcerned with earthly affairs.

N. S.   Where does this belief come from?

I. S.   My mother's Spinozean mysticism, I assume.

N. S.   Did you ever consider the rabbinate?

I. S.   Yes, but my skepticism precluded me from acting upon it. A rabbi should be critical at heart, but deep down he should have no doubts about G-d's benevolence. Otherwise, it is a religion of deceit.

N. S.   So you don't believe that G-d is sheer good. . . .

I. S.   He is beyond ethics. Good and Evil are human categories, institutionalized in order to live in orderly fashion. As far as I'm concerned, they are unrelated to the divine.

N. S.   Leila Avrin, in *Scribes, Scripts, and Books,* claims of the Torah that "[n]o book of any other culture has survived with the same physical form and textual stability. . . . Nor does the book of any other culture have religious strictures as to its layout, the kind of materials that should be used for making it, and how these materials should be prepared."

I. S.   The tyranny of the text. . . . Interestingly, rabbinical literature has a disdain for individuality. Up until the sixteenth century perhaps, rabbis are portrayed as a conglomerate wherein no single person is elevated above others. Names are repeated—Hillel and Shammai, for instance—but do we know about the person who holds them? Next to nothing. . . . Maimonides is an exception, of course. As such, he was the target of animosity: his detractors complained he was "too famous," a rival to the biblical prophets. This endorsement of non-individuality changes with the fellowships that surround mystics such as Isaac Luria and Sabbetai Zevi during the Ottoman Empire, and, eventually, the Ba'al Shem Tov and the Hasidic masters in Eastern Europe. Charisma became a fashion—charisma not as a personality attribute but, in the words of Bryan R. Wilson, author of *The Noble Savages,* "a successful claim to power by virtue of supernatural ordination." Wilson makes this distinction: if a man runs down the street proclaiming that he alone can save others from impending doom, and if he immediately wins a following, then he is a charismatic leader because a social relationship has come to being. If he doesn't win a following, then he's simply a lunatic. This change of approach to the rabbi as leader is dangerous and has a decisively Catholic twist to it. In fact, the textual stability in rabbinical letters derives precisely from the fact that authors are dispensable, never overwhelming the material with their large egos. Once charisma takes over, the rabbi becomes a superstar: he becomes the text. Not surprisingly, the revolutions of Luria, Zevi, and the Hasidic masters all come to us through hearsay. It is thanks to their amanuenses, their apostles and publicity agents so to speak—Haim Vital, Nathan of Gaza, the transcribers of Hasidic tales et al.—that we've come to know them. These transcribers didn't produce history but hagiography. Their account of the masters isn't critical at all; instead, it is predominantly about praise and wonder.

N. S.   You've portrayed the Rabbi Nakhman of Bratslav as one of the "last Chasidic masters and the first modern 'Jewish writer' per se." Your also argue in *The Oxford Book of Jewish Stories* that Jewish authors today serve a rabbinical function. . . .

I. S.   The transition from rabbis to intellectuals took place in the Enlightenment, as religion gave place to secularism. The role of the rabbi in ancient and medieval times was not only that of leader but also that of recipient of the collective angst. That role is performed nowadays by Jewish intellectuals and by politicians too.

As for Rabbi Nakhman, the great-grandson of the Ba'al Shem Tov, in his tales a change occurs that is similar to the transformation undergone by Don Quixote in Cervantes's novel: the protagonists cease to be mere instruments of the author's ideas and become full-size creatures, capable of thought and emotion—that is, characters who undergo a transformation in front of our eyes. That mutation is what modern literature is about.

N. S.   You seem to suggest that modern Jewish letters are Talmudic in their essence: they explain the universe. . . .

I. S.   More than explain, they interpret it. The rules of the game have changed: prayers have given place to novels. At the core, it is the same art of storytelling that is at the fore, though.

N. S.   In the same vein, you've suggested that "Kafka's theological views" are a "reformulation of rabbinical Judaism." But modern Jewish literature might also be antireligious. For instance, Kafka's story "Arabs and Jackals" is an unflattering portrait of Orthodox Jews as jackals.

I. S.   Orthodoxy for Kafka was synonymous with authority, and, as is widely known, his relationship with authority—think of *The Castle* and "Letter to His Father," for instance—is one of pain and obfuscation.

N. S.   From your comments I gather that the position of the rabbi in present times is in crisis.

I. S.   In the United States, the rabbi in a congregation behaves like a priest in a church. Wisdom has been replaced by practicality. [*Laughter.*] The rabbi has become a healer, a psychologist, a business intermediary, and a spiritual guru. . . . There is little to admire in the portfolio-carrying career leaders ordained in the Conservative movement, for instance.

N. S.   Still, are there individual rabbis you admire?

I. S.   Milton Steinberg, for instance, author of the novel *As a Driven Leaf,* about the heretic Elisha ben Abuyah. Steinberg's soul-searching essays on modern Judaism are enlightening. Abraham Joshua Heschel, although at times flaccid in his thought, was an existentialist whose erudition and belief allowed us to understand our place in a heterogeneous, multicultural society. I'm still fond of the youthful biography of Maimonides he wrote in German, which, if memory serves me well, was his doctoral dissertation in Berlin. Joseph

Soloveitchik, whose book *Halakhic Man* left an impression on me in the mid-eighties, is also a model. And then, there's Marshall Meyer, whom I met briefly in the mid-eighties at B'nai Jeshurun on the Upper West Side of Manhattan. He served as a bridge between the North and South Americas. I admired his commitment to justice and equality. He fought against Argentina's military dictatorship in the period of the Dirty War and was responsible for the formation of the Seminario Rabínico Latinoamericano in Buenos Aires. *Prisoner without a Name, Cell without a Number* is dedicated to Marshall Meyer.

N. S.   In the *Nation* [27 November 2000] you reviewed Ruth Wisse's *The Modern Jewish Canon: A Journey through Language and Culture*. In the review you traced the idea of assembling the Jewish literary canon to Hayyim Nahman Bialik. Bialik, in your words, "developed the concept of *kinus*, the 'ingathering' of a literature that was dispersed over centuries of Jewish life." You also explored the concept of a Jewish literary canon in your essay "Of Jews and Canons" [*Forward* (28 January 2000); also in *The Essential Ilan Stavans*]. In that essay you claim, "the duty of our generation is to shape a balanced canon." Do you feel that Wisse's understanding of the modern Jewish canon is shaped by her political convictions (neoconservative, coping with Jewish liberalism)? How unbalanced is Wisse's approach as a "canon maker"?

I. S.   Any committed reader is a canon maker, shaping an imaginary library for the ages. No two libraries are alike: even if the same books appear in them, they are shelved in different locations. I admire the effort by Ruth Wisse. She is an erudite reader and a passionate one too. But she invariably carries her political card in her sleeve, turning literature into an ideological manifesto. She is also weary of popular culture to an extent that I find alarming. Nevertheless, I'm less worried by Wisse's conservative politics—politics is always a comparative exercise—than by her hyper-Ashkenazic (ultra-Yiddishist, Hebraist, and American) affectations. She strikes me as someone with little knowledge of Sephardic and Mediterranean cultures, for instance. Her canon, thus, is a limited *Western* affair.

N. S.   Your own "portable minilibrary"—as imagined though the prism of *The Oxford Book of Jewish Stories*—is much looser in construction, more inclusive and is infused with a polyglot sensibility. I imagine Wisse may bristle at your statement "It was enough, for me, to have a tale by a Jewish writer to make it Jewish." Can you discuss the tough choices that "canon makers" and architects of "portable minilibraries" make? Does being more inclusive necessarily result in wider public acceptance of the canon or does this generous spirit of acceptance meet with greater resistance because it tests preconceived notions?

I. S.   By bringing a distinct Jewish sensibility to it, it is the reader and not the author who makes a text "Jewish." This of course is a position that has its risks. Might a novel by Charles Dickens be "Jewish" simply as a result of a character with Jewish faith or belief who appears in its cast? Of course, the answer is "no": the Jewishness of a book is in neither the characters, nor in the plot, although it might be found in them as well. It is *behind the words,* in the way a page palpitates in front of the reader's eyes. *The Oxford Book of Jewish Stories* originally included approximately one hundred entries. I imagined it as "my own *personal* favorite one hundred Jewish stories." But space and permissions made the inclusion of many entries too prohibitive. It is, in any case, my personal minilibrary.

The part of your question about public acceptance of a literary canon is, I think, disingenuous. What is the true purpose of a literary canon? It isn't about being exclusive, really. Instead, it is merely a list of suggestions that attempts to inspire interest in others. It would be ideal if any average Jew, any place in the world, was acquainted with at least half of Wisse's laundry list, or with a quarter of the authors I included in *The Oxford Book of Jewish Stories.* It never happens, though; literature, after all, has always been for the few, not for the many, especially in this day and age. Still, we should go on dreaming because it is in the human spirit to share what is good with others.

N. S.   You've acknowledged that *Tevye the Dairymen* stands on its own as an undisputed classic of the modern Jewish literary tradition. In recent memory Tevye has been both adapted and served as a source of inspiration for stage and screen. For example, the legendary Maurice Schwartz's 1939 version withstood critical barbs in the press to become a landmark of Yiddish film eventually recognized by the prestigious National Film Registry of the Library of Congress. The year before, the great Solomon Mikhoel and the Jewish Academic People's Theatre of Moscow unveiled a version of Tevye reportedly dressed in Soviet ideology. Years later Israel's film pioneer Menahem Golan got into the act with a 1968 production titled *Tevye and his Seven Daughters*. But it was the 1964 Broadway production *Fiddler on the Roof* that immortalized Tevye's Jewish soul. And the 1973 Norman Jewison film version cemented Tevye's iconic stature. The spirit of Tevye even makes a cameo in the form of Zero Mostel in your childhood reminiscence, published in *Hopscotch* [Summer 2000], entitled "In the Country of Lost Words: Modes of Seeing." You describe your intimate brush with Tevye incarnate during a visit to your father on the set of Mostel's star vehicle, *Once Upon a Scoundrel:* "In my eyes he was simply not only the most accurate, most authentic, and memorable of the Tevye's but, most significantly, the perfect archetype, a metaphorical description of all Eastern European Jewry in a single individual."

In contrast, you assert that veteran Mexican actor Manolo Fábregas' reprisal of the Tevye role, *Violinista en el tejado,* was "fraudulent . . . an imitation of an imitation, a Yiddish archetype turned into an American stereotype and then revamped as a Mexican prototype." Although Fabregas's knock-off performance remains, perhaps thankfully, unknown to the majority of the cultural mandarins on the East Coast of the United States. America is not devoid of such cardboard Tevye imitations. Ruth Wisse similarly targets false American stage and screen versions of Tevye in her work *The Modern Jewish Canon.* In Wisse's estimation, the translation of Tevye into these splashy artistic mediums for an English-speaking audience has stripped the character of his depth and power.

Is today's Tevye an example of American Jewish "pop art" or "kitsch?" Without Sholem Aleichem's original writings as a rite of passage for American teens, does the American Tevye become a forgery? Second-rate, derivative, a hand-me-down? How estranged is today's student of literature from the true Tevye?

I. S.   Tevye is by far my favorite character in Jewish letters. His depth, his compassion, his irreverent yet submissive approach to the divine, are models to me. I've reread the classic by Sholem Aleichem (*aka* Shmuel Rabinovitch) many times over, first in Yiddish, then in Spanish, and more recently in English. I also teach it every other year, a fact that allows me the opportunity to revisit his odyssey with the help of a fresh set of students, most of whom are even ignorant of his mere existence. *Tevye der Milkhiker* fascinates me because it is a chronicle of a profound change in Jewish history: the massive relocation from the Pale of Settlement to America and the Middle East. But its true worth is to be found in the fractured nature of the narrative, in its lacunae of information, which are the result of Sholem Aleichem not quite knowing where he was going with Tevye and how he planned to arrive there. For instance, the number of Tevye's daughters keeps on changing, and so does his approach to authority. I see him, in short, as a Don Quixote of sorts: fragile, ignorant of his own condition, a dreamer in a universe of practicalities.

As for the thousand and one portraits of him in popular culture, I'm convinced they are an essential part of his personality. Ruth Wisse is a pedantic critic with little patience for derivative artifacts. I, on the other hand, am infatuated with nonoriginality. What would American Jews be without the Broadway and Hollywood versions of *Fiddler on the Roof* and *Diary of Anne Frank*? Probably still wandering in their forty-year journey through the desert. I've watched Norman Jewison's kitschy movie scoreless times, and have also seen the Yiddish and Israeli variations of *Tevye*. They are all "readings" of the classic that have helped disseminate its message. In watered-down form? Perhaps, but is there anything really pure in this world? We are all forgeries, hand-me-downs—I, at least, am surely one. (Jewison, by the way, has tried his luck with almost every ethnic group. He directed *Moonstruck* and *The Hurricane,* among other films.)

N. S.   Onward to the genesis of the University of New Mexico Press's Jewish Latin America series, for which you've served as series editor since 1997. What difficulties did you face in launching the project? Were you the first prominent author and cultural critic to champion Latin American Jewish writers for the United States commercial market?

I. S.   The origin of the series is somewhat accidental. In the mid-nineties my editor at the University of New Mexico Press was an adorable woman, Dana Asbury, a convert to Judaism. The wife of a photographer, she was a subtle, humble, highly literate person with whom I forged a strong friendship. You might be shocked to know that Dana and I worked together for almost a decade, yet managed never to meet in person. Anyway, in one of our conversations Dana asked me about my influences and about finding role models in Mexico. I told her about a handful of Jewish authors from Peru, Argentina, and Brazil that I admired. She was ashamed to say that she had only heard of one of them, but not of the others. I told her she wasn't alone: most Americans knew nothing about Jewish-Latin American literature. At that point, one of us, I forget who, suggested that it might be a good idea to introduce these authors to an English-language readership. A few had been translated already but their books were out of print or had been released without any notice. What needed to happen, what we needed to work on, was the building of a context in which these authors, myself included, could be judged. I told Dana a book series would do the job. She agreed. Shortly after, the series was approved. I don't remember being asked to submit a proposal or anything of the sort. The idea was taken to the director of the press, and the response was a rotund "yes."

N. S.   Philip Roth edited the Penguin Books series "Writers from the Other Europe." Might the New Mexico series have been modeled after it?

I. S.   Of course. Roth's series was a model. Through him and his effort I became acquainted with Bruno Schulz and Danilo Kiš, to name only two major Jewish writers. My dream was to replicate, somehow, the effort: to make the "other side of the Americas" available to English-language readers.

N. S.   Did you target a specific audience with this literature series? What obstacles did you face in promoting the series to this readership? Is there a risk that your series title, Jewish Latin America, will cause the public to view these authors as part of an exotic niche, rather than as independent and fully developed artists? How do you evaluate which authors to include in the series?

I. S.   No target was imposed, other than to shape the books in a way so as to make them attractive to a nonacademic audience. My objective was not to produce volumes that would be read by PhD candidates but by a larger readership. So all academic paraphernalia was put aside.

The series immediately caught on. Some books have been more successful than others, of course, and better reviewed too. I don't want to ghettoize any of these authors. Just the opposite, I want to offer a context for them to be understood more fully. It was thanks to

Roth that I encountered Schulz, but to me that was only the first encounter. Schulz is an Eastern European author, but his value is universal. After reading *The Street of Crocodiles* I looked for anything and everything else by him. I realized that Roth had not ghettoized Schulz. He simply made him available to a reader like me.

The process of evaluation is not really scientific, nor is it very sophisticated. The only criterion that matters to me is taste: Do I like a book? If the answer is yes, I look for explanations that will satisfy my inquisitiveness even further. Is the author adventurous? How does he understand literature? Why is this book appealing? What does it say to me? Might it be significant to others too? Good literature is not about quotas but about vistas.

N. S.   This leads us to Jewish letters in the Hispanic world. How accepted are these in the region's literary canon? And what literary traditions do Latin American Jewish writers draw inspiration from?

I. S.   Up until recently, Jewish authors south of the Rio Grande had been marginal in the overall tradition. In colonial times, a tradition of crypto-Jews and *conversos* left an indelible legacy, but few, to a large extent, appreciated it because it was delivered in encrypted code. By the time the Ashkenazic immigrants arrived, in the second half of the nineteenth century, the Sephardic component of the landscape was all but erased. The Ashkenazim began anew, as immigrants. It has taken them two or three generations to move from the periphery of culture closer to center stage. Today there are major writers in Brazil and Argentina who are read by the general population: Moacyr Scliar, Marcos Aguinis. . . . More often than not, they tackle Jewish themes nonapologetically.

N. S.   What role does anti-Semitism play in them?

I. S.   It is an integral part of the environment, and, as such, it confronts Jewish writers constantly. Who are you? What are you doing here? These are the questions that, even as democracy becomes more solid, never fail to sprinkle a Jewish writer's journey south of the Rio Grande.

The so-called "brain drain" is a major problem in Jewish communities throughout the Americas, a problem far more serious than assimilation and mixed marriages. Many intellectuals and artists emigrate, particularly to the United States and, to a much lesser extent, to

Israel too. Still, the young continue to write, even if, at some point in their quest—as it happened to me—departure is the only choice. This creates a fracture, of course. The writer moves along, but never finds a home readership. The result, as is clear nowadays, is not only trans-culturation and multilingualism but also the need to connect with an audience that, by definition, perceives you as "alien" and "exotic."

Saul Bellow and Philip Roth write from the center of culture. To a large degree, theirs is the nation's angst and vice versa. Scliar, Isaac Goldemberg, Ana María Shua, are peculiarities: they write from the margins. Therein lies the essential difference.

N. S.   How have Jewish themes and characters fared in the hands of prominent non-Jewish-Latin American fiction writers?

I. S.   Jewish characters have been present in Latin American literature since time immemorial, either as villains, unexpected guests, or "eru-dite memory carriers." The list of anti-Semitic novels, or bucolic portraits of Jews is long. Among the most incisive and balanced au-thors, and my personal favorite, is Borges. Jewish characters appear in his stories "Emma Zunz," "The Secret Miracle," "The Untruthful Friend," and others. He has poems about Israel, Spinoza, and the Golem. He envied and admired Jews. But Borges was an anomaly in a continent where the Church is powerful, a continent prone to ex-treme animosity against foreigners.

N. S.   What are the roots of Borges's fascination with Jewish themes?

I. S.   Throughout his life, he sought to trace a Jewish ancestor in his genealogical tree, one that would finally make him *un judío*. Among the most emblematic pieces of his on the subject is one barely six par-agraphs long, entitled "I, a Jew." In it Borges reacted with enviable concentration and stalwart conviction, to an accusation, made in 1934 by the magazine *Crisol,* that he was indeed a Jew. The accusation came from an anti-Semitic faction of the Argentine intelligentsia and had as an objective to discredit Borges in public opinion. He, in turn, took the accusation as a compliment: "Like the Druzes, like the moon, like death, like next week, the distant past is one of those things that can enrich ignorance," the Argentine argues. "It is infi-nitely malleable and agreeable, far more obliging than the future and far less demanding of our efforts. It is the famous season favored by all mythologies. Who has not, at one point or another, played with thoughts of his ancestors, with the prehistory of his flesh and blood? I have done so many times, and many times it has not displeased me to think of myself as Jewish. It is an idle hypothesis, a frugal and sedentary adventure that harms no one, not even the name of Israel, as my Judaism is wordless, like the songs of Mendelssohn."

N. S.   In a review of Borges's *Selected Non-Fictions,* edited by Eliot Weinberger, you commented on "I, a Jew" [*Forward* (6 August 1999); also in *The Inveterate Dreamer*]. Might this piece also be seen as part of a larger communal search?

I. S.   Absolutely. It addresses, albeit tangentially, the hunt by Latin Americans for the missing Hebraic actor present in 1492, as the continent was catapulted into modernity. In that sense, it is part of a quest for the crypto-Jew in the mirror. In the thirties, when Borges wrote his piece, the cultural climate was fragile. Today it is a bit easier to "come out of the closet" as a Jew south of the border, although the Middle Eastern conflict always threatens to sabotage that openness.

N. S.   How was Borges's political outlook impacted by World War II?

I. S.   He recognized Hitler as an evil incarnation and opposed him even when a plethora of Argentine intellectuals took the opposite stand. His essays "A Pedagogy of Hatred" and "Definition of a Germanophile" testify to the clarity of his political convictions.

N. S.   Were his views affected by the state of Israel's establishment?

I. S.   In 1948 he applauded the creation of the Jewish state and in subsequent decades he wrote poems about Israel and traveled there twice, the second time, in 1971, to receive the Jerusalem Prize. His approach to Zionism is fascinating, if anything, because Borges's understanding of Judaisim is anything but political. He celebrated the Diaspora Jew: abstract, ungrounded, atemporal. The state of Israel for him ran the risk of turning the Jewish people into one more nation like all others. He never read Agnon, for instance, and knew nothing about Hayyim Nahman Bialik and Tchernichovsky; and the nineteenth-century Yiddish writers—Mendele Mokher Sefarim, Sholem Aleichem, I. L. Peretz—attracted him even less. His Jewish interests lead him to Spinoza, Kafka, and to more recondite sources: the myth of the Golem had an enormous appear to him—"The Circular Ruins" is a retelling of sorts; and Kabbalah intrigued him profoundly.

N. S.   In your book *Prontuario* [1993], you "rewrote" "The Secret

Miracle." Your version is called "Otro milagro secreto" and is almost identical to the Argentine's original. What exactly was your intention?

I. S.   Borges's story is astounding, but it is incomplete. Its main character, Jaromir Hladík, is granted a wish by G-d: to finish his masterpiece "The Enemies." Hladik accomplishes his task mentally—that is, psychologically—and then dies. Physically, Hladik's oeuvre remains partial and in progress. This begs the question: is it possible to have a miracle in the ideal realm alone and not in nature? My version corrects this deficiency by eliminating a handful of stylistic infelicities and adding a concluding line that, in my view, alters the overall significance of the tale.

N. S.   But can any one writer "rewrite" the work of another?

I. S.   And why not? What is good doesn't belong to us alone but to humanity. And humanity is a work-in-progress. [*Laughter.*]

N. S.   In *The Oxford Book of Jewish Stories,* you argue that that a solid number of Jewish writers are polyglots. A few exceptions come to mind, though. I believe Philip Roth is monolingual?

I. S.   Impossibly so, I'm afraid. Roth has lived in London and he has been very close with Milan Kundera who's Czech. He has spent time in Paris, he has also been close for a time with Carlos Fuentes. But to the best of my knowledge, he doesn't speak any other language fluently. His case is unlike those of Saul Bellow and Cynthia Ozick, both of whom are versed in Yiddish and even have translated works from it into English. (For instance, Bellow translated "Gimpel the Fool" by Bashevis Singer for the *Partisan Review.*) Then again, Roth represents a pattern somewhat rampant among American Jews of the second generation, the vast majority of whom are astonishingly monoglot, monochromatic, and culturally monotonous. Unlike most other Jewish Diasporas from the Greek and Roman periods on, American Jews are secluded—imprisoned, really—in their own tongue. They might send their kids to Hebrew school so that after a handful of years they will be able to say . . . what? *Shalom.* Before Bellow and Ozick, the early immigrant authors—Abraham Cahan, Anzia Yezierska, Henry Roth—spoke Yiddish and, at times, Hebrew too. In *Call It Sleep,* Henry Roth has entire sections in Yiddish delivered in English.

N. S.   You reflect on it in your Spanish-language volume *Prontuario.* Are those sections in Henry Roth's book in *Yinglish*?

I. S.   It is a sort of protean Yiddish. Only a native Yiddish speaker somewhat removed from the *shtetl* might be able to invent it. . . .

In the nineteenth century, Yiddish was the Latin of the Jewish people. Today it has been replaced by English. This makes American Jews lazy. They ask: if the French speak English, why should I learn French? Take the English cadence in *Operation Shylock: A Confession*: it isn't mannered, nor is it baroque. Roth's novel proves the extent to which the English language has incorporated the Jewish sensibility. Cynthia Ozick once called Roth's novel "our *Moby-Dick*." I like her sentence: indeed, it is a chronicle of the Jewish hunt for the sperm whale. That hunt is inside us—in the open ocean that is Jewishness. [*Laughter.*]

Some months ago, on a panel of judges organized by the National Yiddish Book Center, in Amherst, Massachusetts, where the selection of "The 100 Most Important Modern Jewish Books" was to be made, I expressed my astonishment not to see *Operation Shylock* included. To me it was an inexcusable omission. In fact, it is easier for me comprehend the world without a Greek island than without this book. I was in the minority, though. Everyone else in the room believed other Philip Roth volumes to be superior: *Portnoy's Complaint, Goodbye, Columbus, The Counterlife, Patrimony*. . . . Although the voice of the majority prevailed, I believe it to be a Jewish literary landmark perhaps unequal only to *Tevye the Dairyman*. It is a fascinating tour de force of ideas, written within a country, the United States, not always comfortable with this type of novel. It is about a *Doppelgänger*, that is, about Philip Roth discovering that there is another Philip Roth. One, the authentic Roth, lives in Connecticut. The other, his double, is suddenly heard about in Israel and is up to mischievous things that the original Philip Roth is not doing, which is going around Israel, taking a political stand by suggesting that Zionism is a disaster, that it never really took off as a political idea and that the Israelis, the Jews in Israel, should be repatriated to Poland. Symmetrically, there are two Demjanjuks: John Demjanjuk, loving grandfather and next-door neighbor, and John Demjanjuk, Ivan the concentration camp guard. . . . In short, a novel à la Dostoevsky, about doubles: Israel functions as a counterpart of the Diaspora and vice versa. It is about good and evil, about the shadowy side in each of us. It is also about free-flowing, unfolding personalities, about impostureship.

In *Operation Shylock* there is a scene where Roth's *Doppelgänger* engages in conversation with Lech Walesa about repatriating the Jews, to revive the Polish-Jewish Diaspora, which, according to the novel, is one of the most fruitful moments in modern Jewish life. The plot is so irreverential, so labyrinthine—I love it. It goes on and on. So the reader is led to believe that this is a delusion concocted in the mind of a man who recently had a bypass operation, is under medical treatment and taking the antidepressant, Halcyon. Thus, the plot might be a drug-induced trip that he is taking. It reminds me of that famous story by Borges, "El Sur," where a man has an accident, goes into the hospital and then leaves the hospital, finds himself on a train in the direction of the southern part of the city. He goes down in one of the stations, enters a bar where there are some gauchos with whom he starts a fight and he is killed; he is killed with a dagger, a knife. Perhaps he never left the hospital and is still in the surgery room, under the doctor's knife, and every image he has recorded is a hallucination. The same happens with *Operation Shylock,* although Roth's book is much more: its plot is about Israeli politics, Jews and Arabs, Israel and the Diaspora. . . .

There is an aspect I dislike about it: an author's note at the end, suggesting that everything in *Operation Shylock* is fiction and not, as suggested earlier, a confession, that is, factual information. Why include it? Obviously, there are no two Philip Roths, unless, of course, the entire world is hostage to a Halcyon trip. [*Laughter.*]

N. S.   You said *Operation Shylock* isn't baroque. Is baroqueness a Jewish attribute?

I. S.   Not at all.

N. S.   Would you say that *Sabbath's Theater* is baroque?

I. S.   The protagonist, Mickey Sabbath, was modeled by Roth on his friend the painter R. B. Kitaj. His paintings, drawings, and prints sometimes appear to me to be grotesque and baroque. As a young merchant seaman he traveled to Cuba, Mexico, Brazil, Argentina, and Uruguay. He was also interested in Spain and the Spanish Civil War. Take, for example, his pieces *Junta, Juan de la Cruz,* and *Catalan Christ.* Even his controversial *The Killer-Critic Assassinated by his*

Widower is a nod to Goya. Kitaj has a propensity to absorb ideas, and then turn them into intense pieces of intellectual art: he considers books as paintings and paintings as books. Each painting is densely woven with iconography, including literary, film, and photographic references. Yiddish theatre, Kafka, John Ford, Ezra Pound, are mixed with autobiographical elements. The prints he produced in the sixties are highly representative of this literary approach to art. His most famous painting about Auschwitz, *If Not, Not,* is a reference to the T. S. Eliot poem "The Waste Land."

N. S.   Let's talk about Moacyr Scliar. You've called his novel *The Centaur in the Garden* "possibly the single most important novel by a Jew in Brazil, and perhaps all of Latin America."

I. S.   For a variety of reasons the presence that Moacyr Scliar has in his own native Brazil—he lives in Porto Alegre—has enabled him to reach an audience that is far wider than almost any other Latin American Jewish writer that I can think of. The exception perhaps would be Marcos Aguinis in Argentina. There isn't anybody else, really. I'm thinking of a writer like Scliar who matures with his audience, and that is a very important thing to consider. Roth has matured *with* his audience: author and reader evolve together. One reads the development of Roth's literary devices as a sideboard against which one might be able to understand how American Jews have been transformed, from parochial Newark, New Jersey, dwellers to globetrotting dilettantes.

N. S.   How can a writer mature *without* feedback from his audience?

I. S.   It happens often: authors finish a manuscript and store it in a drawer for years. Many of the Jewish authors from Latin America who belong to Scliar's generation, and the ones subsequently after that, never found their own constituency in terms of readership. They are scarcely read. In fact, they might be read by more people living in the United States than they are read in Latin America, even though here we don't yet have a big audience for that kind of literature. And so, Scliar is an exception and he has known how to develop with this exceptionality. *The Centaur in the Garden* is a beautiful allegory of life in Brazil that mixes humor and mythology. It blends his unbending narrative with Kafkaesque twists and turns. It is well-balanced, accessible, and, unlike those of other Jewish authors from south of the Rio Grande, it is read widely. Other books by him are equally important: *Max and the Cats, The Strange Nation of Rafael Mendes, A mulher que escreveu a Biblia,* etc. To me it stands at the top of a tradition of Jewish angst in the Hispanic and Portuguese worlds. Its Sholem Aleichem-like humor makes it unique.

N. S.   Where does Clarice Lispector, also from Brazil, stand as a Jewish novelist in Latin America?

I. S.   She is our Virginia Woolf.

N. S.   In *Tropical Synagogues,* the last section is fully devoted to Borges. You appear to consider him one of the most philo-Semitic intellectuals in the Americas.

I. S.   Mine was an honorary mention. Through his stories and essays, such as "Emma Zunz," "The Secret Miracle," "Deutsches Requiem," and "Death and the Compass," Borges has done more to reflect on Jewishness in the Hispanic world than most intellectuals since 1492.

N. S.   You've mentioned before the crypto-Jewish tradition. What kind of literature is the one produced by crypto-Jewish authors?

I. S.   Crypto-Jewish literature is a solid literary tradition. And it always obviously depends on the reader. Because this coded text that we are talking about has various readers implied. In fact Leo Strauss, the father figure behind the neoconservative movement, ignited some controversy by suggesting that *The Guide for the Perplexed* has various readers implied. The reader is the one ultimately who can say "this is a crypto-Jewish text" or "it isn't." One can suggest that a text like *Don Quixote* is crypto-Jewish: there is a rumor around that Cervantes was born into a new Christian family, meaning that there was some Jewish blood in his past. There is a chapter in *Don Quixote* where Sancho and Don Quixote encounter a Moor who has just returned from the Americas. That could well be the story of a foreigner, or of a native who goes foreign but turns native again in the Castile of the time. *La Celestina,* a crucial Renaissance volume by Fernando de Rojas, is also a product of crypto-Jewish culture. And so are poets like Santa Teresa de Jesús and Fray Luis de León. They were descendants of Jews. Their poems, religious tractates, biblical disquisitions, and confessions ought to be read "between the lines." For in the oeuvre of Santa Teresa and Fray Luis, nothing is what it seems. This double façade, of course, is a characteristic of the baroque epoch in which they lived, but their "hidden" selves push them to an extreme. In the Americas, there are novels such as *María* by Jorge Isaac, from Venezuela, with characters that aren't openly Jews—yet the Jewish sensibility is everywhere to be felt. Crypto-Jewish literature is epigrammatic.

N. S.   You highlight a distinction between the idea of the *marrano* as it is understood within Latin America and the new phenomenon of crypto-Jewish studies within the United States. I believe that the epicenter for the study of crypto-Jews is the University of New Mexico. Tom Segev wrote an article in *Ha'aretz* investigating this phenomenon of individuals who claim to be the descendants of *conversos*. Victor Perera's autobiography *The Cross and the Pear Tree* is popular with those fascinated with crypto-Jewish identity. Segev's article also presented several voices critical of this movement. Of course, there are those that remain skeptical of Latinos stepping forward claiming to be Jewish. Critics argue that these Latinos are attempting to distance themselves from their immigrant roots to attain a new status within American society.

I. S.   The obsession that Ashkenazi Jews have with Southwestern Crypto-Jews, in *marranos* who are, to use an image that is both convenient and popular, coming out of the closet. The concept of *marrano* as a metaphor has become quite attractive in the academy, much like genocide studies and Diaspora studies. A *marrano* is taken to be almost anybody who is an impostor: Marcel Proust was a *marrano,* J. D. Salinger is a *marrano,* and so on. In my view, it is less interesting who is or isn't, than why the debate is taking place, especially among Jewish intellectuals. And why particularly now? The answer might have to do with the fact that we've witnessed a total de-ethnitization of American Jews. By the third generation, sometimes by the second generation, the ethnic ancestry was all but erased. The protagonist of *American Pastoral,* Seymour "Swede" Levov, dreams of becoming a full American: he marries Miss New Jersey, he moves to the suburbs. . . . In short, he becomes a WASP. His daughter, Merry, can't stand it, though. It isn't that she's going back to Judaism; for her, her father is a symbol of the renunciation of identity.

This arc is typical. The generation of American Jews that came of age in 1950s and 1960s sacrificed its ethnicity in order to assimilate in full. Their children, nonetheless, are attempting to return to the source today—the want to be *re-ethnicized*. They see Latinos, blacks, and Asians, and they say, "How come they are minorities, whereas Jews in America, approximately six million, are not?" (There are 13.2 million Jews worldwide.) Do you know that there are some 35 million Latinos in the United States? There is envy among young Jews toward other ethnic groups, envy and nostalgia. Therein the secret of assimilation: to become American, my parents discarded their ethnic suitcases along the way. In other words, they whitened themselves, they anglicized their manners. Hence the admiration for the crypto-Jew, an emblem of ethnicity.

On a documentary I watched on TV, entitled *Faces,* narrated by John Cleese, a Latina in California marries a Jew. She desperately wants to belong to the Jewish middle class, and to accomplish her objective, she undergoes plastic surgery: she narrows her nose, de-emphasizes her eyebrows, accentuates her ears, etc. Her face before and after the operation is different: she has traveled from one ethnicity to another. Soon after, she converts, adopts her husband's last name and, eureka, she's a Jew! The journey couldn't be the other way around, could it? Would it be a Jewish girl who desperately want to be a Latina and colors her hair, enlarges her nose, all in an effort to look like a *sirvienta*—a maid. It is the wrong direction. Jewish, hot, Latino up-and-coming, perhaps, but not quite hot, not quite at the center. This dichotomy is a fallacy that the younger generation of Jews is discovering. Okay, people want to be like us, but we want to be like them, too.

There is something they have that we don't. Multiculturalism has trickled down among Jews. People, particularly the young, want to go beyond the Holocaust and Middle Eastern politics as the all-inclusive sources of identity. How have Jews in Africa, Latin America, Australia, New Zealand, and Canada shaped their own identity? Are they different from us in any way? By exploring those questions, are there ways in which we might be able to re-ethnicize ourselves?

N. S.   The act of reclaiming your Jewish roots is ongoing. Not too long ago, I came across Christopher Hitchens' essay "On Not Knowing the Half of It," as well as Tom Stoppard's "On Turning Out to be Jewish." Could you explain for the reader the difference between Sephardic writing and Hispanic Jewish writing?

I. S.   Often the mistake is made that if you are Latin American, you are Sephardic. Latin America has been open to other Jewish migrations: Ashkenazic, Lebanese, Syrian, North African, Turkish. . . . A Jew from south of the Rio Grande might be from any of these provenances, speak Arabic, Ladino, Yiddish, etc. In fact, the vast majority of Jews in Latin America today are Ashkenazic.

N. S.   Which is why Rosa Nissán's books *Like a Bride,* and its sequel, *Like a Mother,* are unique. They are a wonderful example of Sephardic women's writing in Latin America.

I. S.   A Sephardic woman who traces her roots, not to the colonial period, but to the former Ottoman Empire. The novel includes portions in Mexicanized Ladino. The film adaptation by Guita Schyfter is provocative.

N. S.   I also wanted to talk about the theme and the representation of prostitution, both in non-Jewish and Jewish literature in Latin America. Many people do not know or have chosen to forget that at the turn of the century, there was the so-called "Polish" connection in Buenos Aires and Rio de Janeiro. *Polacos,* as the local population called them, were Jewish women trafficked by the Zwi Migdal cartel that controlled the "white" slavery ring in Latin America.

I. S.   Right.

N. S.   The Jewish community isolated the "impure" In turn, the so-called "impure" responded by establishing their own cemeteries and synagogues. This theme of Jewish prostitution appears in *The Fragmented Life of Don Jacobo Lerner.* Samuel Eichelbaum, Mario Szichman, and Moacyr Scliar have also written about Jewish prostitution.

I. S.   Prostitution in modern Jewish literature is a topic worth pursuing in terms of research. The first thing that comes to mind is that famous Sholem Asch play . . .

N. S.   *God of Vengeance.*

I. S.   Yes, the story of the struggle by a couple who have a daughter and run a bordello downstairs to keep their daughter pure in a context of impurity. And it was a very scandalous play in its time and remains scandalous to this day. And Sholem Asch remains also a very embattled, and embittered, writer for that reason, writing about Jesus Christ, writing about thieves and prostitutes and criminals and so on. I use it as a stepping stone to talk about Latin America because you could actually go to Yiddish literature and see how Latin America is represented even before it could represent itself in the perspective of Jewish life. A tale by Sholem Aleichem, "The Man from Buenos Aires," part of *The Railroad Stories,* where lumpen Jews jump onto and off third-class wagons to schmooze, handles the subject lucidly. The protagonist has an uneducated background but somehow strikes it rich. He is back in Europe after a sojourn abroad. What does he do, specifically? And how did he make his fortune? These questions aren't answered directly. Still, his listeners are mesmerized by his adventures. Sholem Aleichem's audience knew that Buenos Aires was a headquarters for the prostitution cartel, so they understand the type well. In short, the protagonist is a *padrote,* one ready to return home to seek a pure, pristine woman to become his wife.

N. S.   Yiddish as a language of the brothel. . . .

I. S.   Of course. Think again of Sholem Asch's scandalous play *God of Vengeance,* where the topic is in full view. It isn't about Latin America, but there is a Yiddish play by Leib Malach about *la trata de blancas,* the so-called flesh trade, which surely is. . . . As you might see, this is an infamous episode in Jewish-Latin American life. The *shtetl* as the source for across-the-ocean brothels? [*Laughter.*]

N. S.   Why are Iberian and Levantine Jewish literatures relatively unknown in the United States, compared to its Ashkenazi counterpart?

I. S.   Earlier we talked about memory. But memory and oblivion go hand in hand. Jewish history as understood by Americans begins with Adam and then moves into Biblical times. From there, you have perhaps snapshots of the Greek and Roman periods and then from there, you literally jump over to the enlightenment, the Maskilim, the Hasidim, the birth of Zionism, nineteenth-century nationalism, the twentieth-century Holocaust, the creation of the state of Israel, and here we are happily in the United States. The whole period of Spanish cohabitation of Jews, Muslims, and Christians is very easily, very quickly sidestepped. Very few people know that a substantial amount of the Makhzor borrows from the poetry of Shmuel Hanagid, Moses ibn Ezra, Solomon ibn Gabirol, and Yehudah Halevi courtesy of the translations by Shmuel ibn Tibbon and the legendary school of Toledo—a period that is crucial to understanding how Jews, much like in America today, are able to coexist with other religions. It strikes me that it is so easily glossed over because it is so close to what we want, the model of democracy, the model of tolerance, the model of cohabitation that we have in the United States today, it's kind of a Babylonian landscape in which identities, ethnicities, languages, and religions coalesce together.

N. S.   Why do we fail to appreciate that period?

I. S.   Because Ashkenazi literature is Eurocentric. Greece and Rome are part of it, as Palestine was before them. In this view, though, Spain is not necessarily part of Europe and the period that existed there is very quickly brushed off. Perhaps with this trickling down of multiculturalism within the Jewish community, we will begin going back to reading and rereading the classic poetry of the liturgy of that period. The interest in Yehudah Halevi by Israeli writers and the entire field of Hebrew poetry has been substantial. T. Carmi produced exemplary translations. Dan Pagis also was close to the whole lyrical period of the *piyyut,* the liturgical poem in Spain. In the United States it's largely left to academics to debate that part. In sermons, American Jews occasionally hear about the dilemmas that the Jews of Medieval Spain faced, but if they do so it is only tangentially. American Jewish identity is mainly about Holocaust survivors, about the *partizaners,* the Haganah, the creation of the state of Israel and those people who participated in it. In Halevi's case, one sees a heart divided, oscillating between the Diaspora and the Promised Land. He has that extraordinary book, *The Kuzari,* which is a dialogue between a Christian, a Muslim, and a Jew about religion. It is a fascinating volume about how we shape ourselves in front of others, written in dialogue. By the way, as a literary genre the dialogue format remains bizarre yet attractive: Miguel Leví de Barrios cultivated it, and, closer to us, Oscar Wilde.

N. S.   Isn't Spain the cradle of the novel?

I. S.   Yes, it is the Iberian Peninsula where *Don Quixote* was written. . . .

N. S.   So why in your view didn't Spain become the ultimate stage for the development of the novel?

I. S.   The first modern novel, in the full sense of the term "modern," is *Don Quixote.* It has precursors, obviously: *The Decameron, The Canterbury Tales,* perhaps *The Thousand Nights and One Night.* [*Laughter.*] Cervantes's narrative offers a pair of characters, the knight and

his servant, who, as they journey through La Mancha, undergo a series of internal permutations. The modern hero is one who reacts to
the environment and is changed by it and changes the environment
in turn. And that is what *Don Quixote* is about. It is a Bildungsroman
par excellence, unlike the storytelling by Scheherazade, where no
metamorphosis takes place. Cervantes was influenced by Erasmus of
Rotterdam, whose skepticism pushed Europe toward modernity. *The
Canterbury Tales* and Boccacio's *Decameron* are not about change but
about the depiction of bucolic life. They are episodic in nature. Of
course, so is *Don Quixote,* but in the Spanish novel, the episodes are
designed to generate change: change in the protagonists, change in
the reader. . . . Parts 1 and 2 appeared in 1605 and 1615 respectively. By
then, the Spanish Empire was in steep decline. The Armada had suffered a terrible defeat at the hands of the British. The fiscal situation
was disastrous, so the exploitation of the colonies became a source of
hope. The *Reconquista* had been achieved by twisting justice and
morality. The Spanish language had already been scrutinized by the
Salamanca grammarian Antonio de Nebrija. Scores of so-called
novels were already available, particularly picaresques like *El lazarillo
de Tormes,* and chivalry tales, such as *Tirant lo Blanc.* Francisco de
Quevedo's *El Buscón,* translated into English as *The Swindler,* dates
back to that time also. None, though, dwells on the fragile frontier
between reality and dream, normality and lunacy, like *Don Quixote.*
Therein, I believe, the door to modernity: it forces us to doubt reality, to question our own existence. Who are we and why are we on
earth? Is this but a dream, like Hamlet and Segismundo suggested?
So why didn't Spain become the ultimate cradle of the novel? How
come England, and subsequently France, get the credit? The answer
is easy: on its road to transformation, the Iberian Peninsula, when
compared to other regions of Europe, didn't make the full leap. It became frozen in time, suspended in its feudal mentality. While Germany, England, Italy, and France already displayed signs of a devel-
oping bourgeoisie, Spain still stuck to a medieval economic system
and set of values. The novel as genre goes hand in hand with the
emergence of capitalism, and Spain plummeted deep into an anti-
Reformation mood, from which it took centuries to wake up. V. S.
Pritchett once said that *Don Quixote* was the book that struck the

dagger into the Spanish heart, allowing it to agonize in a state of sleepiness for too long.

N. S.   Could you explain why the novel has not been a dominant form of literary expression in Sephardic literature?

I. S.   Again, it's a matter of cultural gravitas: Sephardic literature shines through liturgy, whereas Ashkenazi literature shines—it has liturgy and poetry—but it shines in fiction. Sholem Aleichem, I. L. Peretz, Abramovitsh, Bashevis Singer, his brother Israel Joshua, and so on. By the time the Emancipation comes around, we have already the sense that fiction is not only a reflection of reality, it is a way to express emotions, doubt, and uncertainty. The novel as genre becomes for Jews a laboratory of internal angst. One ought to remember that fiction, in and of itself, was forbidden for centuries by Muslims and Jews. It was not until the Jews left the ghetto that they indulged openly and became wonderful fiction writers. Prior to that moment there is no theater per se. Borges tells of the drive by Abul-Walid Muhammad ibn Rushd, known in Latin as Averroës, a medieval Muslim philosopher, to translate a portion of the *Poetics* by Aristotle. Yet Ibn Rushd was incapable of translating key terms, such as "tragedy" and "comedy," because he had never seen a staged performance. On the other hand, in places like England, theater evolved rather freely. Thus, the spark of a genius of Shakespeare's caliber. In fact 1605 marks the publication of the first part of *Don Quixote* and also the original stage production of *Macbeth*. William Blake once said: "Ages are all equal but genius is always above the age."

N. S.   The most lauded Sephardic writer in twentieth century is Elias Canetti, about whom we talked in an earlier conversation. You write about him in the essay "Elias Canetti: Sephardic Master" as "Europe's conscience" [*Forward* (12 February 1999); also in *The Inveterate Dreamer*]. You also included his work in *The Oxford Book of Jewish Short Stories*. Canetti, however, is not known for his fiction.

I. S.   He is an astonishing essayist and memorialist, although his masterpiece, *Auto-da-fé*, is extraordinary. A veritable polyglot, I trust his most inspired work is to be found in his meditations on language and society. This crossroad is at the heart of his multivolume *Memoirs*. Canetti also wrote abundantly for the stage, including the play *The Numbered*. (He even translated Upton Sinclair into German.)

He was the ultimate transmogrifier: an eternal traveler, always on the road, never at home. In his distant past, as a Sephardic Jew, Spain was the fountainhead to him. Happily, he was beyond easy nostalgia. The Iberian Peninsula was not a magnet for him. Instead, he ignored it outright. . . .

N. S.   Similarly, in an essay on Alberto Gerchunoff, you quote from a scene in which the Rabbi of Tolno contemplates returning to Spain. The Dayan of Rabbis dismisses his daydream, saying "Yemach Shemam Vizichrom! May Spain sink in the sea! May she break into pieces! May her memory be obliterated!" You once stated that Spain speaks to you less "as a Mexican than as a Jew." Why is that?

I. S.   The memory of 1492 is alive in me. Spain catapulted the Jews out. In the end, though, who ended up deprived?

N. S.   You talked earlier about the biblical usage of the name of G-d. There is a veneration and guardedness that surrounds the usage of His name. This brings to mind the image of the *genizah,* at center stage in the marvelous story "Xerox Man" [*The Essential Ilan Stavans*].

I. S.   Judaism, in its essence, is a textual—that is, literary—religion. The object of adoration is *the* Book, portable, in constant need of re-translation and reinterpretation. The Book contains the memory of its people. Thus, the *genizah* is a storage room for memory. Every synagogue includes a forbidden room, usually behind the *Aharon Ha-Kodesh,* for ancient, unusable texts to be stored. The rationale is simple: the divine name must be protected from falling in enemy's hands. Therefore, every sacred text and scores of secular ones too ought to be stored away, then either buried or burned.

In 1725 the Renaissance philosopher Giambattista Vico, in his book *La Scienza Nuova* [The New Science], suggested that cemeteries are the authentic foundation of civilized life. His sharp thesis is clear-cut: once we bury our dead, our connection to the land becomes everlasting. With Jews in the Diaspora, the argument requires a special understanding. The itinerant existence of Israel from the first destruction of the Temple in Jerusalem in 597 BCE, onward, suggests that, even though our dead are buried wherever death finds us, not a single portion of land but the entire globe entire is our home. These, I believe, are the roots of our cosmopolitanism: entomb your ancestors, but make memory the perpetual sanctuary.

N. S.   The discovery in 1896 of the *genizah* in Cairo by Solomon Schechter opened up unforeseen vistas to ancient Judaism. These vistas included centuries-old multilingual correspondence from remote parts of the Jewish world.

I. S.   At the textual level, the *genizah* itself symbolized the odyssey of the Jewish people. Solomon ibn Gabirol, Maimonides, Sa'adiah Gaon, Benjamin of Tudela, Gluckel of Hamelin . . .—imagine these disparate figures synchronized in a single space? Not only do you travel from one place to the next, but also carry books along. These accumulated books become the record of the collective travesty. They are dispensable and should never tie the community to the land. The storage room is a microcosm: an Aleph. Quite a lesson in the age of the Internet, don't you think?

N. S.   On a related topic, the Jewish people have for eighteen centuries coped with the *galut* [exile]. Jews have been uprooted many times throughout history: the Babylonian exile (from 597 BCE to 538 BCE), the Second Temple's destruction (70 CE), the English expulsion (1290 CE), the French expulsions (fourteenth century), the Spanish expulsion (1492 CE), expulsion from the German Empire (between 1450–1520 CE), and in more recent memory, the Holocaust. From Adam and Eve to the Exodus from Egypt, Jews have collectively examined the theme of exile. The subject has consumed great writers and thinkers, including Nahmanides, Ahad Ha'Am, Franz Rosenzweig, Maimonides, Yehudah Halevi, and the Maharal of Prague. How has the question of exile enabled the Jewish people's long-term creativity? Likewise, how has the exile of the divine *(galut ha-shekhinah)* and Jews' attempts to end their exile contributed to the richness of Jewish literature? Will the ingathering of exiles *(kibbutz galuyyot),* represented by the state of Israel, spell an end to the Jewish literature of exile?

I. S.   The most accomplished revolution in Jewish history was the composition of the Babylonian Talmud, which, as you know, took many centuries, as well as scores of hands and minds. The Hebrews had gone from a nomadic tribe to become a commanding monarchy in the times of Kings Saul, David, and Solomon. The constant wars against neighboring nations resulted in chaos and, when the Temple was first destroyed, in dispersion. Exile, in those early stages, began as an existential condition, but it was not solidified until the destruction of the Second Temple. It is at that point when the leadership of the people changed: the rabbi replaced the prophet as leader. The role of the rabbi needed to be defined. No longer a speaker for the divine voice, the rabbi became an organizer, a counselor, and the source of communal endurance and continuity. In order to continue to endorse their faith outside their homeland, scores of legal and moral issues needed to be sorted out for the Jewish people. It was left to the sages to shape, in a period of several generations, an atmosphere that was conductive to a life far from home. The sheer idea of *Ba-Shana Havaha be Yerushalaim,* translated into English as "Next Year in Jerusalem," along with the theological justification it required, were then implemented. From a divinity that was obsessed with wars to one that stood by its people in its millenarian journey across space and time, a deeply seated metamorphosis took place.

After some two thousand years, Zionism came along to put an end to the diasporic dispersion. This was, primarily, a political movement, although several rabbis endorsed it, and people like Rabbi Kook even developed a theology to accompany it. Politics, and not theology, is what brought the whole mess along, for Jews had attempted, willy-nilly, to live beyond politics—that is, Jewish-gentile politics—since the Talmud period. But I don't think Zionism is the end of Jewish exile. In fact, some fifty-plus years after the creation of the state of Israel, it is clear that the Diaspora has not disappeared. On the contrary, it is a strong alternative, one that affects the internal life of Israelis on a daily basis. No, Israel was not—is not—the messianic movement the nineteenth-century thinkers wanted us to believe in. It is, instead, a strictly nationalist one, obsessed with borders and flags and patriotic paraphernalia.

Will exile, if it ends at any point, spell death for the Jewish people? No, but a revolution equal in size and scope to the Babylonian Talmud would need to come to pass so that Jewish life would find new meaning in that future, whatever it might be.

N. S.   Along with the *genizah* there is another attractive metaphor: the *sofer,* that is, the scribe in charge of composing the sacred Torah, the parchment for the mezuzahs for the door, as well as the tefillin and other sacred texts. He is obsessed with letters: the shapes of letters, the placement of letters. . . .

I. S.   The *sofer* keeps the tradition afloat by redrafting the Torah again for his generation. No mistake, no typo is allowed. Only the most meticulous and devoted become *sofers*. Every parchment, every scroll must be perfect. . . . A gorgeous lunacy, don't you think? After all, imperfection is our fate. Still, the *sofer* spends endless days building—and burning—sentences.

N. S.   "Burning," you said?

I. S.   Authors are born with a limited number of sentences to use in a lifetime. Once the amount allowed is exhausted, death settles in. The amount has been stamped on our forehead since birth.

N. S.   Like the myth of the Golem. . . .

I. S.   Indeed, according to the legend, the word *"emet,"* the Hebrew term for "truth," was sculpted in the Golem's forehead. To kill him, the mythmaker needed to erase the first letter, turning the word into *"mavet,"* the Hebrew word for "death." Chaim Potok, author of *The Chosen,* once said that the figure of the Golem is a metaphor for the act of artistic creation. "The writer," he stated, "sits all alone. Some of us mutter incantations of a sort. We do all sorts of strange things in order to get the work going and what we are creating in a sense are Golems. Figures that move about on page that are spawned in the imagination, but that are very much alive and sometimes they do get out of hand." For Potok, the act of creation—human, divine—was an attempt to beat the "terrible finality of death." That, exactly, is the purpose of literature: an attempt to defy death. [*Laughter.*]

Index